Igniting the Flame

IGNITING THE FLAME
America's First Olympic Team

JIM REISLER

LYONS PRESS
Guilford, Connecticut
An imprint of Globe Pequot Press

Copyright © 2012 by Jim Reisler

Lyons Press is an imprint of Globe Pequot Press.

Text design: Sheryl P. Kober
Layout artist: Sue Murray
Project editor: Kristen Mellitt

Library of Congress Cataloging-in-Publication Data is available on file.

ISBN 978-0-7627-7848-5

Printed in the United States of America

10 9 8 7 6 5 4 3 2 1

For Tobie and Julia

TABLE OF CONTENTS

Foreword vii

Author's Note viii

Cast of Characters ix

Beginnings: "Nothing More Than a Glorified Pickup Squad" . . . 1

CHAPTER 1: "Games at Athens? What Games?" 19

CHAPTER 2: A Rousing Start 36

CHAPTER 3: The Baron 56

CHAPTER 4: "All Were Stupefied" 67

CHAPTER 5: "Lithe Forms and Springy Steps" 90

CHAPTER 6: "Most Gratifying to Every Princeton Man" 104

CHAPTER 7: "Man of Many Parts" 132

CHAPTER 8: Smoking Guns 148

CHAPTER 9: "A Foreigner Should Not Win This Race!" 156

CHAPTER 10: "Jesu Christo! I'm Freezing!" 177

CHAPTER 11: "Rah! Rah! Rah! Ellas, Ellas, Ellas, Zito!" 184

CHAPTER 12: "A Set of Men That the Nation May Well Feel
            Proud Of" 195

Endings: "Good Feeling and Fellowship Predominated" 205

Appendix: 1896 Olympic Results 223

Acknowledgments .233

Notes 234

Index 274

About the Author .286

FOREWORD

As a runner, I was fortunate to have been a member of several teams—at Lincoln High School in my hometown of Canton, Ohio; at Bowling Green State University; and the United States Olympic team at the 1972 Olympic Games in Munich, where I captured the gold medal in the 800 Meters.

Competing in the Olympic Games is an interesting endeavor. On the one hand, you are competing for your country, while on the other hand, you are competing for yourself. It is an intriguing mix of pride in country and pride in self. While I will always be proud of my accomplishment at the Munich Games, I am just as proud of being a part of the truly special fraternity of US Olympians.

Knowing what it took to win in Munich gives me a real reverence for the Olympians who came before me, and especially for the pioneers who started it all. What Robert Garrett, Thomas Burke, James Connolly, the Paine brothers, and the other members of the first US Olympic team accomplished in Athens went well beyond anything they did at the track or the shooting range. Their memorable performances were integral to creating the American Olympic movement—and making it possible for future generations to become Olympians as well.

So to those first US Olympians, I say "thank you." I hope you'll enjoy getting to know them as much as I have.

DAVE WOTTLE
MEMPHIS, TENNESSEE

Author's Note

The term *Ivy League* is well known, generally referring to eight institutions of higher learning in the northeast United States—Harvard, Yale, Princeton, Brown, Columbia, and Cornell universities, the University of Pennsylvania, and Dartmouth College. Ivy League schools compete in an athletic conference of that name and are best known for academic excellence and selectivity in admissions. So in the spirit of full disclosure, this book refers to "Ivy Leaguers" to describe members of the 1896 US Olympic team, though the term would not appear in print for another three decades. According to *The Yale Book of Quotations*, the 1930s-era *New York Tribune* sports editor Stanley Woodward was the first to use the phrase in print, taking it from Caswell Adams, a colleague. While comparing the merits of Fordham's powerful football team to those of Princeton and Columbia, Adams remarked disparagingly of the latter two, saying they were "only Ivy League." Woodward made note of the term and printed it the next day. "A proportion of our eastern ivy colleges are meeting little fellows another Saturday before plunging into the strife and the turmoil," Woodward wrote October 14, 1933, in describing the football season.

Note that Woodward used the term, "ivy college," not "Ivy League" as Adams is said to have used. So there is a discrepancy in the theory, although it seems probable the terms *ivy college* and the later *Ivy League* came from the sports world, particularly in 1954 with the formal start of the Ivy League conference.

Cast of Characters

The US Team

Arthur Blake (Boston Athletic Association—BAA) Track and Field—1,500 meters, Marathon

Thomas Burke (BAA) Track and Field—100 Meters, 400 Meters

Ellery Clark (BAA; Harvard)Track and Field—Long Jump, High Jump

James Connolly (Suffolk Athletic Club, South Boston) Track and Field—Triple Jump, Long Jump, High Jump

Thomas Curtis (BAA) Track and Field—110-Meter High Hurdles, 100 Meters

Robert Garrett (Princeton) Track and Field—Discus, Shot Put, Long Jump, High Jump

William Hoyt (BAA; Harvard) Track and Field—Pole Vault, 110-Meter High Hurdles

Herbert Jamison (Princeton) Track and Field—400 Meters

Francis Lane (Princeton) Track and Field—100 Meters

John Paine (BAA) Shooting—25-Meter Military Revolver

Sumner Paine (BAA) Shooting—Free Pistol, 25-Meter Military Revolver

Albert Tyler (Princeton) Track and Field—Pole Vault

Charles Waldstein (also known as Walston) (IOC) Shooting

Gardner Williams (BAA) Swimming

Other Influential Athletes

Launceston Elliot (Scotland/Great Britain) Gymnastics, Weight Lifting, Track and Field

Edwin Flack (Australia) Track and Field—800 Meters, 1,500 Meters

Alfréd Hajós (Hungary) Swimming—100-Meter Freestyle, 1,200-Meter Freestyle

Spiridon Louis (Greece) Track and Field—Marathon

George Robertson (Great Britain) Track and Field, Tennis, and Author of the Olympic Ode

Officials and Notables

Eben Alexander: US Ambassador to Greece, Romania, and Serbia

Eugene Andrews: Cornell Archaeologist and Journalist

Baron Pierre de Coubertin: Founder of Modern Olympic Games

Basil Gildersleeve: Journalist

John Graham (BAA): Manager of US Track and Field Team

Crown Prince Constantine of Greece: Olympic Supporter and Benefactor

George I, King of Greece: Olympic Supporter and Benefactor

Burton Holmes: World Traveler, Ace Photographer and Journalist, and Chronicler of the 1896 Olympic Games

Albert Meyer (Germany): Influential Photographer and Chronicler of the 1896 Olympic Games

Olga, Queen of Greece: Olympic Supporter and Benefactor

Rufus B. Richardson: Journalist

William Milligan Sloane: Princeton Professor and Leader of US Olympic Movement

James Sullivan: Director of US Amateur Athletic Union (AAU)

Benjamin Ide: Wheeler Cornell Archaeology Professor and Spectator

"Nothing More Than a Glorified Pickup Squad"

Ellery Clark had an issue. A Harvard student who was aboard the SS *Fulda* on his way to Athens to compete in the 1896 Olympic Games, Clark wanted desperately to practice his specialty, the high jump. But the massive tanker's constant pitching and rolling in the choppy Atlantic Ocean made practicing the event on the ship deck next to impossible. In the turbulence of open waters, a successful practice jump depended on the angle of the ship. "If the deck was going up, about two feet was the limit; if [it were headed] down, there came the glorious sensation of flying through space," Clark said. "A world's record appeared to be surpassed with ease; and your only fear was of overstaying your time in the air, and landing, not upon the decks again, but in the wake astern."

In another part of the SS *Fulda,* James Connolly faced his own dilemma. Clark's teammate at Harvard and headed to Athens to take part in the triple, long, and high jumps, Connolly had strained his back working out in the college gymnasium only two days before sailing. For now, he could do little more to ease his discomfort than take daily walks around deck, sleep in the oversized steamer chairs—and hope he would feel better. So hour after hour each day, Connolly stretched out in his steamer chair, "content with just sitting there and looking out on the blue sea through the open rails," he recalled. At the same time Connolly harbored a desperate fear that the injury would fail to heal in time for the start of the Games, he vowed to maintain an upbeat perspective by absorbing the excitement and reveling in the adventure. "After all, the Games were only part of the voyage," the Bostonian said. "Here I was sailing the high seas, and Athens would be there when I got there . . . It was swell. Just to be gazing out on the deep blue waters was satisfying something deep inside of me."

Acknowledging the cramped conditions and taking a liking to the young Americans, all men, the ocean liner's captain had cleared the lower deck in the rear of the ship most days for an hour starting at 3:00 p.m. so they could practice. "All our fellows could do was to get into a track rig with rubber-soled shoes and bounce up and down on the well deck, where no passengers were," Connolly said. So that became the routine for the entire sea voyage: Before lunch and again in the late afternoon before dinner, Connolly circled the promenade deck six times. It seemed barely adequate for a highly conditioned athlete about to compete in the first modern Olympic Games, but Connolly and his American teammates were doing the best they could.

Most everything about the journey had been arduous. By April 4, 1896, the American athletes and their comrades wanted little more than to land in Athens and get to their hotel and rest. Numbering almost 20, they had been seen off more than two weeks before in Hoboken, New Jersey, by a small group of friends and then sailed across the Atlantic aboard the *Fulda*. Owned by the North German Lloyd Steamship company, the steamship had been anything but plush with no real room for exercise beyond a stroll about the deck—a true impediment for a group of athletes about to represent the United States in the revival of the Olympic Games in Athens.

For eight days, the *Fulda* had been at sea—crossing the ocean and passing through the Straits of Gibraltar across the Mediterranean before docking at Naples. Then the travelers had boarded the local train and headed across Italy to Brindisi, where they hopped on a tiny olive boat and headed down the Adriatic Sea to the Corfu, and then to the port of Patras on the western Peloponnesus in Greece. From there, it had been another train ride—the slow-moving local again, this one taking 10 hours in all—to Athens, where the modern Games were about to start on the site where the Greeks had staged their hallowed ancient event.

The athletes, mostly drawn from Princeton and Harvard universities and accompanied by a trainer, assorted friends, and one wealthy mother and benefactor, had traveled 1,000 miles to run, jump, swim, and shoot as part of a competition about which few Americans seemed to care. Despite their many advantages and the good fortune afforded to those enrolled in prestigious universities, they had sacrificed a considerable amount to be among the first Olympians in more than 15 centuries.

Still, from all accounts, the team had enjoyed their spirited but small send-off back on Saturday, March 21, in Hoboken. For the group of Princeton athletes, it had been the second of two impromptu and celebratory bon voyages among family and friends. Leaving school directly after morning chapel on Friday, March 20, they were seen off at Princeton's cozy rail station by an enthusiastic crowd of students, professors, and townspeople who serenaded them with "cheer after cheer," according to a brief dispatch in the *New York Herald*. The team's immediate destination was Manhattan, where they spent a restful evening at the Murray Hill Hotel before heading Saturday morning on the ferry across the Hudson River to Hoboken. Arriving at the pier in plenty of time before the scheduled 10:20 a.m. departure, the team's four Princetonians basked in a pleasant dose of attention—"mobbed in most agreeable fashion by a bevy of girls, who fixed bouquets and whispered encouragement in a fashion calculated to inspire an athlete of the coldest blood," said a reporter. Maybe it was the attentive women, or perhaps it was all the flowers they received—many in a combination of black and orange for the school colors—but the Princetonians and their admirers were in a chipper mood.

Familiar cheers pierced the morning air at the pier. Launching into repeated football-style orations in honor of their school—"Rah, Rah! Rah! Tiger! . . . Sis! Boom! Ah! Princeton!"—the traveling party and their admirers "woke up the staid residents of Hoboken," according to a reporter. Otherwise, the athletes weren't saying much for the record beyond that they felt "fit and confident." That description applied especially to the shot putter and discus thrower Robert Garrett, the Princeton captain, who, as one wrote, "looked trained to the hour." Cool and understated, Garrett gave the press the perfunctory: "You may rest assured," the captain said, "that we will give a good accounting of ourselves." Pole-vaulter Albert Tyler, better known as a tackle on Princeton's national-champion football team, spoke more brashly, predicting he would return to America as the Olympic champion.

But where were the other US Olympians, the Bostonians? They were late, nowhere to be seen—and concern spread that they would miss the launch. Then, a few minutes before 10:00 a.m., there they were—five athletes in all, and led by the Boston Athletic Association (BAA) trainer John Graham, soon to establish himself as the de facto leader of the American team and its most vocal advocate. At 34, Graham was the right man for the task: A Liverpool native, he had been a teenage running star in Britain before emigrating to Boston and carving a reputation as one of America's top track coaches. In his 20s, Graham had coached at Columbia, then Harvard. In 1889, he had accepted a position in Boston as manager at Charlesbank Gymnasium, the first outdoor gym established and maintained by a US city. Since 1893, the slight, mustached Graham had overseen the BAA, whose well-to-do members were footing the tab for most of the New England athletes.

Graham told reporters all the appropriate things, stating his BAA athletes "could not possibly be in better shape." Recognizing that his greatest challenge was keeping his team fit during the ocean voyage, Graham had shrewdly arranged with the ship captain to set aside a space on the deck for training. His BAA runners would combine a healthy dose of brisk walking with a series of daily dumbbell and chest exercises, and practice starts for the sprinters and hurdlers, he said. Given the unsteadiness of the deck, conditions were a tad tricky for the high-jumpers and pole-vaulters, but as Clark would demonstrate, they would do their best. Graham knew virtually nothing of the competition his athletes would face in Athens, but exuded an air of confidence, particularly about the fortunes of 400-meter runner Tom Burke. A world-class athlete who had triumphed at the 1895 US–Great Britain meet in New York, Burke was ready to take on the world, Graham proclaimed. "[Burke] never enjoyed better health than at present, and if he weathers the trip successfully," the trainer said, "I think he will have no trouble in disposing of all his opponents."

Mounting the gangplank, Graham and his four athletes—Burke and Clark, William Hoyt, and Arthur Blake—headed to the railing near the bow of the big boat, not far from the Princeton contingent who did the same. Here stood the bulk of the American Olympic team, yet their concept of a *national* team was different than today's. Their affiliations lay mostly with their schools and clubs.

Departure was imminent, but not without a final bit of ceremony—more flowers, basketfuls taken on board and presented as corsages to the clusters of athletes. This last, vast floral tribute was courtesy of one Solon J. Vlasto, the cofounder and publisher of the New York-based Greek-American newspaper, *Atlantis*. Though most of America wasn't yet attentive to the revival of the Olympic Games, the coming athletic contest in Athens was already big news in the country's Greek community.

The teams came together, prompting more cheering, namely another few rounds of "Sis! Boom! Ah! Princeton!" from the orange and black contingent and a corresponding "BAA—Rah! Rah! Rah!" from the Boston crew. The ice had been broken between these two separate groups of athletes, whose schools had been rivals for decades. With the big boat pushing off at its scheduled time, the Boston crew gave another cheer for themselves and then magnanimously for the Princetonians, who returned the tribute. A final "bon voyage" roared from the orange and black rooters watching from shore and waving as the boat drew away into New York Harbor, turning east toward the Atlantic Ocean.

What to make of the send-off? After some trepidation that the Bostonians would miss the voyage, the team had left on time, reporters noted. Otherwise, their send-off was loud but small. "The majority of those assembled on the pier were at a loss to account for the vocal pyrotechnics set off by such a small and inoffensive looking group," one wrote. Nearby, an admirer tried putting the occasion in perspective for a group of slightly bewildered women, drawn by the commotion: "These lads, you know, are American college boys going over for the big football match against the Marathon Club," he said. "They are all from Yale, Harvard, University of Pennsylvania, and Cornell, and will simply mop up the gridiron with the Europeans!"

Not exactly. But the gentleman knew more than most. Americans at the time were showing next to no interest in their country's inaugural set of Olympians as they pushed off for Athens. Why even bother to compete in what was perceived as a European creation designed for Europeans? No big-city journalists had seen the team off, and the next day, most of the New York papers buried the two-to-three-paragraph accounts of the team's departure in the back pages. How unfortunate, for this unlikely band of Olympians had come together improbably, on short notice, and in the case of some, at considerable personal risk. Just getting this far was an accomplishment.

Equally remarkable was that the man most responsible for putting the team together—one William Mulligan Sloane—was noted more for scholarship than for athletics. And yet Sloane, the eminent Princeton University historian, had been a tour de force in building the US team. As the American representative of an international committee appointed by the French nobleman Baron Pierre de Coubertin to revive the ancient Greek games, Sloane had worked for two years to assemble a US Olympic team. Overlooked and belittled by US amateur sports officials who showed no interest in the Olympics, Sloane had soldiered on, determined to find a way to get his small band of athletes to Athens.

It hadn't helped that the Games were set during the first part of April, smack dab in the middle of spring semester for the collegians and during their outdoor track season. So Sloane went to work on his fellow Princeton faculty members—and with their buy-in turned to Garrett to secure a kind of in-house US Olympic team. Administrative support for the final collection of Princetonian Olympians— Garrett, Tyler, sprinter Francis Lane, and 400-meter-runner Herbert Jamison—was tepid at best. Jamison was a last-minute substitution for freshman James Colfert, a talented, 50-second quarter-miler whose parents forbade him to leave school. After all, the student-athletes would miss a substantial portion of their classes, some five weeks in all, and make it back shortly before exams. "The trip will no doubt be a good thing for Princeton in the outside world," the *Daily Princetonian* editorialized, but there was concern that a prolonged absence of the athletes "may affect our prospects in the coming contests [in May] with Yale and Columbia. Such a result would be at most deplorable; and if it were anticipated, the trip would hardly be warranted."

To many, the contingent of departing Olympians was an afterthought. On March 25, 1896, the *Trenton Times* devoted front-page coverage to news that the manager of the University of California track team had been invited to join the Princeton-Yale track meet that spring in New Haven, barely mentioning the Olympians at the end of a piece about the Penn Relays. The pervasive lack of interest in the Olympic venture was doubly ironic at a time when major newspapers gave massive coverage to most things Ivy League: That month alone, the *New York Times* devoted nearly half a page to the Harvard-Princeton debate, citing "unusual attention in the struggle," and nearly as much space to a plea by Yale professor Henry Farnam for donations to offset the cost of running the school library. Princeton in particular seemed to enjoy the *Times*'s special attentions, as in another major piece that March heralded the departure of several of the college's professors for a scientific expedition to South America. The *Times* even gave far more attention than it did the Olympic team to the February 29 decision by the Intercollegiate Association of Amateur Athletics of America to add bicycle racing to its annual Games.

About the same time as Princeton's student editors were fretting about the prospects of its tracksters against Yale, the BAA decided to make its own Olympic contribution. After the club's governing board balked at the cost, club members launched a subscription drive, but after two weeks raised only half the amount it needed. Finally, on March 18—only three days before the SS *Fulda* was set to depart for Europe—club member Oliver Ames, a former Massachusetts governor, stepped in and made up the difference. Preparations for both the Boston and Princeton athletes were so last-minute that the US team had no standard uniform, with each group deciding to wear their college and club colors adorned with the American flag.

Most of the Bostonians were current and former Harvard athletes—Clark and Hoyt along with a recent graduate, the distance runner Arthur Blake. Connolly had also been a Harvard student, but withdrew from school after the dean denied him the leave to attend the Games. Paying *his* passage to Athens was another Boston athletic group, Suffolk AC. Meanwhile, Hoyt withdrew from Harvard as well, though he would return and graduate. Connolly, however, would never graduate, his resentment of the dean lingering long after his jumping days. Vowing that he was done with Harvard, he stuck to his guns, never attending another class there. Only decades later when the college awarded Connolly a varsity "H" would he again set foot on campus.

———

Aboard ship, the American athletes wrestled with the logistics of at-sea conditioning. On the first day at sea, the Boston contingent walked about the rear deck. Then, after visiting the captain for clearance to run about the deck for a short time each day, they donned workout clothes and threw together an impromptu open-air, at-sea gymnasium: There were two 25-yard straightaways for the sprinters and a short oval pathway, some 24 laps to the mile, for the middle-distance and distance runners. A day or so later, the captain relented and gave permission to create a more spacious training area that covered the length of the ship through two narrow passages on the bow and back to the stern again, a distance of about 300 yards. Though hardly ideal, it served its purpose and the Boston athletes exercised twice a day— at 11:00 a.m., taking a vigorous walk in regular clothes, and at 3:00 p.m., donning athletic costumes for an hour of more serious training in their makeshift gym. Burke took advantage of the straightaways for the 100- and 400-meter races. Sprinter and hurdler Tom Curtis took a more creative approach, setting up hurdles, jumping rope, jogging, and even hopping in potato-sack races. The swaying ship and a constant southwest wind made things difficult at times, but the athletes did their best, cautioned by John Graham's constant nagging to be careful not to turn an ankle. They had fun too, charming some of the older, more sedentary passengers with their efforts in clearing the deck just for a little exercise. They amused one another as well; when Curtis somewhere found a Napoleonic hat, it naturally found a way to his head, where it remained for an afternoon workout.

Some took a more relaxed approach. Bostonian William Hoyt, the pole-vaulter, did some running and stretched, but little more— after all, how *does* a ship-bound pole-vaulter prepare? Under the weather when he left Boston, Hoyt took full advantage of the chance to sleep long hours and take in the intoxicating sea air. Meanwhile, Arthur Blake, the distance runner, utilized the "track," jumped rope, and ran up and down stairs—prepping as best he could for the hills that awaited him in one of the Games' more intriguing events, the 25-mile marathon. Taking a wholly different approach were the four athletes from Princeton; under Garrett's direction, they limited their training mostly to walking briskly up and down the deck three times a day for a half-hour. That was due in part to the condition of half their contingent—Lane and Tyler were suffering from bad bouts of seasickness.

Entering the Straits of Gibraltar and its celebrated "Rock," the passengers looked forward to four hours ashore before resuming the voyage to Naples. Here before them were the awesome vast limestone cliffs on Gilbraltar's northern and eastern sides rising almost a quarter-mile into the sky. They were passing through the two Pillars of Hercules, a thought that captivated several of the Americans who had spent years steeped in the classics, then a mandatory part of many university educations, and felt fortunate to be headed to the land of Homer and Aristotle. Connolly was feeling downright giddy as the big steamer nosed into port before the looming cliffs on a picture-postcard, sparkling sunny morning. Rising carefully from his deck chair on account of his sore back, he suddenly felt no pain. Just like that, Connolly's ache had vanished with "me feeling loose as ashes," he said. It was a minor miracle and a bit of a mystery—but the triple-jumper would take it. And just like that, Connolly's dream of Olympic glory in Athens took a quantum leap forward.

In Gibraltar, some passengers on the SS *Fulda* hired carriages and local guides to sightsee. But not the dutiful band of American athletes who had done their reconnaissance—having discovered and secured permission for their first substantial on-land training session in more than a week, at a horse racetrack belonging to English officers. Gathering their spikes, the athletes piled into carriages and made their way to the track—all but Blake, who was hoping to squeeze in some miles in preparation for the marathon, an event that was longer, a lot longer, than he had ever run before.

A carriage full of American tourists heading out of town and trailed by a lone runner was quite a sight for groups of small boys along the route. So Blake decided to have some fun, periodically stopping to catch his breath and pretending to collect coins from the ground behind the carriage. Every time Blake stopped and pretended to find a coin, he shrieked with delight, which drew the curious onlookers. "The small boys," said Clark, "were easy victims."

At the racetrack, the athletes got down to business. Some, like Connolly and his fellow Harvard compatriots Clark and Hoyt, stretched and jogged out the kinks from the voyage. Meanwhile, Blake; the hurdler Curtis, an MIT graduate; and Burke, a Boston University graduate, did some running. Joining the workout were the Princeton athletes, led by Garrett, the shot putter who was thinking of entering the discus though it wasn't a part of American track and field competition. Like their Boston teammates, the Princetonians were happy just to get off the boat, with Tyler and Francis Lane perhaps happiest of all to reach solid footing and some measure of relief from their seasickness. Like their counterparts at Harvard, Princeton administrators weren't supporting their athletes, all of them juniors from the class of 1897. But they had been given six weeks' leave, reluctantly, with the firm understanding they would not receive any breaks for the studies they were missing and had better be ready for the really important events of the spring—those track meets against Yale and other rivals of the Ivy League. Just who paid their way to Athens was a mystery at the time. Years later, the truth was revealed: Garrett's mother, Alice Whitridge Garrett, was their benefactor; she was part of the Olympic traveling contingent, accompanied by her maid.

Four other athletes rounded out America's first Olympic team. Gardner Williams, an 18-year-old swimmer from Boston, a member of the BAA, and the team's youngest participant, was aboard the SS *Fulda*. On separate journeys to Athens, meanwhile, were three marksmen: the brothers John and Sumner Paine, former Harvard students and Boston natives, and Charles Waldstein, a native New Yorker who lived in Great Britain. John Paine was headed first to Paris, where he would pick up his brother, a medical student, and Sumner's wife,

Salome. Waldstein, an eminent archaeologist and a member of the International Olympic Committee (IOC), was already in Greece as part of an archaeological dig at Corinth. Of all the athletes, only Burke was a national champion, and he, along with Clark and the Paine brothers, was considered world class. So it went for America's first collection of Olympians, chosen without a tryout, and, as Olympic historian Bob Fulton put it, a team that "was really nothing more than a glorified pickup squad."

— —

Traveling to Athens aboard the SS *Fulda* was another American, not an athlete but a journalist of sorts from Chicago named Burton Holmes, whose dispatches and photographs of the trip and the events in Athens would go a long way toward legitimizing the Olympic Games for skeptical Americans. At 26, Holmes was a dapper, self-assured man distinguishable by a Vandyke beard and a hefty, ever-present box-model camera he carried everywhere like an appendage of his body, and which seemed to dwarf his elf-like frame. At 16, Holmes had been chaperoned by his grandmother to Europe, where he took a lot of pictures, captivated by the power of photography. The next year, Holmes, his camera, and his grandmother returned to Europe, and took in California and Cuba as well. Back to Europe they went in 1890 after which the Chicago Camera Club, of which Holmes was secretary, asked him to display his substantial collection of travel slides with commentary. He was a hit; the Club took in $350 and a career was born. Holmes soon went into business for himself, marking what he would eventually coin as a "travelogue."

Holmes would become a famous and wealthy man. But aboard the SS *Fulda*, he was still a relative unknown, still making a modest living by lugging his camera about foreign lands and taking extensive notes to report his discoveries to audiences back home. "The Olympic Games were the excuse for my intrusion into the land of the scholar and the archaeologist," he said. "I knew too well that I would bring to Greece only a love of travel, an eye not wholly blind to beauty, and a deep respect for the history, the letters, and the art of Greece."

Holmes's commentary could get a bit flowery. Chalk it up to the times and a smidgen of showmanship. His description of life aboard the SS *Fulda* with his new American college friends is a testament to how far from US shores they had traveled. Holmes noticed that the rules and regulations on the ship were printed in four languages. He took delight in the rules, printed in sketchy English, starting with one that "prohibited . . . any passenger to meddle with the command and direction of the vessel, the Captain being the only responsible person." He laughed about another rule, the tongue-twisting "regulation No. 12," which specified, "Passengers having a right to be treated like persons of education will no doubt conform themselves to the rules of good society by respecting their fellow-travelers and by paying a due regard to the fair sex." And he could barely contain his pleasure at another rule, stated with the certainty of biblical prophecy: "Thou shalt not go to bed with thy boots on!"

Holmes was captivated by several of his fellow passengers. The Archimandrite of Vienna, a top official of the Greek Orthodox Church, was aboard, and Holmes took his portrait. He took photos of the stunning Adriatic sunsets, and of shipmates who probably did sleep with their boots on—groups of Albanian shepherds and elderly Greek women with distinctive, lined faces. On April 1, four days out of Gibraltar, the *Fulda* finally reached Naples. After nearly two weeks of travel, the Americans took two days off this time, managing to fit in several more training sessions, mostly by walking. They visited galleries, museums, and the city's celebrated aquarium. It was a restful time until a couple of the Americans caught a headline in an Italian newspaper that reported the Olympic Games were actually due to start April 6—to their horror, that was only four days away—and not April 18, as the team had thought.

The mix-up had happened because the Greeks observed the Julian calendar, and not the Gregorian, as the Americans and Western Europeans did, something that even the scholarly Professor Sloane, and everyone else for that matter, had overlooked. So instead of having nearly two weeks in Athens to prepare and train for the start of competition, the Americans suddenly discovered they would have a day at most. But that thought paled next to the American team's new and paramount preoccupation with just getting to Athens for the "real" start of the Olympic Games. That suited Connolly. Thrilled that his sore back had apparently healed, he kept his sense of humor and relished his fast-developing, newfound friendships with several of his American teammates. Even after a pickpocket lifted his wallet from his hip pocket on April 2 in Naples, Connolly was miffed, but didn't report the loss to either the hotel or the police, lest it keep him from making the trip's next connection—the train to Brindisi. But the police had other plans—and on the morning of April 3 when the team was set to depart town for the railway terminal for the trip to Brindisi, a plainclothes policeman approached Connolly at the rail station and asked in fluent English if he had lost something.

Yes, a wallet, he said, with five sovereigns.

The loss established, the policeman asked Connolly to accompany him to the police station, but the American refused. It was 7:40 a.m., and the Americans' train left in 20 minutes.

"But you must," the policeman said. "The police department is here in the terminal."

So Connolly went. In the station, another policeman, this one speaking virtually no English, conveyed to Connolly that his wallet had been recovered and that he must remain in Naples to prosecute the thief. But that was out of the question; it was now 7:50 p.m. and his train left in 10 minutes.

Asking to be let go because he had a train to catch, Connolly pointed to the clock and refused in his best pidgin English: "No, no, Brin-dee-see train! Otto! Otto!" he pleaded.

Attitudes hardened. Connolly stood and made a motion to leave. Several more policemen entered the room and tried pinning Connolly's arms to keep him there. The American was getting desperate; with his main event, the Triple Jump, the first scheduled final of the Games, his Olympic dreams would be all but dashed if he missed the connection. So eyeing the clock as it hit 7:59 p.m., Connolly made a snap decision he would never forget or ever regret—springing from the policemen's grasp, and bolting from the office in a last-ditch effort to make the train.

Reaching the lobby of the spacious railway station, Connolly frantically tried to determine the correct platform for his train. "Brind-dee-see? Otto! Otto!" he kept yelling, hoping in desperation that somebody, anybody, could point him in the right direction.

A burly porter, presumably used to traveler hysteria, caught his eye. Pointing Connolly in the right direction, he ran with him toward the platform until he was winded. Another porter, younger and thinner, took up the run: "Brindisi! Si! Si" he yelled, leading Connolly the rest of the way. The train was pulling out, and without breaking stride, Connolly thrust his hand into his pocket and came up with two 10-lira notes as tips.

"Dees lire por voo! Dees lire por votre comrade," Connolly yelled to the porter, thrusting the currency in his hands.

But Connolly still wasn't on board. The train was gaining speed and a guard stepped up and tried to stop him. The fleet-footed American sidestepped him and pulled even with the train's running board. Taking a flying stride, he was grabbed by the waist and hauled through an open window by Burke, Blake, and Tom Barry, Connolly's Boston friend who was on the trip.

It had been the closest of calls, but Connolly made his train. Perhaps three seconds more and he would have been stranded in Naples. "I did not realize it then, but if I had missed that train," the athlete said later, "I would not have reached Athens in time for my event in the Games."

Two long days of travel remained for the Americans. From Naples, the train chugged west across the "boot" of Italy, winding through a series of tunnels to Brindisi on the Adriatic Sea. Hopping on a boat headed to Patras, a Greek port on the Ionian Sea, team members got their first, puzzling glimpse of the competition they would face in Athens, a stocky, curly-haired Greek man named Lagoudaki who told Curtis that he too was headed to the Games. Lagoudaki had been studying in France and was returning to Greece to run two events—the 100 Meters and the Marathon, the shortest and the longest event of all things—and earnestly told Curtis that he expected to win both. No way, thought Curtis to himself—figuring that if this man were typical of his opponents, maybe the competition wouldn't be all that steep. "It is difficult to imagine the kind of training he must have been through," Curtis joked.

At least they were nearly there. Arriving in Patras, the team immediately boarded a train for the journey's last leg—another 10 hours—to Athens. On the evening of Saturday, April 4—a grueling 14 days after leaving Hoboken—"we caught our first glimpse of the Acropolis," wrote Clark, "and knew that our journey was at an end."

Despite their initial glimpse at the competition, the odds were stacked against the Americans. Beat tired and out of peak condition after days at sea, they "were not exactly in what today's Olympic coaches would call the pink," remembered Curtis. Not much more than an Ivy League intramural squad, they had been chosen without a trial and more on the basis of availability—and in some cases, against the better judgment of their college officials. For a sports public more focused on the coming baseball season than a European-dominated track meet, interest was minimal.

But then something unexpected happened, and by the time they arrived back in the United States—in plenty of time for Princeton's meets against Yale and Columbia—the Americans had created a national Olympic mania that endures. In the process, the story of this unlikeliest team of college amateurs achieved a level of nobility rarely attained in sports—the pursuit of grace and excellence for their own sake and of competition for the fun of it. How they pulled it off and became one of the most influential sports teams in history is a story for the ages.

CHAPTER 1

"Games at Athens? What Games?"

"GAMES AT ATHENS?" BOOMED THE VOICE OF HARVARD TRACK COACH James Lathrop in reply to an unusual request by James Connolly. Harvard's freshman long- and triple-jumper had just asked how best to go about competing in the recently announced Olympic Games in Greece.

"What Games?" Lathrop asked, and signaling with sarcasm exactly what he thought of Connolly's request, "What Athens?" Lathrop's tone let Connolly know that a trip to the first Olympic Games with the university's backing was as likely as a walk on the Moon. In Lathrop's mind, the discussion was over.

It was early 1896 and Connolly, having read of Princeton professor William Sloane's efforts to put together America's first Olympic team, was testing the waters. From the moment he had seen an article in the December 7, 1895, edition of the Harvard student newspaper, the *Crimson*, detailing Sloane's intentions, Connolly had been smitten with the idea of being an Olympian.

The 27-year-old athlete had figured his enrollment at Harvard would be an advantage in getting to the Games in Athens. For starters, the article had reported Sloane's assertion of "such great interest in this country that it bids fair that a team from the different athletic clubs and colleges will be sent to compete in the different events."

Moreover, the bigger and the more elite colleges, ones with track programs like Harvard's, were expected to foot the costs of the US athletes, all of whom would have to be amateurs, just like Connolly and his college teammates.

Connolly was surely heartened by the news that notable men affiliated with the elite schools made up the American contingent of the Olympic Games' Honorary Committee. They included not only President Grover Cleveland but several Ivy League presidents, such as Harvard's Charles Eliot. Certainly he would favor sending athletes from his own school—or would he? For Connolly, a man born with an insatiable appetite for adventure, a trip to Athens in the middle of spring semester would be much more meaningful than going to class.

Actually, the Olympic buzz on the Harvard campus had started even before Connolly arrived in Cambridge in the late summer of 1895. The previous winter, the *Crimson* had published a long letter from Demetrius Kalopothakes, Harvard class of 1888 and a native Athenian, which extolled the virtues of competing in what would be the first Olympic Games in more than 1,500 years. Kalopothakes "venture[d]" as Connolly put it, "to Harvard men . . . to find their way hither in April 1896 to Athens."

"It is no doubt an unfortunate time of year for a college man, and especially at Harvard, where I have no doubt that April is now the month of extra grinding or the Finals as it was in my days," Kalopothakes wrote. "But there are a number of men who are able to get away—at any rate, a few athletic men could doubtless obtain permission for a five weeks' absence, especially as the Easter vacation (which I hope has not meanwhile been abolished by the Overseers) will cover two of these weeks. Harvard must by all means be honorably represented, as the oldest and greatest of American universities; and her athletic circles must begin to consider the matter from now. It would

20

be a great pity if Princeton should carry off the honors for America; and it would be a great disappointment to the few Harvard men, that I know will be present, not to see the dear old 'crimson' represented in the fight."

Another article in the *Crimson*, on January 28, 1896, further stoked Connolly's competitive fire. These new Games, the article said, would revise "as nearly as possible" the ancient Olympics, a heady thought for a recently declared classics major. What wasn't to like? Imagine running and jumping on the same hallowed grounds as ancient Greeks. "The king and queen and all three princes are showing great interest in the work," the article went on. This wasn't just another track meet, but one with romance and a connection to the Olympic Games of ancient times, slated to take place where it had all happened centuries ago. And it was significantly more appealing than Connolly's only major Harvard track meet to date—back in October at the Freshman Athletic Meeting, during which he easily captured the long jump at 19 feet 8 inches.

— ❦ —

It was no surprise that Coach Lathrop mocked Connolly's Olympic obsession. The five weeks it would take to get there, compete, and get back *was* a long time to be gone from school, particularly for a freshman enrolled for less than a year. On the other hand, how curious that the Harvard track coach was so thoroughly dismissive. This from a representative of a top university, one that led the way in educational reform and took considerable pride in developing its young men's minds, spirits, *and* bodies?

But Lathrop's opinion wasn't the one that mattered. The real decision-maker was Charles Eliot, Harvard's longtime president whose view of most competitive sports was profoundly negative. The

62-year-old Eliot was a formidable intellect, an educational reformer, and a towering leader of the university for the past quarter-century. Armed with a Harvard degree at 18, Eliot returned to the college campus at 19 as a math tutor and embarked on a storied academic career. Appointed an assistant professor of math and chemistry four years later, he was named the university's president at the astoundingly young age of 35 and began turning longtime American educational practice on its head.

Eliot's educational vision collided violently with America's predominant mid-19th-century ideal, which was still dominated by clergymen. For the most part, tradition dictated a curriculum focused on the classics and largely irrelevant to the real-world needs of matching the sons of a growing industrial power to more practical courses of study. Few colleges of the era offered courses in history, science, political theory, and modern languages. Even fewer supported graduate or professional schools.

Appointed president in 1869, Eliot plunged into the vortex of a full-blown crisis in higher education. Having endured three short-term presidencies in the previous decade, Harvard was at a crossroads. Boston business leaders, many of them Harvard graduates, worked to make the university a leader in curriculum expansion to modern, pragmatic courses. Eliot agreed, and set about reforming a system with a plan set forth in a two-part article, "The New Education," that appeared early in 1869 in the *Atlantic Monthly*. "We are fighting a wilderness, physical and moral," Eliot wrote. "For this fight, we must be trained and armed."

Eliot's vision fused elements of his New England background—Unitarian and Emersonian self-actualization ideals that emphasized a reliance on character development. Eliot believed that a college education should provide students with a broad knowledge of science, math, political economy, and languages. A complete education, he believed, prepared students with the skills to make smart choices in this new society—often blending specialized training and a commitment to public service.

At the root of Eliot's philosophy of higher education was giving young men the confidence to explore and discover their passions. "Thereafter, he knows his way to happy, enthusiastic work, and God willing, to usefulness and success," Eliot declared in his inaugural address. "The civilization of a people may be inferred from the variety of its tools. . . . As tools multiply, each is more ingeniously adapted to its own exclusive purpose. So with the men that make the State."

Eliot's leadership revolutionized American higher education, turning Harvard into an incubator of sorts for the "new" university. When he spoke, other university presidents listened and reform spread. As chairman of a national committee that represented secondary school students, Eliot pushed an agenda with uniform standards and a more thorough and modern study of English. He was the first educator to suggest cooperation among colleges through holding common entrance exams and lobbied secondary schools to provide deserving students with scholarships.

Eliot's reforms were most apparent at his home campus of Harvard. He hired world-class faculty, modernized the curriculum in the law and medical schools, expanded classrooms and labs, and built specialized academic libraries. And when Eliot raised the admission standards for Harvard's incoming students, the ripple effect shot through secondary education.

For Harvard students, Eliot's reforms were liberating. Out the window went many of the school's petty disciplinary rules. Eliot pared the university rule book from forty pages to five. But despite the accelerating pace of reform, Eliot was not well liked on campus.

23

Perceived as stiff and humorless—New England's "topmost oak," one called him—he was often grim and given to eccentricities. Looking to prepare his students as businessmen and as leaders, Eliot wanted Harvard men to be strong of mind and of body. His ideal, historian David McCullough wrote, was the student who "ought to be able to row a boat and ride a horse, swim a mile and hike 25 miles."

Under Eliot's watch, Harvard put up athletic facilities and steadily expanded its sports offerings. In 1862, the college started a baseball team, and a year later laid out a field on Cambridge Common. Two years later, Harvard played its first intercollegiate game, besting Williams College 35 to 20. But the opinionated Eliot wasn't thrilled about certain forms of athletics. He had developed an intense dislike for most team sports and particularly baseball, which he considered unfit for a gentleman. Earning most of his wrath was the pitcher, whose success depended on deceiving the batter. How unseemly, said Eliot, to throw a pitch and fool the batter, especially with a curveball.

In 1874, Harvard played its first football game and launched a track team. In a vote the next year for the school colors and nickname, students overwhelmingly selected Crimson—which beat out the more purplish shade of red, Magenta. By 1880, Harvard's track team was the best among America's colleges—winning the first of its seven straight national titles. In 1886, Wendell Baker set a world record for the 440 with a time of 47.75 seconds despite considerable challenges—a standing start on a straightaway dirt track and losing his shoe 50 yards from the finish. (Accurately tracking world records was a challenge in the era of the 1896 Olympic Games. Only in 1912 with formation of the International Association of Athletics Federations [IAAF] as the international governing body for the sport of athletics were track and field officials finally able to tabulate world records with precision. So even though events like the 100 and 400 Meters as well as the High Jump, Long Jump, Pole Vault, Discus, and Shot Put were Olympic sports from the very first Olympiad in 1896, it would take another 16 years for records in those events to be catalogued with certainty.) Into the 1890s, Harvard's track team, led by frequent winners like Hoyt and Clark, remained among America's top college programs.

Eliot approved of track and other specific sports like tennis and crew. Marksmanship passed muster and so did lawn tennis, fencing, and for some reason, cricket, a team sport, which at least was the province of gentlemen. But he never overcame his hatred of baseball, and he loathed football, declaring it "more brutalizing than prize fighting, cock fighting, or bull fighting" in his widely circulated 1894 diatribe, "The Evils of Football." There was absolutely nothing Eliot liked about football, though he headed a university that regularly fielded one of the country's best teams. "[Football] sets up the wrong kind of a hero," he wrote. "The man who uses his strength brutally, with a reckless disregard both of the injuries he may suffer and of the injuries he may inflict on others.... [Football is] unfit for colleges and schools." How much better the sport would be, Eliot argued, if the ball carrier in football acted honorably and ran toward the toughest part of the opponent's defense, and not its softest part.

Perhaps no man personified Eliot's ideal better than Theodore Roosevelt, Harvard class of 1880. Wealthy and socially connected, young Roosevelt could have breezed through Harvard with his Brahmin classmates, but instead set a frantic pace—starting with membership in all the right clubs like the satirical Hasty Pudding Club, the "Dickey" or DKE fraternity, and Porcelain. Along the way, Roosevelt drove himself physically by rowing on the Charles River in a one-man shell, wrestling, boxing, and taking long hikes, a significant accomplishment for a man who had overcome a sickly and asthmatic childhood. He also joined the Rifle and Art Clubs, and worked hard at his studies, which included German, Italian, metaphysics, philosophy, and natural history. In his senior year, Roosevelt began work on his study of the naval battles of the War of 1812, which became his first book. "He was always ready to join anything," recalled Richard Saltonstall, his closest college friend.

By 1896, Theodore Roosevelt was two years from winning election as governor of New York, and four years from the Presidency. In the meantime, Harvard remained a bastion of the privileged; for instance, most of the class of 1897 had grown up within a 100-mile radius of Boston, and attended one of New England's notable public or prep schools like Boston Latin, Roxbury Latin, Andover, or Exeter. But driven by reform, the doors had been thrown open to growing numbers of students from modest circumstances able to pass the entrance exam—"the very best part" of the college in Eliot's words. The Harvard student body of the era wasn't a portrait of diversity in the modern sense; according to a survey of the class of '97, in the group of approximately 400 students were 16 Roman Catholics, 14 Methodists, seven Jews, a single Mormon, and no African Americans. It was a start, at least.

Clark and Hoyt were part of the prep-school crowd, and so were most of the Boston group's other Olympians—Burke, Curtis, the Paine brothers, and Williams—all of them members of the city's upper and middle classes. James Brendan Connolly, however, was not; his neighborhood was *South* Boston, the city's working-class, Irish-Catholic enclave and the source of his lifelong preoccupation with sports. And athletics were about all he shared in common with his more generally privileged classmates.

At 27 years of age, Connolly was nearly a decade older than most of his Harvard '98 classmates, nor had he ever graduated from high school, despite his first-rate mind, a gift for language, and a healthy dose of chutzpah. One of 12 children of John and Ann Connolly, Irish immigrants from Galway, Connolly acquired a fierce pride of his heritage and a healthy sense of adventure from his fisherman father.

In later years, Connolly relished telling stories of his youth in South Boston, where sports were central to the community fabric, something "all of the men [are] interested in," especially hurling, bowling, and wrestling, all popular back in Ireland. "You could find the old unable to read or write (but) could argue keenly, intelligently on any outdoor sport whatsoever," Connolly said. "And among many of those old men were many who had been athletes of some fame." For Boston's Irish immigrants, sports were a true democratic outlet; you were judged on your agility or speed or ability to break off a curveball, and not your heritage or connections. "They were a hot-blooded fighting lot, but also a clean-living, sane, and healthy lot," Connolly recalled. "The children growing up healthy [and] rugged just naturally had a taste for athletics. Among the boys I knew, it was the exception to find one who could not run or jump or swim, or play a good game of ball."

By the 1890s, if a young man excelled at sports, he could potentially make it a living. Within a half-mile of the Connolly's home lived six big-league baseball players. Local sports heroes were here, there, and everywhere, none greater than John L. Sullivan, the "Boston Strong Boy" crowned in 1882 as boxing's heavyweight champion and reigning for a decade. A man about town, Sullivan dressed well and could often be seen strutting the streets, which Connolly, as a boy with a bit of brazenness himself, exploited.

"'Hello John!'" Connolly often bellowed.

"'Hello kid!'" the great man answered.

"He didn't know me, but never quizzed me," Connolly said, "[I was] a boy that had a right to salute him familiarly, a boy of the district."

Another neighbor named Gallohue, spelled in some sources as Gallahue, had made a name as a circus acrobat and was probably more responsible than anyone for triggering Connolly's interest in track. Gallohue spent a lot of time on the road, so when he got home to Boston, it was a happening. At 6 feet and 190 pounds, the circus man stood out at a time when most men were considerably shorter. Also, Gallohue had a distinctive style, dressing in $60 suits, a significant amount in those days, especially in South Boston. Gallohue had earned it, too, winning a bet from a circus manager who believed he couldn't jump over a baby elephant. Apparently, he could.

With public parks few and far between, Connolly and his neighborhood chums played ball in the streets and vacant lots. As teenagers, they gravitated to a more spacious place—the State Flats area, a roughly 45-acre plot of reclaimed land that hugged the city's central railroad close to Boston Harbor. The Flats weren't pretty, but gave many of the city's top sportsmen the space to train; its sun-baked clay track became the center of great summer festivals run by Boston's Irish and Scotch societies.

It was at the Flats that Connolly developed into a multi-sport regular. Fast and sinewy, he played football and baseball and ran track. Connolly had plenty of smarts, though school took a distant second to his interest in games. He attended the Lawrence Scientific School and then South Boston's Notre Dame Academy, but his heart was elsewhere; at 15, he dropped out, moving to a series of jobs that would always seem to end up back where he was meant to be—connected to sports.

Finding work as a clerk at an insurance company, Connolly continued to balance his training in several sports, but track in particular. His promise was revealed in 1890 when he won the US amateur championship in "hop, step, and jump" (or triple jump) as a member of South Boston's Trimount Athletic Club, a predecessor of the Suffolk Athletic Club. In an 1892 letter, Connolly detailed his personal training regimen for track. "Practice easily but regularly," he advised. "Overtraining is worse than under-training . . . Do not run the day before a race . . . From 4 to 5 in the afternoon is the best time to exercise and about five times a week usually gives best results . . . Eat plain food you like . . . drink as little liquid as you can during the day of a race, outside of your usual allowance of tea or coffee."

In the early 1890s, Connolly "got the family itch to rove," as he put it, and followed an older brother, Michael, who had ventured south to Savannah, Georgia, with the US Corps of Engineers. Michael was ambitious and took up law—specializing in maritime law—and would become admiralty commissioner for the port of Savannah. Through Michael, James also landed a job with the Corps of Engineers, and while in Savannah, continued to pursue a variety of sports—not only as an athlete, but as a coach and an administrator as well. In 1891, he put together a football club for Savannah's Catholic Library Association (CLA), serving as business manager. Surviving are a series of business letters from the era that shed considerable light on his character.

Looking to arrange a game with the University of Georgia, Connolly described his team as a blend of attorneys, bankers, retailers, clerks, and an undertaker. In a March 1892 letter to the editor of the *Macon News* before a game against Mercer College, he responded to criticism that his team included not just professionals, but—gasp!—Jews and day laborers. Labeling the charge "a willful distortion of the real truth," Connolly appealed to reason, wondering why anyone would have a problem with a teammate, a "Mr. Coningham," because he "worked with his hands for a living."

In another letter mailed three days later to the captain of the Mercer College team, Connolly described his team in detail. "[They're] all classes of people," he wrote. "Wealthy and poor, Christian and non-Christian." Addressing the presence of a Jewish teammate named Fred Myers, Connolly specified, "All of the team are not Catholics. . . . They pay the same dues that their Catholic brethren pay and are treated with the same consideration." And just so it was understood how strongly he bristled against the apparent elitism and blatant anti-Semitism of his potential opponents, Connolly wrote that Myers "moves in the highest social circles here . . . [and is] a member of the Young Men's Hebrew Association."

The exchange, which comprised many letters, demonstrated a lot more than Connolly's ease of expression and organizational abilities. It revealed an ease in his working class roots, a deep sense of decency and fairness, and a rage against discrimination and arrogance. In Connolly's view, the members of the Mercer College team were abject failures, not only for their unfortunate attitude, but for recruiting non-student players, spying on his team at practice, and faking injuries.

Connolly's work as an athlete and an organizer made him a big deal in Savannah's thriving sports community. A busy man, he became a sports columnist for a Savannah weekly newspaper and captain of the CLA Cycling Club. He promoted the Savannah Wheelmen, and with Fred Myers, bought a bicycling shop. Connolly quickly realized he had no grasp of business, and sold his share; later, he joined the Savannah Baseball Club and the city's independent gun club. By the winter of 1892, he was also captain of the city's football team. A year later, Connolly even became manager of a local prizefighter named Pat Raedy.

But Connolly missed his hometown of Boston. He moved back and picked up as if he had never left—falling into his old crowd of sportsmen, who included John Graham, the former director of the Charlesbank Gymnasium and now managing the Boston Athletic Association. Urged by a mentor, Nathaniel Shaler, dean of the Lawrence Scientific School, to aim high, Connolly decided to apply to become one of President Eliot's bright young working-class recruits at Harvard. So in October 1895, the high school dropout took the college's entrance exams at Lawrence, and passed four of the test's five subjects to secure admission to one of America's bastions of learning. He enrolled with plans to study the classics and play sports.

Football beckoned. Joining 144 others with hopes of making the freshman team, Connolly was minutes into his first scrimmage when he was walloped head-on by a classmate. The collision broke his collarbone, ending his season and his football career. But the unfortunate accident had a silver lining, for it was then and there that Connolly figured his sports future lay in less violent pursuits—track and field for one.

———

Stopped cold by Coach Lathrop in his request for support to get to Athens, James Connolly turned elsewhere. He went to see Dean LeBaron Briggs, who endorsed his plan and suggested he put in a formal request for an eight-week leave of absence with Professor William J. Bingham, chairman of the Harvard University Committee on the Regulation of Athletic Sports.

Connolly approached Professor Bingham not as a brash athlete, but rather as a humble student. "I piped down on any talk of violet-wreathed Athens, or marbled Athens, or the bard Homer chanting his sonorous period before the customers of the market-place inn," Connolly remembered years later. "[But] one peek at the chairman's puss told me that here was no friendly soul."

Professor Bingham got right to the point. "Athens! Olympic Games?" he cried, echoing Lathrop. "You know you only want to go to Athens on a junket!"

Connolly played it cool. *A pilgrimage to ancient Greece [is] a junket? he thought to himself. Competing for my country for an Olympic championship [is] a junket?*

The chairman prattled on anyway. "You feel that you must go to Athens?" he asked.

"I feel that way, yes sir," replied Connolly, soberly.

Whereas Coach Lathrop was concerned that Connolly would miss a sizable part of the spring track season by going to Athens, Bingham cited his freshman status and mediocre academic performance as reasons that the university would deny a request for leave. Apparently, Connolly was struggling in a machine shop course and already faced the prospect of making up a significant amount of work in summer school.

Student and professor had reached an impasse. "Then here is what you can do," the chairman told Connolly. "You resign and on your return you make re-application for re-entry to the college, and I will consider it."

Connolly held strong. "I am not resigning and I'm not making application to re-enter," he told the chairman. "I'm through with Harvard right now. Good day!"

At least that's how Connolly remembered the exchange nearly a half-century later in his memoirs. It's a good story, but most likely a tad embellished. By then a best-selling author, Connolly was a spell-binding orator and, according to Jonathan Shaw in an article on the first Olympians for *Harvard Magazine*, afflicted with "a lifelong habit of bending [the truth]."

Chances are that Connolly did appeal to Professor Bingham, but the university archives have no record of such an exchange. There is, however, a letter from March 18, 1896—only three days before the SS *Fulda* was due to sail for Europe—in which Connolly requested a leave of absence. While the information in the letter is not as colorful as Connolly's tale, it provides another perhaps more reliable recording of events.

"I contemplate making a trip to Europe," Connolly writes. "The opportunity is before me to make the trip now at little expense to myself, an important consideration with me. I may never be in the position to take such a trip in later life. Inasmuch as I shall try to keep up my text book work while away, my work in shop only would suffer. This work could be made up next July, should I find myself in a position to return to college next Fall which in frankness I must say, seems improbable now. I consider the educational advantages of such a trip would be of value to me."

As expected, the administrators were unmoved by the educational advantages of a trip to Athens. They denied Connolly's request. But he had made up his mind, and on March 20, wrote a follow-up note to Dean Shaler asking that he be given leave to withdraw honorably as a student from Harvard. Shaler obliged, and the official record gets right to the point: "Withdrew March 19, 1896. Reason: To visit Europe."

That's different from the way Connolly spun the story a few years later. "I had been kicked out of Harvard even though I stormed out of the place," he wrote in 1944. "And all because I kicked up a bit of a fuss when they wouldn't let me miss school for a few weeks so I could go to Athens." In any event, the experience bruised Connolly's feelings about the school forever. He would never re-enroll or graduate. A decade would pass before Connolly set foot in a Harvard building for a speech on literature to the Harvard Union.

Suddenly free of academic obligations, Connolly felt liberated; there was nothing to keep him from what he considered his Olympic destiny. How he signed up and managed to join his eventual teammates on the SS *Fulda* is unclear, though it's almost certain that he did a lot of travel planning for Athens well in advance of his rejection for leave; most likely, John Graham secured him passage on the *Fulda* with the other Bostonians. And though Connolly would insist later in life that he paid his own way to Athens, that wasn't the case: his parish in South Boston footed most of the bill.

So the only question remaining was what athletic club Connolly would represent in Athens. Hard as it is to fathom today, the athletes of America's first Olympic team were at first more focused on competing for their clubs and in the case of the Princetonians, their school, than for the United States. For Connolly, representing the BAA seemed a likely choice, but he quickly ruled it out; despite its name, the BAA wasn't as much a sports organization in those days as a social club for the prosperous that sponsored a number of Boston-area sports events. The Manhattan Athletic Club of New York was another possibility; one of the country's top track programs, it had happily taken in Connolly some years back. But Connolly had never actually competed for it and harbored a resentment for the big clubs, which, he said, didn't typically offer athletes much support—"always taking promising athletes away from poor clubs and keeping them like stables of horses, paying their way and giving them a good time so long as they brought prestige."

So bypassing the Manhattan AC, Connolly made what in retrospect was an apt choice. With his heart very much in Boston, he would don the singlet of his hometown Suffolk AC with its golden stag emblem adorned with a silk American flag. "Still the little hometown club for me," Connolly said. What a match: Within weeks, much of America would recognize the names of "Connolly" and "Suffolk AC."

CHAPTER 2

A Rousing Start

THE OLYMPIC GAMES WERE SET TO BEGIN THE MORNING OF
Monday, April 6—and America's team had made it to Athens just
under the wire. With fewer than 48 hours before the first events,
worn out from the long journey, they needed rest. But that would
have to wait.

During the trip's last leg, the 10-hour train trek to Athens, word
had been telegraphed ahead to Greek Olympic authorities that the
Americans would soon be arriving. Pulling into the Athens train station early Saturday evening, the Americans stared out the windows
of their car, thunderstruck at the pressing crowd there to meet them:
two musical bands and hundreds of enthusiastic well-wishers "welcoming us instantly, overwhelmingly," Clark said. Above the crowd
was a truly astonishing sight, one that Clark would never forget—a
blue-and-gold banner in honor of the BAA contingent, and another
in orange and black, for the Princetonians. Where in the blazes had
they come from?

There was cause for this celebration. The arrival of the American team instantly transformed the Olympic Games into a nearly
global event. No longer were the Games a collection of Europeans,
but rather an event that went a long way toward fulfilling Baron de
Coubertin's vision of worldwide sport.

But the Greek hosts were just warming up. Pushing their way to the front of the crowd were a committee of men, dressed formally in frock coats and tall hats, who intercepted the Americans as they were about to leave the station. Several of the men in frock coats gently and politely prodded the visitors into a single line with one band in front and the other trailing and marched them toward a mystery ceremony of some kind. "We found ourselves engulfed, marched away—we knew not whither—and the quiet of the hotel became a distant dream," Clark said.

No one in the Greek welcoming party spoke English, and only a few of the American contingent spoke more than a pidgin version of Greek. But eager to be liked and not having much of a choice anyway, the Americans went with the flow, basking in the attention of the crowd and curious about what came next. Soon, they were in City Hall, where athletes from the other dozen or so nations competing in the Olympic Games were already seated. People made speeches—in Greek—with white wine passed around and toast after toast made to the contestants' health.

Sitting together, Connolly, Burke, Blake, and Hoyt hesitated at their host's insistence on the ceremonial drinks. The four Americans were teetotalers, at least until the end of the Olympic Games, and found themselves risking a diplomatic dilemma should they not imbibe. Amidst the wide-scale toasting, it wasn't until the German team stood up, and facing the Americans with glasses held high, gave three loud "Hochs!" followed by "Amerikansiche!" and drained their mugs that the Americans acted decisively.

"The honor of our country demanded that something be done *now*," recalled Connolly. So filling their mugs and giving the Germans a series of "Rahs!" and an accompanying Salut, they raised and swallowed their beer. Any potential international diplomatic incidents had been averted.

The festive welcome amused and befuddled the Americans. And as with Curtis's encounter with the Greek runner on the boat, it revealed that they knew more about training than many of their European competitors—or at least took it more seriously. Everyone seemed to be knocking back drinks without a worry in the world. "The idea that this form of reception was perhaps not the best thing for athletic training never seemed to occur to the local authorities," said Curtis. The attitude puzzled Clark, as well: "Our hosts scarcely understood," he said. "'Training? What did that signify? A strange word. Come have a glass of wine to pledge friendship. No? Very well then, so be it. Strange people, these Americans!' Yet they forgave us courteously enough; we had a welcome of the finest."

Close to 9:00 p.m., the Americans were finally able to duck away. Herded back into line, they wended their way through the still-crowded streets, accompanied by the two bands, and marched to the Hotel D'Angleterre, their quarters for the next two weeks. After dinner, they finally had an opportunity to relax. Yet, still giddy with excitement, most were unable to bed down until about 1:00 a.m.

The sounds of the bands and the cheering crowd still lingering in their heads, Connolly, Tom Burke, and Tom Barry wouldn't fall asleep until 2:00 a.m. In the aftermath of their long journey, how encouraging it would have been to report that the Americans enjoyed a restful few nights heading into the start of competition. At least they had Sunday—and spent a relaxing day seeing Athens for the first time and working out at the Olympic Stadium. But any sense of quiet vanished promptly at 4:00 a.m. Monday when a burst of martial music from the street jolted the Americans awake. So they got up, figuring any hope of more sleep had been dashed. With the Hotel D'Angleterre across the square from the Royal Palace, marching bands were a fact of life for hotel guests.

Taking their time, the Americans shaved, washed, and had a leisurely breakfast. Shortly before noon, they piled into a fleet of low-built cabs and threaded their way through streets clogged with spectators as they headed to the stadium for the scheduled 2:00 p.m. start of the Olympic festivities. Hopping aboard was the intrepid Burton Holmes, box camera at the ready and quick with first impressions. Driving through the streets, "we are at the same time surprised and disappointed," Holmes said, "surprised to find the handsome shops, clean pavements, fresh facades; disappointed to observe that no reminders of the past are visible and the inhabitants are dressed like those of any European city."

Holmes should not have been so disappointed. Several centuries separated modern Greece from its heyday of antiquity, and Athens in the spring of 1896 was a thriving city of 123,000, packed with merchants, small manufacturers, and public servants. Once and forever Greece's largest city and national capital, Athens in the late 19th century was experiencing modest industrial development, particularly in the port of Pirareus, to the south at Metaxourgio and north toward Neapopoli and Exarchin. Yet reminders of its glorious past were everywhere in Athens, including the crumbling steps of the Parthenon and other relics from long ago.

Holmes was mostly interested in capturing modern Athens anyway, creating a snapshot in time that still honored the many reminders of antiquity. Little escaped his attention, from the open-air cafe below the windows of his room at the Hotel D'Angleterre to the "coquettish little tram-cars . . . drawn like playthings across the public square by tiny horses, big enough for toys." The Athenian bootblacks seemingly positioned "at every corner in every square" fascinated him.

"Judging from the magnificence of their outfits [or kits], they must do a thriving business," he wrote. To be sure, those elaborate bootblack kits were a thing of wonder, jammed with blacking, polish, oils, and dressings—enough, he said, "to treat every existing kind of leather from delicate patent-leather to a piece of Attic beefsteak."

Holmes took to Athenian cafe society. There, he wrote, "sipping coffee and cracking pistachio-nuts, we observe the passers-by with interest." He found the men as a rule dressed as most would in any land—"that is, badly . . . in the most convenient and hideous garb ever devised." He praised Athenian women in their imitation of the latest fashions from Paris, for dressing well. But Athens's snazziest dressers, Holmes thought, were the "Evzonoi"—the dazzling Greek military officers, "a delight to the eye" in their handsome red fezzes with distinctive blue tassels, embroidered jackets, and fustanellas with big pleats. Even their feet were memorable, adorned in red leather shoes or tsarukias with red tufts on turned-up toes—shined, most likely, by an Athenian bootback.

Holmes's photographs would be widely circulated and published—and represent a sizable chunk of the slightly fewer than 100 or so surviving shots of the Games in Athens. Seven photographers—Holmes, five Greeks, and a German—are known to have worked the first Olympics, the most notable being Albert Meyer, a 39-year-old Dresden native who took more than half of the extant photographs. Unlike Holmes, Meyer was already well established at the time, with more than a dozen assistants and three thriving studios, including one in the well-to-do Potsdamer Strasse section of central Berlin. Accompanied by his wife, Elizabeth, Meyer had sailed to Athens with the German team, and like Holmes, was a busy man at the Games, easily recognizable in and around the Olympic venues as he lugged his bulky, "box-studio" studio and travel cameras, essential tools of the trade in the days prior to motion-friendly, light-weight, handheld cameras.

Meyer's work in Athens lives on mostly because he stuck to sports—not travelogues. With the equipment years away from being able to capture more than blurry "action" shots, Meyer made the most of circumstances and churned out a series of memorable photographs, including the first known shot of Olympic competition—sprinters poised for the gun in the heats of the 100 Meters on the morning of day one. In the following week, Meyer took other shots, some "action" and some posed, of gymnasts, cyclists, the marathoner Spiridon Louis in a Greek army uniform, and even a high-jumper in "mid-jump." Also, he utilized classical features of the Olympic stadium as back-drops to memorable individual shots of Connolly, Clark, and Curtis, each gripping an American flag; and group portraits of the US team's Princeton and Boston contingents.

But for all his success in Athens and the multiple awards he earned at international exhibitions during a long career, Meyer's later years would be difficult, beset with personal tragedy and financial tra-vails. His son, a soldier, was killed in World War I. Then, in 1923, Meyer lost everything in Germany's postwar depression. The next year, the first great Olympic photographer died, impoverished at 67.

Thomas Curtis's initial impression of Athens, the celebrated city of antiquity, was comprehensive and matter-of-fact. "A small city built of very white houses with white streets," he called it. But his feelings would turn to awe as the Americans made their way through the cramped streets to the stadium for the start of the Games. Athens was in full-throttle festival mode, the streets jammed with people, bands everywhere and thousands of colorful flags fluttering from lampposts in the cool, overcast breeze of early spring. Businesses and stores, meantime, were shut tight, with seemingly all of Greece out and about, and many of the men donning native finery: puffed-out, white-frilled shirts, full-length tight-fitting white woolen drawers, and black velvet coats that stopped just short of the waistline.

The Greeks had been celebrating for several days. The streets of Athens had been filled evenings since Good Friday with processions of various parishes, making it slow going for pedestrians. Priests led the majority of the processions, trailed by candle-toting men, women, and children, many of them singing and chanting, and assorted collections of bands and choirs. Watching the lines of the devout from a balcony at the Hotel D'Angleterre, the American writer Maynard Butler was startled to see Queen Olga, clad in black, walking incognito amidst the crush, leaning on the arm of her relative, the Grand Duke Georgius of Russia, betrothed to Princess Marie. "The perfect simplicity and evident unconsciousness of the act quite won one's heart," Butler wrote.

All that Saturday, shops had remained shut tight and church bells tolled at regular intervals. Though it rained a good portion of Easter Sunday, Athenians donned their best clothes to attend mass and then take in another religious parade or two before returning home for the traditional holiday meal of lamb. The pomp was multiplied because the Greek and Roman Easters fell on the same day in 1896. In addition to Easter, generally the happiest and perhaps most important part of the Orthodox calendar, the Greeks were celebrating the eve of the 75th anniversary of national independence.

The Olympic organizers had planned well in this regard—matching the Games' start to Independence Day to take advantage of what had become a true explosion of nationalistic pride. On Easter Sunday, organizers held a ceremonial unveiling of a statue at the stadium plaza. The work portrayed the Games' biggest benefactor, the Greek philanthropist George Averoff. Doctors had forbade the frail 82-year-old Averoff from attending the ceremony, but it drew quite a crowd that not even a steady afternoon downpour held back. The leaders of the city's two major Christian faiths, the bearded Metropolitan of Athens in his black robes and Père Didon in the white robes of the Dominicans, were there. And so were members of parliament, foreign officials, Baron Pierre de Coubertin, and members of the IOC. Many trade union members were there too, accompanied by more bands. Then Crown Prince Constantine pulled the canvas off the statue, and everyone trudged home, soggy but satisfied.

Still, it wasn't until Monday, as their carriage drew close to the stadium amidst the ever-thickening throngs, that the true pageantry of this historic international event dawned on the Americans. "Up to this very moment, we had not the slightest idea of what the Games meant to Greece," Clark said. "We did not know whether the huge stadium would contain 1,000 spectators or 10,000. Yet, as we drove through the city, slowly the magnitude of the whole affair began to dawn upon us."

One look at the enormous horseshoe-shaped stadium was all the Americans would need to convince them of the magnitude of the event. Nearing the long, sharply proportioned structure of pure white marble that rose over the ruins of the Stadium of Herodis, built in 330 BC, on the very spot that the ancient Olympians had competed, all those drafty indoor New England and New Jersey gyms suddenly seemed far, far away. The Americans had never seen anything remotely like it. "This stupendous structure should number among the 'wonders of the world,'" a dazzled Tyler said. A line of soldiers held up the vehicles 200 yards from the stadium, allowing only the athletes to drive to the entrance.

Averoff had spared little expense in building the stadium, the finest and largest in the world. The architects had done quite a job, fashioning row upon row of easily accessible seats into a kind of natural amphitheater. The stadium came together in all of 18 months, and had enough architectural flourishes to evoke the glories of the ancients: Chiseled mostly from marble, the structure was dotted with reproductions of statues and columns of ancient heroes, and stands with orderly rows of wooden benches that from the middle of the stadium floor seemed to rise to the sky. Circling the infield was the cinder, oval track—and within the track were various "stops" or areas for gymnastics and field events like Shot Put, Triple Jump, High Jump, and Long Jump. And to think the stadium wasn't completely finished, with painted wood substituted in a few places for marble, and still a few of the antique decorations, statues, and columns to be put in place. When that happened, pondered a delighted Pierre de Coubertin, "Athens will in truth possess the temple of athletic sports."

Heading into the tunnel that led to the locker room, the athletes took advantage of accoutrements worthy of a modern-day, big-league baseball clubhouse: a refreshment booth with food and drink for the athletes on request, a score of attendants, lots of clean towels, and a big bathroom with silver-mounted plumbing. The locker room was actually a series of small open dressing rooms surrounding a graveled oblong court where the athletes could warm up. It was there that the Americans encountered another curious sign that some athletes were more interested in libation than competition—the sight of two German wrestlers, who in seeing the Americans, raised large tankards of beer and saluted them with a guttural "Hoch!"

All morning, carriages had delivered Athenians to the Stadium. Advance ticket sales had been practically nil, but catching the Olympic bug late, city dwellers swamped the ticket vendors who had dotted the surrounding streets throughout the morning. It was more orderly inside the stadium where assigned seats were marked by section and row. Prices were reasonable—one drachma to sit in the upper section and two for the lower sections close to the field. Some 30,000 others, including a boisterous contingent of US sailors from the USS *San Francisco*, peppered the surrounding hills, content to watch from afar.

Those lucky enough to be there would never forget the panorama of the start of the modern Olympic Games. The big stadium was filled to the rafters, all 60,000 or so of the seats occupied. Many were still dressed in their Sunday finest, just like Easter, and there were sailors in uniform and lots of soldiers with medals pinned to their chests. Countless others donned native costumes with stylish red fezzes adorned with tassels. Flags of most of the 13 competing nations flapped in the wind, as nearly 250 athletes from Greece, the United States, Austria, Bulgaria, Chile, Denmark, Germany, France, Great Britain, Italy, Sweden, Switzerland, and Hungary gathered in the center of the track. Notably absent was anyone from Holland, which hadn't sent a team because the country's strict code of amateurism required its athletes to pay their own way. In some cases, the athletes came from nations that were not represented in the ceremony—the Australian, Edwin Flack, for instance, was living in London and competed for Great Britain (Australia wouldn't became a commonwealth until 1901); while tennis player Dionysios Kasdaglis represented Egypt. The stands were full, and the infield had drawn a throng as well. The gathered athletes were joined by a 200-piece group of classical musicians and a choir of 300, performing under the direction of Greek composer Spiro Samaras his majestic "Overture to the Olympic Games." Created for the occasion, the Overture's music and words were an elegant mix of modern and ancient; to this day, it is a constant at Olympic opening ceremonies. "Immortal spirit of antiquity—father of the true beautiful and good—descend, appear, shed over us thy light upon this ground and under this sky which has first witnessed the imperishable flame," the chorus sang. "Give life and animation to those noble games! Throw wreaths of fadeless flowers to the victors in the race and in the strife!"

Stirred by the tribute and the many references to Greek antiquity, the crowd stood and cheered. Remaining on their feet, they peered toward the field as though they were expecting somebody. Just before 2:00 p.m., the Greek royal family came through the main gate and onto the stadium infield. Perfectly choreographed and trailed by a procession of family members, ministers, senior military officers, and bureaucrats, they climbed into the box they were to occupy for a good chunk of the next two weeks, with the queen and king seated on cushions of red velvet. Headed to the center of the infield was Crown Prince Constantine, who belted out a speech that few could hear. Then the king arose from his box and announced in a voice that was unmistakable: "I hereby proclaim the opening of the First International Games in Athens!" Everyone stood for the Greek National Anthem, after which a loud bugle call heralded the start of competition. The Games were off to a rousing start.

For the athletes, everything began moving with increasing speed. As the track was cleared of people, they heard the call for heats of the 100 Meters, which meant the start of competition for Tom Burke, Thomas Curtis, and Francis Lane, all in different heats. Moments later, on cue from the bugler, the three American sprinters—clad in spiked shoes and light, sleeveless shirts—headed out to face competition they had never seen and knew virtually nothing about.

The six-lane track was soft by American standards, mostly likely from lack of use. That would account for the relatively slow times of the athletes throughout the Games. The track also had extra-long straightaways, narrowing the infield and making the turns so sharp that they felt like right angles. For the Americans running events of 400 meters and up, there was an additional challenge: races were run clockwise or European style, the opposite from US tracks. But one of the most striking aspects of day one at the Olympic Games for the American sprinters was their first look at the starting positions of their twenty-one European competitors. In the days before starting blocks, they presented quite a contrast to the Americans' classic, hunkered, heads-up position with both hands on the track, similar to the universally accepted posture of today. The Europeans had nearly as many postures as athletes; some stood, others crouched.

Angling into position for his heat, Curtis peered at the next lane and spotted a familiar face—Lagoudaki, the confident Greek student he had met on the boat to Patras. While noting that Lagoudaki was using a standing start, Curtis saw that he was wearing something unusual—a pair of white gloves. Later, he explained it was "because I . . . run before the King." The Greek runner was serious—later in the week, he would don his gloves again in the marathon.

The pistol cracked and Curtis leapt into the lead, staying there and easily taking the heat. Lane won his heat as well, despite his weakness from the lingering effects of seasickness. So did Burke, whose finishing time of 12.0 seconds was tops for the day, about a fifth of a second faster than his American teammates, establishing him as the immediate favorite in Friday's final. Three heats had generated three victories for the Americans. Finishing far—*really far!*—off the pace was the overmatched Lagoudaki, some 40 yards behind Curtis but forever brimming with confidence, companionship, and unusual theories. Finding fellow marathoner Arthur Blake, he confided that his footwear (which was white, like his gloves) had accounted for his lagging behind the American sprinters in their spikes. "These shoes have no nails in them," he told Blake, pointing to his own feet. "Your shoes make you go fast, my shoes are like glue. If you and I will be close in the marathon, we will finish hand in hand and show that the Americans and the Greeks are good friends."

After each heat, the Greek organizers had added an unexpected flourish of ceremony, soon to become a standard of the Olympic medal awards. To honor the victor, the flag of his country was hoisted to the top of the flagpole at the stadium entrance, with the winning time or distance posted on a nearby chart visible to all corners of the stadium. The prompt posting of results is routine at track meets today, but it was radical for the 19th century and very much appreciated. "The Committee in charge of the Games deserve to be greatly commended for the prompt and excellent manner in which the events were carried off," said Tyler. "The long delays [at US collegiate meets], which are so tiresome to the audience and trying to the athlete, did not have to be endured."

In the coming days, the American flag scooting up to the top of the pole would become a common sight. And just like that, the American athletes who had left Hoboken more focused on representing their clubs or universities had become *American* winners, suddenly aware that *country* came first at the Olympic Games. Assigned to a box, perhaps 50 feet from the royal box, the other American athletes cheered and whooped as their sprinter teammates beat all comers, stirred at the site of the American flag fluttering in the breeze. Springing to their feet, they gave Lane a Princeton cheer, and a few moments later, yelled with gusto the Boston Athletic Association cheer—"BAA—Rah, rah, rah! BAA—Rah, rah, rah! BAA—Rah, rah, rah! Curtis! BAA—Rah, rah, rah . . . Burke!" But with their impromptu celebrations, heads turned. "What *is* this?" many of the crowd seemed to be saying, "this odd kind of war cry emitting from the Americans?" What the Americans quickly and delightfully realized is that loud and somewhat organized demonstrations of fandom were unknown to the Greek crowd, who presumably had never attended baseball games at the Polo Grounds.

For a few moments, the stadium grew so quiet that the Americans thought they might have violated international etiquette. Hardly. In fact, the Greeks were absorbing this American war-cry, and captivated, they were only trying to figure out how to match this strange sound. "Then, all at once, they seemed to grasp the meaning of our effort," said Clark. "We had, by good fortune, chanced to please the popular taste. Their efforts to join us produced a composite discord of sound such as I never heard before," said Clark, "and surely never expect to hear again."

From that moment until the Americans left Athens, their cheers would be in constant demand inside the stadium and all around Athens. The rest of the day, eager-to-learn fellow spectators attempted to match the Americans' "BAA—Rah, rah, rah!"s though their initial efforts came out more as "B-ah-alis!" Even the king was transfixed, and at one point during the afternoon when the Americans had not sounded a "BAA—Rah, rah, rah!" for an hour or so, a special aide to the king was dispatched to the Americans with a royal request. Touching his hat in greeting, the aide said in a solemn voice that His Majesty requested "once more, you will make . . . that peculiar noise?" They would be honored, responded the bemused Americans. So their next effort was a particularly rousing version of "BAA—Rah, rah, rah!" to which the king stood, and looking their way, touched his cap in acknowledgment.

Amidst the canopy of sound rolling around the stadium at the end of the 100-Meter heats, the bugler appeared and announced the next event, a final. It was the Triple Jump, James Connolly's specialty. He would be the last of 10 competitors and the only American to participate.

Overshadowed by its athletic cousin, the more-glamorous long jump, the triple jump dates to ancient times. The event was likely a part of the ancient Games, though it was recorded as long jump. Historians conclude there had to have been a form of triple jump—or some series of jumps—because there were recorded distances of more than 50 feet. The triple jump again received its due when in the 12th century the Irish "Book of Leinster" described the *geal-ruith*—Gaelic for triple jump—as part of the Tailteann Games held at Telltown, County Meath from 1829 BC until at least 554 BC.

The early Irish involvement in the event must have appealed to Connolly. A triple-jumper since his days competing in the Hibernian and Caledonian Games around Boston, he had grown up using the event's traditional style of taking two hops and a jump, which emphasized spring and rhythm. But at the insistence of US track officials, American athletes had been required to adopt the more modern hop, step, and jump, built for the kind of speed used by long-jumpers. Connolly regretted the change, sorely missing the hop, hop, and jump technique of his youth. "I was marked by spring rather than speed," he said. "For rhythm, meaning timing, the fellows back home had it that timing was the best part of my hop, step, and jump."

But Connolly had caught an unexpected break in Athens: European judges were permitting the jumpers to use either technique. Competing last would be another break, giving Connolly a chance to size up his competition and think about which technique would serve him best. Watching carefully, he took stock of each of his nine opponents: Only three used the modern hop, step, and jump, while the other six resorted to the more traditional "hop, hop, jump" approach. Thinking fast, the American decided to go with his strength after all—two hops and a jump. It was risky—Connolly hadn't jumped that way in competition for several years. But he would stick with his gut.

There were still a couple of other challenges. Officials had prohibited the athletes from taking a measured run, forcing Connolly and others to take a guess at the proper length of their takeoffs. And in contrast to most other events, the final distances would not be posted until each athlete had taken his allotted two jumps.

Meanwhile, it wasn't difficult for Connolly to quickly figure out his stiffest competition: That would be Alexandre Tuffère, a Frenchman living in Athens, and the class of the other nine with a distance of 41 feet, 8 inches. So jogging up the runway, Connolly threw his cap off to the side in the grass to mark the spot where Tuffère had taken off.

Some in the crowd objected to the American's measurement technique and what they perceived as arrogance. An article, filed by *Boston Herald* reporter Beverly Cronin, told a more fanciful tale, almost certainly apocryphal. According to Cronin, Connolly walked up to the line in front of Prince George of England and Prince George of Greece, acting as chief judges for the event, and hurled his cap down, yelling in a fit of emotion, that "Here's one for Old Galway!" The story went over fantastically back in Boston, but was probably fictitious since Connolly's memoirs tell the story of the Triple Jump but never mention any such thing. Though George of Greece was chief judge for the event, Prince George of England was not, and did not even attend the Athens Olympics.

A more likely explanation is that Connolly put his cap—some say it was a sweater—as a takeoff marker because he was nearsighted. The gesture still nearly touched off an international incident when Prince George of Greece, acting in his role as referee and perhaps responding to jeering from the crowd, kicked the cap aside. Up jumped Bill Hoyt, the American pole-vaulter turned peacemaker, who tapped the prince on the arm and explained that Connolly needed the cap as a marker because of his poor vision. That got the crowd really riled. Who was Hoyt to challenge the prince?—though poor Hoyt thought he was dealing with a track official and had no idea he was challenging royalty. Into a brimming controversy stepped a nearby American spectator, the Greek-speaking Cornell professor Benjamin Ide Wheeler. Recognizing what had happened, Wheeler briskly and gingerly descended the stadium steps to the infield, collared Hoyt, and introduced him to the prince-turned-referee. Hoyt quickly apologized, later explaining he had mistaken the prince, in his admiral's uniform, for a policeman.

Score one for the prince. Deftly grasping the situation, he acknowledged no hard feelings and ruled that yes, Connolly, presumably because of his nearsightedness, could use his cap to mark the spot where he needed to plant his lead foot in starting his jump. Finally exonerated, Connolly squeezed his lucky rabbit's foot, given to him back in Boston by a friend, Jim Murphy. Then he headed to the top of the runway, took a look around and absorbed the extraordinary tableaux of humanity gathered for the first Olympic final of modern times. "I looked up and around," he said. "There was color aplenty in the stadium and on the hill slope outside . . . [including on] the highest slope . . . [against] a patch of blue sky . . . a man's head and shoulders . . . outlined. Just that one man. He stood balanced there by himself on the very pinnacle of the hill."

Almost ready to start his approach, Connolly checked carefully to make sure his shoelaces were tied—and not, as a Greek journalist would write, "bow[ing] his head in a short American prayer for success." Then he breathed on his hands, rubbed them dry on his jersey and took off, steaming down the runway. As close to his cap as he could, Connolly hit the takeoff perfectly, stretched with his hop, stepped, and then straining with all his power, sailed to an unblemished part of the pit, well beyond where the others had landed. Connolly had nailed it. It had taken all of a few brief seconds, but it was a big moment. Spectators leapt to their feet in excitement. "It's a miracle!" one yelled. "A miracle!"

Connolly had a feeling his jump had been a good one, but wanted to know just how far he had gone. Turning to a track coach of the London Athletic Club, a man named Perry, who was smoothing the earth in the pit between jumps, he made his appeal. "They ought to tell how far each man jumps," pleaded Connolly, the Irishman to the Englishman who could have been an Irishman. "Then a fellow won't be breaking his back when there's no need of it."

Perry saw the logic. "As far as you're concerned, you can go on back to your dressing room and take your bath," he said. "You have this event in your pocket right now." Connolly had jumped 44 feet, 11¾ inches, which was more than three feet beyond Tuffère's effort. No one else, including two Greeks, had come anywhere near his jump and wouldn't on their second jumps either. Perry was right. With a single, supreme effort, Connolly had erased the need to even make another jump. It was enough, and just like that, James Brendan Connolly, who could no longer run for his college track team, had become the first Olympic champion since a boxer named Barasdates of Armenia in AD 369. Finishing second was Tuffère, and crowd favorite Ionnis Persakis of Greece was third. The judges conferred and left it to Prince George, who spoke English, to officially break the good news to Connolly. "You are the victor," the prince told him. "You have beaten the second man by a meter."

Connolly was pulling his sweater and trousers over his track uniform when the final results were posted just as Spiro Samaras's 200-piece band boomed into action. Snapping to half-dressed attention, Connolly peered high above the stadium into the hills and noticed the crew of the USS *San Francisco* standing in rapt attention, as were the 60,000 spectators inside the stadium.

It took another moment until Connolly realized what the orchestra was playing. "The Star-Spangled Banner" played as two Greek soldiers in blue jackets hoisted the American flag to the top of the flagpole. Then it was another fraction of a second before it dawned on him that the ceremony, the flag raising and the National Anthem, was *for him*—the skinny kid from South Boston who had accomplished something no one else had in 1,527 years. "You're the first Olympic victor in 1,500 years," Connolly said to himself. "The gang back home will be tickled when they hear of it!"

Connolly and the other Olympic victors would earn silver medals for these Games, not gold. Though Coubertin had lobbied for gold, silver, and bronze medals for the first-through-third-place finishers as would happen in future Games, Crown Prince Constantine had overruled him in Athens. With gold coins the standard currency at the time in many nations, Constantine reasoned that gold medals would make it seem that athletes were being paid. So for these Games, a handsome *silver* medal designed by the celebrated Parisian sculptor and medal engraver Jules-Clement Chaplain would go to the victors. Chaplain drew on the classics for his design: On one side was the laurelled head of Zeus, holding a globe on top of which was a winged Victory clutching a laurel branch; on the other was a view of the Acropolis and the Parthenon. The king himself would present victors with their medals, along with diplomas contained in sizable pasteboard rolls and, just like the ancients, a branch of olive from the sacred-grove of Olympia, in a ceremony after the Games.

But the attention had only just started for the modern Games' first champion. The anthem finished, Connolly shook hands with his competitors and headed to the tunnel toward the locker room. A handsomely dressed man in the first row of the stadium got his attention and waved his program at him in an informal salute. Next to him sat a woman in white gloves who waved, too. Connolly waved back—to the king and queen, he later learned.

"I went floating—not walking—across the stadium arena on waves of what sounded like a million voices and two million hands cheering and applauding," Connolly said. At the tunnel entrance, a half-dozen bearded Greeks grabbed him, offering their form of congratulations—one after another, kissing him on both cheeks. Then five of the six beckoned him to stick around while they sketched him. Too excited to oblige, Connolly was offered wine by the man at the refreshment booth—thanks but no—and dipped into the locker room and showered. Afterwards, two attendants with 12-foot towels helped dry him off, crying "Nike! Nike! Victor, Victor!" the whole time. Dressing, Connolly thought to himself: *Am I glad I made this voyage! And you are lucky! Supposin' you missed that train to Brindisi!*

CHAPTER 3

The Baron

TAKING IN THE SPONTANEOUS CELEBRATION ACCOMPANYING JAMES Connolly's victory, Baron Pierre de Coubertin couldn't have been more pleased. The canopy of noise was the achievement to which the slight, 36-year-old French nobleman had dedicated his life.

In photos, Coubertin is unsmiling, his face dominated by a magnificent mustache that, when carefully combed, extended perhaps a half-foot in each direction, well beyond his ears. "A whiskered cat destined for a long life," Olympic historian Richard Mandel wrote of him. Best to look beyond the mustache into the baron's eyes. "Dazzling and aggressive," Mandell noted, "they were the eyes of a man continually gauging the possibility for action, assessing the nature of the present in order subtly to form the future."

Little in Coubertin's background marked him as his era's crusading sportsman. Born in Paris, Charles-Pierre Frédy de Coubertin was the fourth child of wealthy parents with a noble lineage. Growing up in a home crowded with works of art and shelves filled with leather-bound books, the young baron rode horses from the family stable and accompanied his family each year to Rome in a horse-drawn coach. Coubertin took great pride in his ancestry, men who had served France for generations as army officers, lawyers, and judges. His father, Charles, was a painter of moderate success, and his mother, a musician dedicated to good works. Both parents were passionate Royalists, still mourning the departure of the Bourbons and despondent over France's humiliating defeat in the 1870 Franco-Prussian War. Honoring the birthday of the Bourbon claimant to the French throne, the exiled Henry V, known as the Count of Chambord, the family, including a 16-year-old Pierre, trekked in 1879 to Austria. There, they met the aging count, who at the time had been in exile for a half-century.

A Jesuit education at the Collège Saint-Ignace in Paris gave Coubertin grounding in ancient history and in particular a lifelong admiration of the classical Greeks. Adhering to the Greek belief of the balance of mind and body, Coubertin boxed, rode horses, and rowed in school, becoming a passionate sportsman. Destined to study law, the baron did so half-heartedly, and found himself caught up by current events and a growing belief that educational reform was the key to restoring French pride. He soaked up the writings of Locke, Darwin, Mill, and Rousseau. At 20, the young aristocrat rebelled against his family's belief in the traditional order of things by thoroughly absorbing and endorsing the aggressive republicanism of leading intellectuals like Léon Gambetta, Sadi Carnot, and Jules Ferry. This was more radical thinking than it may appear, particularly in the baron's willingness to defy the extreme nationalism of the day and look to other European nations as models of reform.

French nationalism manifested itself largely through hostility toward German culture—making the baron a bit of an iconoclast when he suggested that his country would do well to emulate Germany's public educational system. But it was England's educational system that Coubertin admired most of all. The British Empire was perhaps at the peak of its power—admired for its success in foreign policy, its industrial might, its navy, monarchy, and even its fashions, hunting dogs, and racehorses. The more Coubertin studied Britain's resounding domination of the world stage of the late 19th century, the more he was convinced that a strong and vibrant society started with British-style education.

Coubertin's convictions were sealed when he read a remarkable book, *Notes sur l'Angleterre*, by the French historian Hippolyte Taine. Based on research from visits to England in 1859 and 1862, Taine wrote that English students actually worked an average of three hours a day *fewer* in studies than French students, devoting those extra hours instead to exercise. "It is against nature to force him to be all brain, a sedentary bookworm," Taine wrote. "Here [in the public schools], athletic games, fives, football, running, rowing and, above all, cricket, take up a part of every day. . . . Pride plays an important part; each school tries to beat its rivals and sends teams of players and oarsmen, picked out and trained, to play and row against the others."

The baron had found his muse. Taine linked the "ambition and regimen" of British athletes to an embracing of the Greek ideal—one that featured "a special diet [and] abstain[ing] from all excesses of eating and drinking." And he celebrated Thomas Hughes's famous book, *Tom Brown's School Days*, first published in 1857 as *Tom Brown's School Days at Rugby by an Old Boy*, in creating his model. Though Coubertin had read the book years earlier, he eagerly re-read the tale of a young lad at the famous Rugby School during the era of its famous headmaster, Thomas Arnold, as part of his new, consuming interest. Arnold is the model for Hughes's depiction in *School Days* of "The Doctor," Rugby's stern but fatherly and cherished leader of boys.

In 1883, the baron traveled to England for a firsthand look at its educational model. Speaking flawless English and aided by impeccable manners and an insatiable curiosity, Coubertin was cordially received at Oxford and Cambridge, where he drank a lot of wine, made acquaintances, and took notes. Visits to preparatory schools from Tom Brown's Rugby to Eton, Harrow, Wellington, Westminster, and Charterhouse affirmed the baron's admiration of the English model. A generation of young men was being educated as students *and* as citizens, in stark contrast to the decadence or "boredom and weakness" as Coubertin put it, of the French state schools. In Britain, wrote the baron in his 1888 book, *L'Education en Angleterre,* were the roots of "le regime arnoldien," the useful, practical curriculum, which integrated with sports, created the modern ideal of education.

Coubertin cared little that Thomas Arnold, who had been Rugby's headmaster in the 1830s and died in 1847, was no sportsman. As historian Michael Llewellyn Smith notes, free time for Arnold was better spent looking at nature or hiking than rowing and playing cricket. Nor did it matter to the baron that Arnold in his 15 years as headmaster at Rugby was not the father figure as portrayed, except to seniors who helped him discipline the younger boys, or that his relations with the local town were often strained. None of that mattered: Arnold had become Coubertin's spiritual role model.

But for all his lofty ideals, the baron was far from perfect himself. He could be arrogant, choosing to deal with only the men of his class. He overlooked many of the imperfections of English public schools, like flogging. He didn't seem to notice that the kind of educational opportunities he espoused were accessible only to the elite, and that the costs of such an education were far beyond the rank and file. Back in France, he had to confront the predictable criticism that he was an "Anglomaniac." "Well then, we are agreed," the baron countered. "We hate the English and they hate us."

Armed with his rock-solid belief in the English educational system and an ever-widening circle of acquaintances, Coubertin was just warming up. Back home, he became a forceful proponent of balancing academics with sports. "I am convinced that experience will quickly show, better than any arguments, that the true remedy for overwork or rather the effects which we attribute to it does not lie in the weakening and slowing down of studies, but in the counterweight which sport can provide for intellectual fatigue," he wrote. "It is sport which will re-establish the broken equilibrium; it should have a place marked out for it in every educational system."

Coubertin laid out his plan in lectures, at banquets, and in op-ed pieces for influential newspapers. His vision was bigger, much bigger, and much more detailed than building a gym or teaching students to row or fence. Schools needed playing fields and locker rooms, he urged. They should offer several individual and team sports from football (soccer) to tennis and fox hunting, he added. Coubertin even recommended cricket, a sport the French loathed as too "English." Think again, argued the baron: "[Cricket] is a superb game of the greatest interest," he wrote, "demanding discipline and fostering esprit de corps."

Among the baron's lofty suggestions came some wacky ones. He became a proponent of nudism, believing that it was best practiced in hot air baths and in waters scented with "virile" perfumes. "I just cannot understand the pedants who pronounce a sort of excommunication against perfumes in general," he wrote, "and against the so-called 'degenerates' who use them." In a larger sense, Coubertin believed that well-rounded students were a valuable counterweight to the era's preoccupation with vice. The devil could be kept at bay with details, and the baron devoted considerable thought to things like the organization of beds in a boarding school, and the need to lock the dormitory doors from the outside to ensure proper conduct. But the baron insisted that this path of reform was quite separate from advocating military service. "It is not militarism that our education needs," he wrote. "It is freedom."

In the summer of 1889, Coubertin traveled to the United States to absorb the latest thinking on American education and exercise. While compiling his findings in a report for the French Ministry of Education, the baron took seven months to travel about the United States and Canada, nations he described as being "of fantastic contradictions." As he had done in England, Coubertin visited universities and made numerous contacts, making a name for himself next to that of another French traveler in the United States more than six decades before: the social scientist Alexis de Tocqueville, whose 1835 book, *Democracy in America*, is a penetrating portrait of the Jacksonian era. The baron attended a physical education conference in Boston and met Theodore Roosevelt—then the US Civil Service commissioner—and would remain a lifelong admirer of the future president. Squeezing in a trip to Canada enabled him to draw comparisons between the traditional Catholic education system in Montreal and the more modern Toronto.

At some point during the next three years, the Baron embraced the idea of reviving the Olympic Games. Here was a concept that seemed to exemplify much of what he believed in so deeply: a sports festival that fused the spirit of the ancient Greeks with fit young men from around the world competing for honors that would "re-establish the broken equilibrium," as he put it. Fortified by a zealot's passion and a healthy bank account—the baron never really had to work—he was just the man to put the Games in motion. For the time being however, the baron was only the latest in a series of 19th-century dreamers with similar ideas.

It is unclear precisely when and how Coubertin arrived at his Olympic plan. Chances are that he put things together after reading about other periodic festivals throughout the 19th century that incorporated aspects of the ancient Games, sometimes even being called the "Olympics." One of the most prominent mid-century Olympic-style annual festivals was the invention of an Englishman. William Penny Brookes resided in the rolling countryside of Shropshire in central Great Britain near Wales, the same area A. E. Housman celebrated in a series of poems, *A Shropshire Lad*. A photo of Brookes in middle age at one of his sports festivals reveals a bearded, hefty gent leaning on a cane, donning a top hat and a frock jacket pinned with medals. Brookes had the look and bearing of a retired military hero, but he wasn't: Born in 1809 in the village of Wenlock, Brookes was the son of a physician, who became one himself, assuming the practice when his father died. Brookes became a community pillar in Wenlock, serving for a time as justice of the peace and commissioner of roads and taxes. Throwing himself into good works to benefit working men, he founded a reading room for farmers and agricultural laborers, and in 1850, established the "Wenlock Olympian Class" for the "moral and physical improvement" of the locals.

Brookes's Games were based on his belief in the benefits of exercise and a vague, romantic idealization of ancient Greece. The annual Wenlock Games flourished. There was track and field, just as in the original Games, but competitors also partook of more contemporary mid-19th-century games like soccer, cricket, quoits, and "tilting of the ring" with cash prizes awarded to the winners. There were children's events ranging from spelling bees to art, reading, and knitting, and all the traditional marks of an English country fair filled with the requisite eating, drinking, music, and games of chance. What distinguished the Wenlock Games was its embrace of many of the symbols of the ancient Olympians. To the victor of Brookes's favorite event, the tilting of the ring in which a galloping, mounted horseman speared a narrow ring with his lance, went a crown of laurel, bestowed by a young maiden. Brookes added other medieval and ancient flourishes like jousting and using a herald to make announcements.

Then, in the mid-1850s, a prosperous Greek businessman named Evangelis Zappas proposed *his* Olympics—one that would stick to his country's past glories by staging events on the very spot his forbearers had staged theirs. Zappas was a stickler for tradition—looking to sprinkle the competition with events from centuries past, like track and field, wrestling, horse races, and quoits. And he looked to do it by adopting a four-year cycle, just like the ancients. Inspired by Zappas's efforts, Brookes became an admirer of the Greek games, so much so that the Englishman passed along via the British ambassador in Greece several program suggestions and 10 pounds for a prize to the tilting winner.

Zappas had quite the resume, having served in northwest Greece and southern Albania as an officer in the Greek war of independence, and then turning to a lucrative career as a shipping magnate and trader. Viewing an Olympic revival as a way of fulfilling an ardent pride in his Greek heritage, Zappas had formulated his grand plan with the help of poetry of all things. An ardent nationalist, Zappas had been inspired by works in the 1830s of the Greek poet Panayiotis Soutsos, whom historians have come to generally credit as the first serious advocate of mounting a revival based on the ancient Olympic Games.

Soutsos was interested in capitalizing on the Greek victory in their war of independence from the Ottoman Empire in 1822, when after centuries of foreign control, they became an autonomous nation. The growing pains were considerable; years of harsh Turkish rule had left Greece well behind many of its more advanced Western European neighbors, leaving Soutsos and other Greek intellectuals of the era to ponder how to help their struggling nation honor its independence and begin earning the respect of their more modernized neighbors. Writing to Greek minister of the interior John Kolletis, Soutsos proposed that April 6 or March 25 on the Greek calendar be declared a national holiday and feature a big celebration with an Olympic sports festival as its centerpiece.

Kolletis was captivated, and proposed the idea to King Otto. But it would take more than two decades until the wealthy Zappas took up the call. In 1856, Zappas wrote to King Otto offering to foot the bill for an Olympic revival with dividends from the sale of his share in a steamship company. So three years later, in November 1859, Zappas launched *his* Games—not precisely on the site of the ancient stadium, but nearby on Athens's Ludwig Square, now known as Koumoundourou Square. Neither chariot racing or tilting made it into the Zappas Games, but discus, javelin, long jump, and pole climbing did. So did three footraces—one of about 200 meters, another of about 400 meters, and the last one just short of a mile. It was an all-Greek Games with the event winners celebrated throughout the country and well compensated for their efforts. Taking the long race, the *dolichos,* was one Petros Velissariou of Smyrna, who was awarded a prize of 10 pounds, the equivalent of 281 drachmas. King Otto's portrait adorned the medals.

Poor King Otto wasn't to last, exiled from Greece in 1862 and replaced by a more stable ruler, George of Denmark. Zappas didn't last either—he died in 1865. But his Olympic Games lived on, as did Brookes and the English Games—creating for a time what were essentially dueling Olympics, each one open to its own nation's citizens only. In 1866, with Brookes serving as president of the organizing committee, Britain hosted its Olympic Games at the famous Crystal Palace indoor area in London. Taking the 400-meter hurdles was an 18-year-old future doctor named William Gilbert Grace.

Better known as "WG" Grace, he wouldn't practice much doctoring or much more hurdling for that matter; instead, he would become Britain's version of Babe Ruth, his country's greatest cricketer.

Not until 1870 was there a second Zappas Games—this time held on the actual site of the ancient Games in a stadium built of wooden bleachers. Athletes turned up from all parts of the Greek world, thanks to the organizers who footed the bill for those who couldn't afford passage to Athens. The policy was a revelation, democratizing the Games and helping a manual laborer from Crete win the wrestling championship and an extremely fast butcher take the 200 meters. Most everyone liked these more open Games, according to Olympic historian David Young, except for a few influential university professors. The professors were elitists—believing that the presence of working-class athletes diminished the Games. Their collective funk was enough to limit the next Greek Games, in 1875, to university students—killing off much of the interest and essentially sweeping the Zappas Games into the dustbin of history.

But the impact of the Zappas Games endured, serving as a critical step in the evolution of the modern Olympic movement. Zappas demonstrated that there was a future in the concept of a nationwide sports festival—if anything for the buildings it produced. One of the venues of the 1875 Games served as the Olympic fencing venue at the 1896 Games: Today, the so-called Zappeion remains a big-event conference center in the heart of Athens, having served as the site of the European Council during Greece's first Presidency of the European Union, and the first home of the 2004 Greek (Olympic) Organizing Committee.

After Zappas's death, a committee was formed to manage his Olympic legacy. Chaired by future prime minister Stephanos Dragoumis, the committee reestablished the four-year Olympic cycle of ancient days. But after the 1875 Games, the reality was that neither Dragoumis nor Greek prime minister Harilaos Tricoupis nor many committee members were truly committed to the idea of a giant sports festival. The Zappas Games were simply "too early" in the words of Olympic historian Michael Llewellyn Smith. Drawing on the Hellenic model, the Games and its focus on the ancient Greek model were not the intelligentsia's most effective way of connecting to the West. National progress, Greek leaders believed, would be achieved through commerce and science—not sport. It would take the more modern Olympic concept, one connected to an international cast and led by a charismatic pan-European, to create a revival that would last. Just such a leader was the French Baron Pierre de Coubertin.

CHAPTER 4

"All Were Stupefied"

THE CROWD IN THE OLYMPIC STADIUM WAS STILL BUZZING ABOUT the triple-jump triumph of James Connolly, but Robert Garrett stayed calm. Princeton's reserved, long-faced track captain kept mostly to himself as he focused on the Games' next event, the Discus, another final and perhaps the crowd's most anticipated event of the afternoon. So quiet that he practically escaped attention, Garrett was about to do something truly astonishing.

The Discus was the pride of Greek athletics, an event with roots in the ancient Games and commemorated by classical depictions of nude young men preparing to launch the "disc." Most famous was the British Museum's *Townley Discobolus*, a Roman marble copy of Myron's lost Greek bronze original. *Townley Discobolus* had been discovered in 1781 on the property of the Massimo family on Rome's Esquiline Hill. It was restored by the family and placed at their residence in Palazzo Lancelotti. Italian archaeologist Carlo Fea then identified the sculpture as a copy of the original, completed during the height of the Greek classical period between 460 and 450 BC. Today it is named for the British collector Charles Townley, who eventually acquired the statue and in 1805 sent his collection of marbles to the British Museum.

Myron's *Discobolus* is magnificent—a study of grace and athleticism. The figure's head is down, knees bent and body coiled, preparing to unleash a throw. Classicists consider it a masterpiece of the ancient Olympic ideal of rhythm, harmony, and balance. But for all the attention lavished on the discus by the ancient Romans and in Greece, the event was virtually unknown outside those countries. Neither Princeton, Harvard, nor any other university in the United States or any other non-Greek country for that matter included discus at track meets, practiced the event, or even knew anything about it beyond the impressive statues in museums. But that hadn't stopped Garrett from an abiding curiosity in the discus and his decision to give it a try in Athens. Raised in considerable wealth in Baltimore, Garrett took an extended trip through Europe and the Middle East as a boy. At that time, he developed an abiding passion for classical studies and the glories of the ancient times, to which the discus was an intriguing connection.

Strong and sinewy with unusually long arms, the 6'2" Garrett excelled in field events at Princeton. In early 1896 as he and Sloane worked to recruit a team of fellow Princetonians to compete in Athens, Garrett was filling the Olympic entry form—quickly checking off his specialties, shot put and high jump—when he came to the "discus throw, (which) stopped me momentarily," he said. "It seemed to me I had read about the discus in Greek history, but I had no idea what it was. Nevertheless, I checked that one too, figuring if it was simply a matter of throwing something I was big enough and strong enough to try."

How exactly to prepare for an event he had never performed or even seen? To the rescue came Sloane, the classics professor, with a suggestion for his young classicist: Look up Lucian, a second-century Greek writer who described the discus as "a lump of brass, circular, and not unlike a small shield, but without a handle or thong." From the available information, Sloane and Garrett figured the discus was an object of metal or stone, about 12 inches in diameter and an inch thick. Garrett then carried the dimensions to a blacksmith in a Princeton machine shop and ordered a custom-made model.

Stopping by to pick up his discus a few days later, Garrett was in for a surprise. Grinning, the blacksmith delivered his new implement with a message: "If you can throw that thing," he bellowed, "I'll give you a medal myself!" Garrett quickly understood what he meant. This discus was as heavy as a boulder—about 25 pounds, or about five times the weight of the actual 2-kilogram (4 pounds, 6.55 ounces) Olympic model. It had sharp edges, making it difficult to hold and even harder to throw. "I was baffled," Garrett said of his homemade discus. "How could the Greeks hurl such an object?" So right then and there, Garrett dropped the idea of competing in the discus, though he had already posted his entry. Not a problem, Garrett figured: He would cancel when he arrived in Athens and focus in the meantime on the high jump and shot put.

Much later, on the Sunday before the Games started, fate intervened. Venturing to the Olympic stadium for a quick workout— "part of a little outing after our long journey," Garrett called it—the Americans got the lay of the land. The runners circled the track, getting the kinks out from their sea voyage. The field men found the various parts of the infield where their events would take place, acclimating themselves to the surroundings. Everyone admired the venue and its marble columns as athletes from other nations did the same. Eyeing a rounded, plate-like object on the ground that looked like a considerably smaller version of the discus from Princeton, Garrett picked it up. It was "light as a feather." This discus was the four-and-a-half-pound Olympic model—so light because it was made of wood, not metal or stone, with a brass core and iron rim. Observing Garrett as he inspected this lighter-than-expected

Olympic discus, a Greek thrower offered to show the American the proper technique for competition.

Garrett was game. "Not hard to handle," he thought to himself, fingering the discus. Watching the Greek get off a few throws, Garrett then stepped in the circle and sampled a few throws himself. "It felt good," he said, "and I could tell by the way the Greeks were nodding approvingly that my distance wasn't bad either." So having just hurled a discus for the first time ever, Garrett resolved to take part in the event the following day after all. "I didn't expect to become a competent discus thrower overnight," he said. "But since I was already entered in the event, I thought I might as well compete—if only for the exercise."

Connolly had already taken the Triple Jump, but the Discus was the Olympic opening day's main event, and the Greeks expected to win it. They had invented discus and considered it their own, much the way Canadians regard hockey or Norwegians do ski jumping. "It was a perfectly natural interest," Garrett the young classicist reasoned. "They had been hurling it for about 14 centuries [and] figured that no man in the world could beat a Greek with the discus."

—◆—

Asked as a middle-aged businessman what he would have done differently in his college years at Princeton, Robert Garrett said he would have changed very little. He would have tinkered a tad with his course selection, focused "all my subjects in the broad field of the humanities, beginning with the classics," in part perhaps because he had spent his student days in the sciences "struggling with chemistry, physics, and mathematics." But Garrett had absolutely no doubt that the time he devoted to sports was worth every minute. "Athletics were among the most valuable experiences of my college life," he said.

Unlike Connolly, for whom sports were a cradle-to-grave preoccupation, Garrett wasn't raised to be an athlete. Born into a prominent Baltimore family of industrialists, Garrett grew up in luxury, surrounded by tutors and servants at the family's 48-room mansion— a bona fide symbol of the Gilded Age with a magnificent art collection, Tiffany hangings, and even a 23-karat-gold toilet seat. Garrett's great-grandfather, also named Robert, was the man who set the family fortune in motion, one fortified in future generations by heavy investments in the railroads.

The Garretts were Baltimore aristocracy. Arriving in America from Ireland as a boy, great-grandfather Garrett joined the city's early-18th-century business elite by exploiting the city's strategic position as a seaport and building superior transportation networks west to the frontier. Dramatically improving the slow method of shipping produce by pack horses over the Allegheny Mountains, Garrett made his name by establishing fast-moving trains connecting to the Pennsylvania Canal. When businessmen began planning construction of the Baltimore & Ohio Railroad, Garrett signed on, becoming an enthusiastic supporter.

But Robert Garrett I had bigger plans. Recognizing the potential of frontier trade and building direct connections to Latin America and Europe, he established a banking arm, which became hugely profitable and soon dwarfed the company's shipping business. Back in Baltimore, Garrett helped organize the Western Bank and built Baltimore's largest steamship to that time to link the trade of the city with San Francisco.

Garrett's two sons expanded the business. Joining the company's diverse operations gave Robert Garrett III's grandfather, John, a thorough grounding in shrewd decision-making, most notably during a severe recession in 1857 when his recommendations to the B&O

Railroad, of which he was a stockholder, were so well received that he was elected railroad president. During the Civil War, John Garrett firmly allied himself with the Union cause and offered the use of his railroad as an early-warning system for an attack on Washington, DC. In 1863, the B&O became a part of history by facilitating the first military rail transport—the transfer of 20,000 Union soldiers from Washington, DC, to Chattanooga.

The war ended and business soared. Like his father, Garrett continued to diversify the company, putting up wharves at Baltimore's Locust Point and creating an alliance with ocean liners of the North German Lloyd, the line that one day would help his grandson and his Olympic teammates get to Athens for the Olympic Games. John's two sons, Robert Garrett II and Robert III's father, Thomas, also joined the family business, but not without some family turmoil. Robert II was a rebel, literally, and at the age of 16 ran away during the Civil War and joined Robert E. Lee's Army of Northern Virginia, despite his father's firm support of the Union. But after his father convinced him to return home, young Garrett did and entered Princeton, the first in a string of his family to do so.

A Confederate veteran winding up at a prestigious Ivy League university in the North wasn't as farfetched as it may seem. For years, Princeton was a pipeline to the students from Southern states, particularly Virginia—and into the early 20th century was thought to attract more Southerners than any other university in the North. The Civil War itself was devastating to the university, and a marble memorial on the west wall of the War Memorial Room at Nassau Hall on the Princeton campus honors the 62 student soldiers killed in the conflict—31 from each side. Of the Princeton Confederates who perished, two were brigadier generals, two colonels, and 10 captains.

Robert Garrett II graduated from Princeton in 1867, meaning he probably didn't attend history's first intercollegiate football game on November 6, 1869, when Princeton traveled to New Brunswick, New Jersey, to take on Rutgers. Rutgers won 6–4 despite Princeton's best efforts to intimidate their opponent by adopting the blood-curdling "yip hoohah" of the Confederates, the "Rebel Yell" of legend. Maybe it helped; the following week Princeton took the rematch, 8–0 at home. In doing so, the team asked their fellow students to yell for them in what is thought to be the start of the American sports world's organized cheering.

———

Robert Garrett's youthful escapade with the Rebel Army paid dividends. In 1871, he succeeded none other than Robert E. Lee as president of the Valley Railroad in Virginia, extended the line into Staunton, Virginia, and made it a branch of the B&O. After his father died, Garrett succeeded him as B&O president and quickly established himself as a business visionary. For the rest of the decade, Garrett directed the railroad's greatest expansion—successfully fighting off frantic competition and extending the B&O into Philadelphia and, in perhaps his greatest business coup, building up the B&O telegraph system, which became a formidable business in itself. The business was eventually sold to Western Union.

With Robert Garrett II running the railroad, his brother Thomas Harrison followed a more sedentary path. Thomas didn't kick up the fuss of his older brother; he too graduated from Princeton, in 1868, and then went to work running the family's banking business. Thomas's passions weren't flashy: He collected rare coins and married the wealthy Alice Whitridge with whom he had three sons, John II, Horatio, and Robert III, born in 1875, and resided with his family

in the big house, a gift of his father. Garrett's numismatic infatu-
ation was triggered at Princeton when he spotted a rare New Jersey copper coin from the 1780s—and had to have it. Inspiring his
sons to be enthusiastic collectors themselves, Garrett built one of the
world's most impressive coin collections. He collected other things
as well—autographs of the signers of the Declaration of Independence, manuscripts, prints, oriental rugs, and Chinese and Japanese
art—and he and his family continued to donate to worthy causes.
Their dollars and influence founded hospitals and service organizations throughout Baltimore. They bought land and gave it to schools.
In 1888, Thomas joined a group of benefactors donating a collection
of valuable Greek and Roman coins to the archaeological museum at
Johns Hopkins University.

That same year, tragedy struck when Thomas Garrett died at the
age of 38. Thinking a change of pace would do her family good, Alice
departed with her three sons for an extensive journey through Europe
and the Near East. It was the privileged family's version of the Grand
Tour as Alice and her sons, accompanied by tutors, wended their way
through many exotic ports of call, including Athens. The teenage sons
benefited in different ways. For John, the interest he took in different
cultures would lead to a diplomatic career. Robert used the journey
to fuel his passion for the Greek classics and all its heroes and myths,
and in collecting, especially old manuscripts.

Returning to the United States in 1891, the family prepared
for what was expected of all Garrett males—entering Princeton.
With Alice taking up residence in Princeton at 1 Bayard Lane, the
two oldest Garrett sons, Horatio and John, graduated in 1895. By
then, Robert, class of '97, was also at Princeton and already excel-
ling in track and field, so much so that he would be elected team
captain for the first time in 1896. Given his growing prowess in

sports and thirst for antiquity, it was almost ordained that Robert would thrive there.

From its earliest years as a training ground for the Presbyterian clergy, the shady, Gothic-spired campus was, along with Harvard and Yale, in the troika of America's finest colleges, the choice for sons of the elite. By the late 1890s, Princeton enjoyed a special advantage with particular appeal for young Robert Garrett—a century-long relationship with the Greek government, making it America's unofficial academic mecca for Greek culture. Nicholas Biddle, class of 1801, was the man most responsible. The second American to travel to Greece after US independence, Biddle became the leader of America's philhellenic movement to aid Greece's struggle for independence from the Ottoman Empire.

Biddle was integral in developing a Princeton tradition of granting scholarships to deserving Greek students, the first of whom graduated in 1840. For the remainder of the century, classics professors such as Sloane took the mantle and successfully lobbied the university to require that all Princeton men take ancient Greek, which would remain mandatory through 1919. In the late 19th century, Princeton was the first American university to establish the teaching of classical archaeology and in 1881 was among the founding institutions of the American School of Classical Studies in Athens. No wonder Garrett and Sloane needn't have strayed beyond the university library for those illustrations of ancient discus throwers. To this day, Princeton's vast libraries, with a collection of several thousand classical Greek editions, are one of the world's leading centers for ancient Greek culture.

A late-19th-century snapshot of Princeton and other elite Ivy League universities suggests not a single impression, but many. They had the scholarship, the vast libraries, and student bodies that produced future captains of industry, philanthropists, and presidents. History hung from every lamppost along Prospect Avenue, which runs through the heart of Princeton's campus. In 1896, the university celebrated its 150th anniversary—its founding dating to 30 years before American independence—and celebrated the occasion by officially changing its name to "Princeton" from the College of New Jersey. The history of Nassau Hall itself could fill a book; completed in 1756, it housed for half a century the entire college—classrooms, dorms, the library, chapel, dining hall, and kitchen. The Continental Congress met there in 1783, making it America's capital for four months that year. It was fitting; nine members of the Continental Congress of 1787 had gone to Princeton, more than any other American or British institution.

University legend, lore, and tradition were important and seriously followed by many alumni for the remainder of their lives. The orange and black that Garrett, Francis Lane, Herbert Jamison, and Albert Tyler wore on their uniforms in Athens dated to the 1860s when Princetonians donned orange ribbons in athletic competition, most likely a reference to England's King William III, the Prince of Orange, or the House of Nassau for which Nassau Hall is named. When students began writing class numerals in black ink on their orange ribbons, the two colors became associated and a tradition was born. No one cared much that the House of Nassau's real colors were orange and dark blue; they weren't about to change the title of the much-loved late-19th-century song, "The Orange and the Black."

F. Scott Fitzgerald's debut novel, *This Side of Paradise*, published in 1920 when he was all of 23, was all about Princeton and gave both the university and its eating clubs a battering. Fitzgerald had entered the university in 1915—just 19 years after Princeton athletes competed in the first modern Olympics. But Fitzgerald dropped out to join the army and never graduated. In his view, Princeton was a bastion of snobbery, filled with shiftless rich boys gliding through with their futures secured by connections. Fitzgerald's portrayal of a sharp but unfocused charmer named Amory Blaine was somewhat autobiographical: Like Fitzgerald, young Amory was from Minnesota and attended an Eastern boarding school followed by Princeton, where he studied with indifference. "I think of Princeton as being lazy and good-looking and aristocratic—you know, like a spring day," Fitzgerald said. "[It was] the pleasantest country club in America."

The novelist's description was accurate to a point. The *Daily Princetonian* regularly featured ads for the dashing young gentleman—Brooks Brothers at the corner of Broadway and 22nd Street in Manhattan ran frequent notices, as did Wanamaker on Chestnut Street in Philadelphia ("Golf and Bicycle Clothing; Fancy Shirtings; White Shirts; Collars and Cuffs; Sweaters"). And unlike Harvard, Jewish or African American students were unknown at Princeton at the turn of the century; the university's first African Americans wouldn't graduate for another half-century.

Princeton differed from Harvard in another important way. While both adhered to the concept of Muscular Christianity or a student's excellence in mind and body, Princeton—unlike Harvard—encouraged team sports. About the time that Princeton played the first intercollegiate football game, the university's new president, James McCosh, argued strenuously in his inaugural address that organized athletics should have a prominent place—"a gymnasium for the body as well as the mind." So it did—and in the ensuing 24 years of his presidency, McCosh turned Princeton into a national sports power.

In 1873, four years after Princeton and Rutgers first played football, Princeton blanked Yale 3–0 in a game that still looked more like rugby or soccer. Most significantly, the Yale game launched the longest continuous rivalry in American collegiate football. Three years later, in 1876 on Princeton's initiative, representatives from Columbia, Harvard, Princeton, and Yale formed the Intercollegiate Football Association, which adopted modified rugby rules for the evolving sport.

In 1878, with two underclassmen named Woodrow Wilson and Earl Dodge directing the student-managed Princeton College Football Association, Princeton won all six of its games. Through the 1880s and '90s, Princeton's football team was regularly among the nation's best. In 1885, the team went undefeated, outscoring its nine opponents 637 to 25. Undefeated again in 1889 and in 1893, great players like Hector Cowan and a group of brothers named Poe (cousins of Edgar Allan) were the team's anchors and became national figures, the ideal of those Muscular Christians.

Princeton track rarely drew headlines. But as with football, the university was an innovator in track, hosting in 1873 the first collegiate track contest in the United States. It was an intramural affair called the Caledonian Games, so named by George Goldie, Princeton's Scottish-born director of the gymnasium, for the circuit of mid-19th-century East Coast summer track meets in which he himself excelled. One of America's great track athletes, Goldie arrived at Princeton in 1869 as McCosh's choice to run the Princeton gym and in little time almost single-handedly gave American collegiate track a blueprint for doing college sports right.

The 28-year-old Goldie was a driven multi-sport dynamo, already well known as a trackster, a gymnast, and even as a circus performer. Athletic excellence ran in the family; he had plunged into the summer circuit of the Caledonian Games at the encouragement of older brother, John, a star of track and baseball in New York. After John died unexpectedly in 1871, George assumed the family mantle among America's thriving track and field circuit, one of rudimentary ovals and makeshift arenas, which were often little more than drafty horse barns. With a popularity rivaling that of today's team sports, early track and field events drew big crowds in a nation hungry for entertainment.

A peppering of talented, often colorful and now largely forgotten stars fed the excitement. Topping the list was the great Lon Myers, the first man to run 440 yards in less than 50 seconds (49.2 in 1878) and who from 1880 to 1888, set world records in the 100, 220, 440, and 880. There was Lewis "Deerfoot" Bennett, a member of the Snipe Clan of the Seneca Indians, who in 1863 covered 18,589 meters or 11.5 miles in one hour, and often competed clad in wolfskin and a feathered headband. And who couldn't help but be moved by the poignant tale of one Malcolm Ford? In 1885 and 1886, Ford took National Championships in the 100, 200, and long jump, a "triple" not matched again until Carl Lewis did it in 1983. But Ford's literary family—Malcolm's middle name was "Webster" after his great-grandfather, Noah Webster—had other aspirations for him. Strongly opposing their son's participation in track, they disinherited him for refusing to give up competition. Ford faced other troubles, as well, enduring several scandals for competing as a professional, which banned him from amateur competition. Then, his marriage fell apart and his publishing ventures went bankrupt. In 1902, Ford went to the residence of his brother, the novelist and biographer Paul Leicester Ford, and fatally shot him before taking his own life.

While Ford's star rose and fell, Goldie became a track and field heavyweight. At 5'11" and 180 pounds, the Princeton professor was well suited for his role—using his gymnastics background to set world marks for the standing high and long jumps and vaulting 9'9", among the best in the world. Representing the New York Caledonian

Club, Goldie continued to devote his summers to the Caledonian circuit. Taking off right after Princeton commencement, he racked up loads of victories and career prize money—more than $1,000, quite a haul for the day. On July 4, 1873, in Pittston, Pennsylvania, Goldie entered 10 events and won 9. That summer, he started 104 events, placed in the top three in 93 of them, and won 51. In 11 weeks, he won several hundred dollars in prize money, at least as much as his coaching salary. A year later, he took 10 of 12 events at the International Caledonian Games in Auburn, New York.

Back on campus, Goldie gave the Princeton Caledonian Games the feel of the Caledonian circuit, which took its cue from centuries of track meets in the Scottish Highlands. And so late-19th-century American collegiate track had its blueprint: There was pole vaulting, the standing long jump, and the forerunner of the high jump—the running high leap, hitch, and kick. Just like the old days in Scotland, Goldie's games were chock-a-block full of heaving heavy objects—the 56-pound weight for distance and another for height, the 22-pound hammer throw, and something called the Sheaf Toss, a 16- or 20-pound burlap bag stuffed with rope, straw, or mulch, and tossed over a cross bar with a pitchfork. For the most part, American collegiate track evolved to include versions of those events.

Princeton would carry on its on-campus Scottish-based affair for more than 70 years. In the meantime, Goldie developed a reputation as a developer of champions. At the first Intercollegiate Amateur Athletic Association (IAAA) meet in 1877, Goldie's Princetonians swept the field. That same year, after Andrew McCosh took four firsts and a second at the Princeton Games, his proud father, university president James McCosh, introduced him to a friend, saying, "This is my son, Andrew, whose brains are in his heels." He was kidding; McCosh graduated with honors and became a surgeon. Some years later, Francis Larkin, class of '79, took back-to-back intercollegiate championships in four events—shot put, hammer throw, standing high jump, and standing broad jump. He was the first four-time Intercollegiate Association of Amateur Athletes of America (IC4A) single-season victor, the only in school history.

Goldie spent several years at the New York Athletic Club (NYAC), where one of his charges was Malcolm Ford. But at heart Goldie was a professor, and he returned in 1893 to Princeton, where he stayed for good. Ever the innovator and mentor, Goldie encouraged sprinter Luther Cary to try a crouch start and the Princetonian became the first intercollegiate champion to run the 100 in 10 seconds and the 220 in less than 22 seconds. Recognizing Garrett had been tutored and had never run organized track, Goldie regarded the young man's long, lanky frame and surprising strength, and suggested he focus on shot put and high jump. He even found time to invent a rowing machine.

But Goldie wasn't a total miracle worker. Next to Yale, Harvard, and the University of Pennsylvania, his Princeton tracksters lagged, mostly from a lack of depth. At the 1895 IAAA Games, the Tigers fell behind all three. As the year's collegiate champion, Yale earned the right to take on Cambridge University as part of a United States vs. Great Britain meet that September at Manhattan Field in New York. The international meet was a triumph for US athletes, who swept the 11 events. The day included five world records from the Americans—including a "double" in the 100 and 220 by Georgetown University's Bernard Wefers. Though Thomas Burke of the NYAC did not set a world record that day, he used "an electrifying dash," as the *New York Times* put it, to win the 440 in 49:0.

Of Princeton's four Olympians in 1896, Garrett appeared to have the strongest chance of medaling in Athens. The Baltimorean was particularly well suited to the position. "He is thoroughly positioned in all matters pertaining to track or field, and moreover is acknowledged to be a most careful trainer and instructor," the *Trenton Times* wrote of Garrett in the February before the Games.

By then, Garrett had filled out to 6'2" and 178 pounds. Under Goldie's helm, he added weight training to his regimen, and the results were beginning to show. "Previous to this year, he has continued his attention to the jumps, and pole vault," the *Trenton Times* reported, "but early in the winter he began to work with the weights and has met phenomenal success." On February 9, 1896, at the sixth annual Boston Athletic Association annual amateur handicap games in Mechanics Hall, the hard work began to pay off when Garrett took the shot, throwing 39 feet, 9½ inches, only about three feet short of the world best. On February 22 at Princeton's annual indoor winter games, he cleared 6 feet, 1 inch in the high jump—and by early spring, was long-jumping well beyond 21 feet, 4 inches, among the nation's best collegiate marks. Garrett was winning admirers, and said to be improving every day. An observer credited his "fine courage, perseverance and sound judgment." Along the way, he became Goldie's most prominent protégé, faithful to hard training and a role model among his fellow students. But the idea of medaling at the Olympic Games in the discus, an event he had picked up the day before? It was a stretch.

To Greeks, the Discus was not just the most important event of the day, but possibly of the entire Olympic Games. National pride was at stake. Those second-century statues of athletes throwing the "discobolus" were Greek, and Greek competitors ever since had mimicked the grace and form of their ancient countrymen. Maintaining the event as an all-Greek affair over the centuries had its advantages: No competitors from other countries were familiar with the discus and the rules of the competition, or had the foggiest notion of the technique required to throw one. Among them was Garrett, who in choosing to enter the event for the fun of it crossed a barrier of sorts in Athens as a foreigner who dared take on the Greeks at an event they considered their own.

Records vary on how many competitors entered the discus in the 1896 Olympic Games, the first time the event was a part of international competition. It may have been nine or as many as 11. At least three were Greek, including the lithe national champion Panagiotis Paraskevopolus, who in photos displayed a form so magnificent that it sent his countrymen into a swoon. Also entered were two Danes, Viggo Jensen and Holger Nielsen; a Swede, Henrik Sjoberg; a Frenchman, Alphonse Grisel; and a striking Englishman named George Stuart Robertson. A classical scholar at Oxford, Robertson, like Garrett and other Americans, had chosen to compete at Athens because, well, why not?

Robertson had learned of the events to be held in Athens in the winter of 1896 while strolling the Strand in London. Spotting a sign in the window of the travel agent, Thomas Cook, which urged passersby to drop their cares and book passage for Greece to watch and even participate in the first Olympic Games of the modern era, the Oxford man signed on. Many years later when he had lived to be 91, a whimsical soul celebrated for his art criticism, Sir George reminisced about his decision: "Oh, it all seemed a bit of a lark," he said. "The Greek classics were my proper field at Oxford, so I could hardly resist a go at the Olympics, could I?"

Like Garrett, Robertson had never thrown the discus but was happy to give it a go. At Oxford, Robertson was a hammer thrower—"a proper hammer with a wooden handle and a leaden head, not some confounded ball on a string like they throw now," he said in retirement. But since there was no hammer throw in Athens, he chose to do the other weight events, including Shot Put, and also compete in Tennis—"a bit of a pit-a-pat," he called it. All in all, Robertson would have a grand time in Athens, in part because "there wasn't any prancing about with banners and nonsense like that," he said. Robertson's enduring Olympic legacy became apparent a few weeks later at the closing ceremony, when he recited his hastily composed Olympic Ode, written in ancient Greek language and meter. It remains a part of the Olympic closing ceremony.

In the Discus, athletes would get three turns, with contestants recording the top three distances qualifying for the finals. Displaying his classic form in the preliminaries, Paraskevopolus uncoiled a throw of 28.51 meters (93.54 feet). Another Greek discus thrower, Sotirios Versis, better known as a weight lifter, would send the discus 27.78 meters (91.14 feet), nearly matching his countryman. As expected, both qualified for the finals and both looked exceedingly good in doing so. "The Greeks almost tied themselves in knots in preparing for a throw, and then suddenly stretched out, and the discus sailed through the air," Albert Tyler wrote. Meanwhile, Robertson, the hammer thrower, uncorked the discus 25.20 meters (82.67 feet), a worthy effort but not enough to reach the final round of three. Garrett qualified, too—the only non-Greek to do so—but it took some doing.

Clutching the discus in his right hand for his first attempt, he settled into the circle and focused hard on the rhythm required of his body. Bending his knees, Garrett brought his right arm around and let go, but not yet with all the force or form he needed. The discus slipped a bit from his hand, but Garrett reached a distance of 27.53 meters (90.32 feet) anyway, a respectable opening toss for a first-timer. Recognizing that he was neglecting the fluidity of form and old-fashioned strength needed to achieve an optimal distance, Garrett decided right then and there to use his second and third throws to work on form. He was a work in progress; his second toss was also crooked and not as far as the first. "Miserable duds," an exasperated Garrett said to himself. In the stands, Eugene Andrews shook his head: Garrett's form was "so clumsy and awkward," the Cornell archaeologist noted, "that everybody just laughed." But the American's first throw had outdistanced everyone but Paraskevopolus and Versis—and was enough to reach the finals, setting up a showdown against the two Greeks. Considering he had only picked up a regulation discus a day before, his Princeton teammates were thrilled. "You may imagine [the] joy" of the moment, reported Tyler.

The odds were heavily in the Greeks' favor. Paraskevopolus and Versis were veterans, experienced practitioners in the art of the discus. "Men of magnificent physique," Lane called them. They performed with a precision of motion and a grace that looked effortless—and behind them was a passionate, "hometown" crowd led by King George imploring them to bring glory to Greece. Each finalist would have two throws, with Paraskevopolus set to go first. So he did, and rose to the occasion, like an actor nailing his lines: The Greek champion unleashed a throw that traveled 28.88 meters (94.75 feet), the best distance of the day. The crowd unleashed a hearty roar. But would it be enough for victory?

It would be for now. Next up, Garrett sent the discus almost as far, but only enough to slip into second at 28.72 meters (94.23 feet), well back of Paraskevopolus. But the American was encouraged: He was starting to get comfortable, and in doing so achieved a personal best by a whopping 1.19 meters (3.9 feet). Garrett was catching on quickly, a realization that took an immediate psychological toll on the

Greeks. "So provoked" by the sudden success of his opponent, Lane observed, was Versis, that he sent the discus only 27.48 meters (90.16 feet), well back of his two opponents.

The three finalists each had one throw remaining. The judges placed the Greeks one-two in order with Garrett to go last. First up and seemingly oblivious to the American's steady progress, Paraskevopolus got right to business as if he were stamping out a quickly forming brush fire. Utilizing what the American photographer and writer Burton Holmes called "classic gestures," he picked up the discus, strode rapidly to the circle, and "with the grace of an animated antique statue," launched his final throw of 28.952 meters—95 feet on the button—and topping his best. Scarcely had the discus touched the ground before the partisan Greek crowd recognized another good effort and jumped to their feet, shouting and waving hats and flags. "For the first time, the victory seemed theirs," Holmes said, "and we [Americans] may readily imagine their great joy." It barely mattered that Versis, the next man, sent the discus 27.78 meters (91.175 feet), well off the performance of his teammate. Victory by a Greek seemed imminent.

It was Garrett's final turn. The task before him was simple to understand and exceedingly difficult to execute: Muster the form, technique, and strength needed to send his final throw beyond 95 feet and he would be an Olympic champion. Fall short and he would earn applause for a worthy debut. Stepping into the circle, Garrett focused, set, and began swinging his discus-laden right arm slowly as if he was revving up an engine. Bending his knees, he rocked his body rhythmically, and in all of an instant, captured one of the essential truths of being an Olympian: In contrast to a football or a baseball player who has many performances over years to make a mark, Olympians often get one shot, a glorious single moment in which to excel and make their years of training worthwhile. Do so and you're remembered forever; otherwise, it's a pat on the back with best wishes for a good life.

In the discus, flawless coordination is essential, everything channeled into a precise burst of strength at release. On Garrett's side was a quiet confidence in his own abilities, a payoff from those workouts in the musty Princeton gym, along with a healthy dose of plain old American moxie. "By this time, he had caught the knack of hurling the discus and had complete confidence in himself," Lane said. Pivoting his body, Garrett marshaled everything into the last throw—a solid transition from technique to strength—and sent the discus, spinning tightly this time, on an upward arc into the air far above the stadium infield. So intent on the flight of the 4.5-pound wooden discus, the stadium throng of 70,000, thunderous only moments ago had gone "silent," Tyler remarked, "as if the structure were empty." All eyes focused on the discus as it sailed over the infield. Seconds later, the discus landed, just beyond the spot Paraskevopolus had reached.

Garrett had done it; he had hurled the discus 29.15 meters (95 feet, 7.5 inches) to win the Olympic title in an event he had taken up the day before. "All were stupefied," recalled Holmes, among the tiny clump of American expatriates sitting in the stadium, a few rows back of the royal box. "The Greeks had been defeated at their own classic exercise." Bursting into applause, the Americans led the celebration, letting loose a Princeton cheer in recognition of another memorable moment in an Olympic Games that had only just started. For Thomas Curtis, "no one was more surprised than Robert Garrett himself." Looking back more than a half-century later, Garrett was still bemused: "Surely by name and tradition and physical perfection, [Paraskevopolus] should have won," the old champion said, "but a cheeky, scrawny American managed by accident to win the event."

Cheeky? Perhaps. But scrawny? An accident? No and no again. Garrett's enduring modesty aside, what had really happened? "Simply this—the best of the Greek throwers was not really good at all," reported George Robertson in an appraisal of the event for the British magazine *Fortnightly Review.* "Ninety-five feet is an absurdly short distance to throw a flat missile of under four and a half pounds. Had English or American athletes practiced the sport, the records would have been nearer 130 feet than 95 feet. The American won simply because he was accustomed to the throwing of weights, and knew how to bring his strength and weight to bear on the missile. The Greek had brought the knack of throwing to greater perfection, but one could see that he did not know how to apply any large portion of his strength to the throw." Robertson was right on most counts, but he didn't have to be so smug about it. In short, Garrett had used his smarts—figuring out how to best combine his strength, long arms, and fitness with harnessing centrifugal force, probably the only competitor to effectively do so. Gaining confidence with each throw, he had expanded his sculpted Greek opponents' focus on form *and* athleticism. In short, Garrett gambled with his on-the-spot changes and triumphed, a marked improvement on Versis's lumbering strategy. "Lovely to watch but weak," wrote Richard Mandell in *The First Modern Olympics* of efforts in the final by the Greek discus thrower. Painfully short on technique, Versis "simply took a little hop and then just let it go," Mandell wrote, whereas "Garrett devised an individual style of wind-up for the throw."

Tyler's comments in the *Princetonian* were part of the wire report that flashed the startling news around the world. On Tuesday morning April 7, Americans opened their newspapers and absorbed the stunning triumphs of Garrett and Connolly, who overnight became household names. Meanwhile on the Princeton campus, the reaction to news of Garrett's remarkable performance was electric. Returning to campus from Easter break on Wednesday, April 8, students were summoned by the track team's manager, Ed Turner, to a meeting where the news was shared. Cheers rang out for Garrett and the school's other Olympians. In the clipped language of a cablegram sent to Garrett, the students shared their enthusiasm: "Mass meeting students," it read, "Princeton University, send heartiest congratulations to Princeton team." Sending their own best wishes were professors Andrew West and Allan Marquard. Both Garrett and Connolly would lead long, rich, and varied lives, but they would be forever lionized for what they did on an overcast April 1896 afternoon, far from home.

CHAPTER 5

"Lithe Forms and Springy Steps"

ONE DAY INTO THE GAMES THE NEWS OF THE OVERWHELMING American success in Athens broke on the home front with sensational force. In its Tuesday, April 7, 1896, edition, the *New York Times* ran a page-one story headlined AMERICAN ATHLETES WON—featured top of the fold and center, between news of National City Bank's $800,000 shipment of gold to Germany and a fatal train wreck in Wales.

Excitement was particularly high on the East Coast, in New York and Boston. AMERICANS WIN AT ATHENS led another page-one piece, in the *New York Tribune*. In Boston, both the *Globe* and the *Herald* devoted sizable articles to its hometown heroes for days on end and the big crowds that filled Olympic Stadium to watch them. At a time when photos were still rare in daily newspapers, several ran column-wide pen-and-ink headshots of America's newest idols. Of the major papers in New York, only the *Post* missed the story that Tuesday, realized its oversight, and quickly came around and for the rest of the week featured prominent articles on the doings from Athens.

Elsewhere around the country the Olympic story was prominent. Throughout the week of April 5, the *Galveston Daily News* ran daily dispatches from the Olympic Games, and featured prominent drawings of Curtis, Clark, and Burke. Scores of other papers did as well— from the *Daily Northwestern* in Oshkosh, Wisconsin, to the *Daily*

News in Salem, Ohio, the *Morning Herald* in Titusville, Pennsylvania, the *Oakland Tribune,* and the *Weekly Wisconsin* in Milwaukee. At a time when the World Series was still seven years away, the unlikely band of Olympians, so recently relegated to the back pages, was stirring something deep in the national psyche.

A sports story had to be big, very big—on par with big college football games or a championship fight—to earn page-one coverage in the *New York Times.* The other prominent sports item that week, the stalled contract negotiations of the New York Giants' star pitcher Amos Rusie, was buried inside. Included in the Olympic coverage were the details of Garrett's improbable victory, Connolly's mastery of the triple jump, and even details of the heats. Just who put together the information for the newspapers is a mystery since the articles didn't carry bylines. But the Olympic coverage in the *Times, Globe,* and *Herald* included considerable detail and times on the performances, ruling out most of the American spectators, who were not necessarily track savvy—and making the likely source either John Graham or one of the American athletes.

The correspondent understood the nuances of track and field and had access to the officials for the times and distances. So was it Graham, whose reports to the *Globe* would earn a considerable space in the coming weeks? Probably not, since the BAA trainer was busy coaching, making sure his athletes were ready to perform. Most likely it was Albert Tyler, he of the long letter to the *Princetonian,* and because the pole vault competition wasn't until Friday, he certainly had the time. Moreover, Tyler had field privileges and therefore access to officials for times and distances of the events. Included in the Francis Lane scrapbooks in the Mudd Library Archives at Princeton is an intriguing item: an April 7, 1896, telegram from the London bureau of United Press International (UPI) addressed to 10 US athletes and John Graham, care of the US minister in Athens, asking that somebody "cover [the] remaining Olympic contests" and that the information be sent "giving names, times, distances [of] Americans immediately after events." Most US papers were vague about attribution; as was the custom in those days, there were no bylines, and several papers sourced the dispatches as from "special correspondence" or by "telegraph" or "cable." Whether it was Tyler or not, the correspondent thoroughly knew the sport and filed a series of reports loaded with detailed information about the dominance of Connolly, Garrett, and other US athletes. Combined with the front-page placement, the daily reports became important elements in establishing the importance of the Olympic Games in the American mindset.

For Burton Holmes and the tiny collection of expatriate spectators at Olympic Stadium, the American team's stunning success was giving them a special status as witnesses to one of the biggest international sports sagas of the era. Holmes and the other American onlookers were nothing like the leather-lunged baseball aficionados of the Polo Grounds.

A scholarly lot, they were the late-19th-century version of a Mensa meeting—accomplished academics, artists, and government officials infused with a broad worldview and a dose of healthy wanderlust. Most of the American spectators were in Athens for the long Orthodox Easter holiday—four days that stretched to two weeks—for r & r, and were attending the Olympic Games for camaraderie and out of curiosity. But even though most were not sports fans, the Americans quickly grasped the magnitude of what they were watching, and got cracking—churning out magazine pieces on the Games for mainstream publications that would capture the color and pageantry of the first modern Games for a large audience back home. In an age when print dominated journalism, their work went a long way toward glorifying the Games—and describing a dressed-up Athens as *the* place to be. The American Olympic movement was only in its infancy, but would get a big boost from this unexpected band of influential advocates.

Of the bunch, Rufus B. Richardson, an archaeologist, would have perhaps the biggest impact. A former professor of Greek at Dartmouth and Indiana University, the 50-year-old Richardson was among several Americans in the region as part of the excavations at nearby Corinth. In his lengthy 20-page piece in the September 1896 issue of *Scribner's Magazine*, Richardson detailed how his initial skepticism about the Games quickly turned to admiration once he got to Athens and experienced the festivities. "It seemed a hazardous experiment to institute a series of international athletic contests under the name of Olympic Games," he wrote. "The sun of Homer, to be sure, still shines upon Greece, and the vale of Olympia is still beautiful. But no magician's wand and no millionaire's money can ever charm back into material existence the setting in which the Olympic Games took place. It is only in *thought* that we can build again the imposing temples and porches, set up the thousands of statues, make the groves live again, bring back the artists, musicians, poets, philosophers, and historians, who came both to gaze and contribute to the charm of the occasion. Never again will athletes move in such an athletic atmosphere, winning eternal glory in a few brief moments."

Richardson was prepared to be underwhelmed by the Olympic Games, but fortified by the American success and the outgoing kindness of his hosts, he quickly changed his mind. "The American athletes were the heroes of the hour," Richardson wrote. "They were lionized and followed by enthusiastic crowds wherever they went in the evening."

At the stadium, Richardson was sitting two rows in back of an elderly priest who kept turning and asking the American visitor, "Is that one of yours?" when Garrett, then Connolly and others started the US victory parade.

"Yes," Richardson would nod, followed by another "yes" and another. "Yours are doing well," the priest graciously responded. Captivated by the success of his young American compatriots, Richardson wanted to give a whoop or two, but the priest's graciousness got him thinking that he had better stay humble. "If the few American spectators made too much demonstration," he wrote, "this good-will might be turned to envy."

Richardson was on the money. Envy was in the air. A Greek journalist was already grumbling at the American success, accounting for their victories by claiming "they joined to the inherited athletic training of the Anglo-Saxon the wild impetuosity of the red-skin." But Richardson's *Scribner's* piece was about much more than the doings from the Olympic stadium. Little escaped his notice from the festive straw hats worn in the streets by Hungarian athletes to the comings and goings of the Greek royal family. Richardson's enthusiasm shines through, a ringing endorsement for just about everything that happened in Athens, all except for the wind-swept rain that blew in off the coast. "It seems the Olympic Games . . . have become the prize in an international contest," Richardson wrote approvingly.

Accompanying Richardson's article were a series of remarkable illustrations of the inaugural Olympic Games by New York artist Corwin Knapp Linson. Along with Holmes's photos, the illustrations are an important record of what happened in Athens—and reveal the budding talents of a young artist on the rise. The Brooklyn-born Linson, though still in his early 30s, already had earned a considerable reputation as a bright light of the Academie Des Beaux Arts in Paris, where Paul Gauguin was a classmate. But Linson's most enduring fame stemmed not from art, but from a close friendship with the American literary prodigy-turned-novelist, the 24-year-old Stephen Crane. They had met on a wintry day in January 1893 at Linson's studio in New York City through Linson's cousin, and became fast friends and roommates in the Greenwich Village section of New York. In 1894, they went to Scranton, Pennsylvania, to investigate the appalling conditions in the coal mines for *McClure's Magazine*. Linson illustrated the August 1894 article by Crane, "In the Depths of a Coal Mine," a true muckraking expose syndicated throughout the country.

Visiting Linson at his studio in New York, Crane would squat on the floor, Indian-style, while chatting and flipping through decades-old issues of *Century Magazine* stored in an oak bookcase. Devouring several of the magazine's stories about the Civil War, the great battles and the recollections of veterans who fought them, Crane had an epiphany: "These fellows spout eternally of what they did, but they never say how they feel," he said. "They are as emotionless as rocks." Fueled by his revelation, Crane wrote *The Red Badge of Courage*, his great novel of the Civil War. Published in 1895, the book traces the development of a young Union recruit, Henry Fleming, through fear, illusion, panic, and cowardice to a humble heroism. This vivid account of the emotions of a common soldier in combat is all the more remarkable because Crane had never even been in the service. Tragically, the brilliant young writer would succumb to tuberculosis in 1900, at only 28 years old. Linson then turned a magazine recollection of his late friend into a memoir, *My Stephen Crane*.

In Athens, Linson was here, there, and everywhere, supplementing Richardson's piece in *Scribner's* with 20 illustrations that captured the excitement and pageantry of the Olympic Games. The detail of Linson's work is remarkable, revealing not just action studies of

Garrett readying to launch the shot put, Curtis hurdling, and the classical forms of the Greek discus throwers, but the sweeping "stadion" scenes of the opening ceremonies and the Athens street parade of dapper gents in hats and women in bonnets. Linson also displayed a piercing eye for city scenes: flags draped across Hermes Street and the evening panorama of the illuminated Place de la Constitution and Royal Palace. It was the late-19th-century equivalent of the ESPN documentary, giving many Americans their first real-life sense of the drama of the Olympics.

Two other men from the small American collection of spectators were a couple of Cornell archaeologists, Eugene Andrews and Benjamin Ide Wheeler, the man who had helped straighten out Prince George during the Triple Jump. Like Richardson, they had headed to Athens from the Corinth excavations for the long Easter break. Their tenure in Greece was a continuation of a Cornell tradition of sorts, one that started in the 1870s when university archaeology students took to studying in exotic places far from home. In 1882, Cornell was part of the founding of the American School of Classic Studies in Athens, ensuring that generations of students would get the chance to study in Greece.

Both found their way to the Games while stationed at the American School of Classic Studies. The 41-year-old Wheeler was one of the few Americans *not* to record his impressions of the Games; three years later, he would begin a 20-year career as president of the University of California. But Andrews would record his impressions of the Games—and his magazine piece about the events would be widely quoted for decades. The eventual head of Cornell's Archaeology Department, Andrews was also a collector; more than a century after the Games, his Olympic ticket stubs were part of a Cornell museum exhibit.

96

All in all, the presence of American academic expatriates in Athens would become one of the intriguing under-the-radar details of the 1896 Games. Another visitor, Eben Alexander, was in Athens as ambassador to Greece, Romania, and Serbia, or according to his official title, "Envoy Extraordinary and Minister Plenipotentiary/Consul General," which sounds like something from a Marx Brothers movie. A former professor of ancient languages, Alexander would later teach Greek at the University of North Carolina. Still another American was there, Charles Fairchild, who had been the US secretary of the treasury during the first presidential administration of Grover Cleveland. Then president of the New York Security and Trust Company, Fairchild was in Athens to represent President Cleveland, an honorary member of the American Olympic Committee, and at the time serving his second term in office.

Meanwhile, the grandly named American, Basil Lanneau Gildersleeve, almost never made it to Athens. A true classicist who looked the part with a bushy beard that gave him a resemblance to Charles Darwin, Gildersleeve was in the Richardson mold—an intellectual-turned-modern-Olympics' skeptic, so much so that he dithered in Italy before reaching Athens just before the closing. What a shame he didn't get there earlier, for Gildersleeve was instantly captivated—and like Richardson, would wax poetic about the glory of the modern Games and this new set of heroes for an influential magazine. Gildersleeve's piece, "My Sixty Days in Greece; The Olympic Games, Old and New," ran in the February 1897 issue of *Atlantic Monthly*, and was a tour de force in selling the glory of the modern Olympic movement to Americans.

Among the most brilliant classical scholars of his era, the 64-year-old Gildersleeve didn't care much for sports, preferring the life of the mind. The son of a Charleston, South Carolina, Presbyterian minister, Gildersleeve graduated from Princeton in 1849 at 18 and was teaching Greek at the University of Virginia when the Union fell apart. Like many faculty members of Southern universities, he resigned and joined the Confederate Army as a part-timer—serving in a staff position in the summers and returning to teach each fall. Delivering orders to the front in 1864, gunfire shattered his leg. "I lost my pocket Homer, I lost my pistol, I lost one of my horses," Gildersleeve wrote, "and, finally, I came very near to losing my life." He walked with a limp for the rest of his life.

In March 1896, Gildersleeve was on his way to Naples aboard the SS *Fulda*, when he ran into the bulk of the US Olympic Team with whom he became fast friends, particularly those from Princeton— "my *own* college," he noted proudly. Headed to Italy to tour Pompeii and then Sicily, Gildersleeve became so enamored by his new group of 20-something fellow passengers and their Olympic task that he pledged to meet up with them in Athens. "Any one would have been proud of such representatives, so modestly, so becomingly did they bear themselves," Gildersleeve wrote. "I watched their lithe forms and their springy steps, as they exercised on deck, with a delight that was somewhat tempered with bitterness as I thought of the universal neglect of athletics in the collegiate America of my time."

As much as Gildersleeve enjoyed the company of his new acquaintances, he still hadn't expected to really enjoy the Games. He was a classicist, convinced that the sacredness associated with the ancient Olympics would be lost in 1896 Athens, and he feared the modern iteration would amount to just another athletic event, a pale imitation of the spiritual celebration it was in ancient times. "Religion hallowed athleticism; it hallowed the Olympic Games," Gildersleeve figured. "The Games were part of the worship of the Gods; victory was a token of their favor. . . . Is there anything left of the old spirit, or can anything of the old spirit be evoked?"

Gildersleeve did prattle on in his *Atlantic Monthly* piece. "The life of the Olympian victor was a term of comparison, not for happiness merely, but for blessedness, which is more; and this blessedness had not lost its significance even in the time of Plato," he wrote. Overall, the article is a tough read, wordy and hard to follow without a solid background in the classics. But for all his verbosity, Gildersleeve was a man of his word—eventually reaching Athens and finding himself instantly swept up by the infectious enthusiasm of the Games. "Everything was wild with excitement," he wrote. "The streets were thronged; there was joy on every face."

Gildersleeve had missed a chunk of the Games but made the best of things. Overall, he had a grand time in Athens, taking in the swimming in the Bay of Zea—"well worth seeing, not for the match itself," he wrote, "but for the setting, for the landlocked harbor of Zea and the crowds of spectators." Roaming the streets of Athens, he reveled in the warm reception he received as an American, thanks largely to the success and popularity of his US Olympic compatriots. "The popularity of the American contestants was unbounded," Gildersleeve noted. "Treating is a Greek vice, and the American visitors were treated and toasted everywhere. As a fellow citizen of the victor with the discus [Garrett], I was received with distinguished consideration wherever I made the fact known." Meanwhile, Gildersleeve quickly grasped the positive change that the modern Games had unleashed on Greece. "Every square, every street in Athens, was alive with young people, running races, jumping, putting the shot," he wrote. "Gymnastic societies flourished. ... Grace articles were written as to the expediency, nay, the necessity, of remolding the educational system of Greece on the basis of physical culture. A new era had dawned for Hellas."

There was another American in Athens, overlooked in the history books, but perhaps the most influential behind-the-scenes figure of the inaugural modern Games. He was the brilliant, enigmatic professor Charles Waldstein, later Walston, renowned for scholarly, enduring contributions to archaeology, but only now gaining recognition on both sides of the Atlantic as a bona fide Olympic pioneer-turned-athlete.

Like other American scholars and artists at the Athens Games, Waldstein published books and chaired prestigious academic posts. Britain even knighted him, befitting a life of achievement. After his death in 1927, the obituaries in the newspapers were long and laudatory, but neglected to mention his significant Olympic contributions. And yet, he joined Richardson and Gildersleeve in writing an influential piece about his experience at the Athens Olympic Games—not in an American publication, but with the article, "The Olympian Games at Athens," in the May 1896 issue of the *Field*, a British sports newspaper.

Waldstein's article is mercifully more to the point and far more readable than Gildersleeve's, and it is every bit as laudatory about the Olympic experience. "The first celebration of the Olympic Games has ... been a stupendous success," he wrote. Like Gildersleeve, Waldstein was overjoyed by the American success, writing that Prince George, presumably speaking on behalf of other nobility in Athens, confided in him that "'We all love the American athletes.'" After all, as the prince confided to Waldstein, "'They behaved so well, and are such good fellows. They taught our people a lesson with their true interest in sport itself. They would sit down and discuss sports with them without any idea that they were rivals.'"

That Prince George was chatting up Waldstein underscores the good professor's status as a bona fide Olympic wheeler-dealer, perhaps more than any other American in Athens. Born in 1856 in New

York City, Waldstein was a formidable intellect, graduating from Columbia and earning a doctorate at the University of Heidelberg. In doing so, he followed his older brother, Martin, to both universities. Older than Charles by two years, Martin became a prominent chemist and leading contributor to scientific journals. Charles chose a different path, turning a budding interest in antiquities into a prominent career. Waldstein was a lecturer in classical archaeology at Cambridge, when in 1886, he met Coubertin, younger by seven years, during one of the baron's research excursions. The two unusual men struck up a friendship, sharing a passion for scholarship and sport.

Details of Waldstein's evolving relationship with Coubertin are sketchy, but recent research by Dr. Don Anthony in the *Journal of Olympic History* indicates the two men were real partners in building the modern Olympic Games. According to Waldstein's diary, Waldstein in 1894 attended a dinner in London in Coubertin's honor. And Waldstein's name appears in Coubertin's letterhead list of dignitaries for the 1894 Sorbonne Congress, a crucial stepping stone to the Games.

Meanwhile at Cambridge, Waldstein's star was rising quickly. He became a university reader, then a professor, and named director of its Fitzwilliam Museum. In 1889, Waldstein accepted a position as director of the American School of Classical Studies in Athens, affording him access to important archaeological excavations. In Greece, he directed excavations by the Archeological Institute of America at the site of ancient Plataea, Eretria, where he took credit for unearthing the tomb of Aristotle and the Heraeum of Argos. Why Waldstein was teaching in the UK and not at home in the United States was likely due to the strident anti-Semitism of the day; Jewish professors weren't welcome in the halls of American academia.

Waldstein's presence in Athens gave Coubertin a valuable ally in a country where he badly needed connections. The Frenchman asked his friend to use his influence in Athens to make contact with and gauge the interest of the Greek royal family in hosting the Olympic Games. While some historians suggest Waldstein wrote many letters but ultimately wielded little influence, author David Young believes Waldstein's role was considerable, beginning in April 1894 when he met the Greek royal family during their visit to excavations in Argos. According to Waldstein's correspondence, the royals spent four hours in Argos, time enough for the American to collar Prince Constantine and lay out Coubertin's plans for the Olympic movement. Captivated, the prince agreed right then and there to serve as an honorary member of the Olympic Congress, handing the baron a crucial breakthrough. Later, Waldstein contributed another important idea—suggesting to Coubertin that he invite the influential Greek writer Dimitrios Vikelas, a Royalist and a friend of Constantine, to attend the Paris conference. The baron took Waldstein's advice, and did him one better—naming Vikelas, who lived in Paris, to represent Greece at the Congress's 1894 meeting at Sorbonne.

It all paid off. "Not only was the remarkable Charles Waldstein a powerful wheeler-dealer behind the scenes in the organization of the first Olympic Games in Athens in 1896, but he was a distinctive cultural influence on Coubertin throughout the critical years of development of the modern Olympic Games," Anthony wrote. "Waldstein's profession made it possible for him to marry both sport and art, and the ancient and modern Olympic ideas."

At the Games, Waldstein was a jack-of-all-trades. For starters, he joined the Paine brothers as America's third marksman. How Waldstein joined the American team is lost to history, as are details of his Olympic performance, which none of those lengthy and laudatory obituaries ever mentioned. Just where Waldstein learned how to shoot is another mystery; it's unlikely he did so growing up in New

York City, but rather on his wooded farm and estate in Newton Hall, just outside Cambridge. There is no record of the process by which he made the team; most likely, Waldstein asked his friend Coubertin, who made sure it happened.

Olympic competition would have fit the American archaeologist's healthy appetite for adventure. Little is written about Waldstein, the private man, but a 1927 obituary in the *Times of London* offered some insight into his personality. "No one who knew him could be in any doubt as to his affection his generosity, and his loyalty to his friends," the newspaper wrote. "Those who knew him best would be the first to say that there was something essentially childlike and lovable about him. . . . He was neither shy nor reserved, and he talked eagerly and with animation on any subject that was uppermost."

In Athens, Waldstein spent a few days sick in bed, and then got cracking, as if he were making up for lost time. There was the shooting. Also, he umpired cycling and tennis, and served on the gymnastics subcommittee. Waldstein even found the time for some more "wheeling and dealing" as Anthony put it—getting Coubertin and Vikelas to lunch with the Greek royal family, where they discussed strategy for future Olympic Games.

As a marksman, Waldstein competed in the 200-Meter Military Rifle, among the Games' five shooting events. Held April 8 and 9 at the Olympic shooting range at Kallithea, the event was dominated by Greeks, who took the top five places. Forty-two shooters from seven countries competed in the event—the Paine brothers did not—but only scores of the top 12 finishers were recorded. Waldstein was not among them. At least his place as a footnote in the record books is secure: At 40 years, 10 days, Waldstein was the oldest Olympian of the 1896 Games, barely beating out another shooter, Sidney Merlin of Great Britain. For the record, Waldstein was 23 days older.

CHAPTER 6

"Most Gratifying to
Every Princeton Man"

WHEN THEY HAD EYED THE COMPETITION IN THE 100 METERS, THE Americans—Francis Lane, Thomas Curtis, and Thomas Burke— knew immediately that these Olympic Games would be different from any of their previous track meets. Absorbed in the magnitude of the moment, they had headed from the dressing room to the track on Monday, April 6 for the heats of the inaugural event of the modern Olympics, preparing to face a blank slate, a group of runners unknown to them. Despite the uncertainty, all three had qualified for Friday's final.

Of the three, Lane had faced perhaps the biggest impediment. Still feeling wobbly from the after-effects of a bad case of seasickness, the 21-year-old native of Franklin, Ohio, had risen to the occasion. As the lone American in heat one, he easily took the race on the soft track in 12.15 seconds, with Hungarian Alajos Szokoly finishing second. It was well off his best time of 10 flat, set back the previous summer in Ohio. The time, however, didn't matter; he had qualified for the final, earning the honor of winning the first race of the modern Olympics.

By taking the second heat, Curtis, a 24-year-old MIT graduate, had matched Lane's time. Alexandrous Chalkokondilis of Greece took second in the heat. Curtis was satisfied; he was using the event as training for his specialty, the 110-Meter High Hurdles, in which the heats would be Tuesday. So even before the opening-day heroics of Connolly and Garrett, the American sprinters had already started making a statement. They set down the opposition with machine-like precision—and with the help of a technique that Europeans had never before seen. Their "crouch" start, which accounted for an opening burst, had thrust them forward with more power than their opponents' variety of standing starts.

More remarkable is that both Lane and Curtis were not even among the elite of American sprinters. Members of the New York Athletic Club and the world's top sprinter, Bernard Wefers of Georgetown, must have been kicking themselves to realize there was Olympic glory for finishes in the 12-second range. Though Americans generally competed in the 100-yard dash, about eight feet shorter than the 100 meters—the top sprinters had been running in the "10s" for most of the decade. That went for John Owen Jr. of the Detroit Athletic Club, generally acknowledged as the first American amateur to officially run "even time" or at 10.0 seconds for the 100 yards. Owens ran his record-smasher at the AAU championships in 1890, pressed by a top field, including Princeton's Luther Cary, and the NYAC's Fred Westing, to finish in 9.8 seconds. A week later, Cary lowered the record, running the 100 yards in 9.5 seconds, despite suspicions that he had "retired to a lonely Jersey byroad near Princeton, and accompanied by two alleged timekeepers, made up the record," as the *New York Times* reported. The Amateur Athletic Union didn't recognize the mark, but Cary was no fluke, blazing 100 meters in 10.75 seconds, for real, the following summer in Paris. He was the first man to break 11 seconds, a time so fast that it stood for five years.

In the third heat of the 100, Burke's performance became an exclamation mark for the dominance of the American sprinters. Like Curtis, the 21-year-old Bostonian was in the 100 to prepare for another event, which in this case was the 400 meters, at which he was the best in the world. The previous September at Manhattan Field, Burke had taken the 400 as a member of the US team that easily outclassed a Great Britain team comprised mainly of Oxford and Cambridge men. It was among the first big international track meets, and the Americans dominated, winning 8 of 11 events. Using a smooth, efficient stride, Burke nipped the British champion, Gilbert Jordan of Oxford, in 49 seconds flat. "The quarter-mile run furnished the most exciting finish of the games," the *New York Times* wrote of Burke's victory. "Not 20 yards from the tape Burke made a wonderful burst of speed, caught Jordan, who looked to be a sure winner, ran with him until the last two strides, and then, with an electrifying dash, he forged ahead just far enough to break the tape, and won by a couple of inches. It was a beautiful finish."

The September 1895 contest was typical of Burke's racing strategy. "Winning was more important to him than the making of fast time," John Hallahan of the *Boston Globe* would write a few years later. "He never cared what style of pace was set, and he could go out front and race just as well. . . . He never sought records. . . . Efforts were made to have him try for the quarter-mile record on one of those horse tracks, but it never appealed to him." The son of a West End undertaker, Burke was an unlikely athlete, having grown up as a child with a serious case of rheumatism that made it likely he would walk the rest of his life with a crutch. Tall and gangly, "he looked anything but a runner," Hallahan wrote. Not only that, but Burke didn't start running competitively until 1893, at age 17. He took that first race, a novice 440-yard race, in about 55 seconds at the Suffolk Athletic

Games in Boston, and kept winning. A year later, representing the BAA, he was a national champion—taking the national AAU title in 50.6 seconds at Travers Island, New York. Understated and reserved, he was well liked by teammates and admired for going about his business with workmanlike humility.

In one of Albert Meyers's photos, Burke crouches at the start of his heat in the 100; both his hands rest on the starting line with his feet settled in the holes in the dirt to support his takeoff. The photo is memorable for several reasons: It is the first Olympic "action" shot to survive, and Burke is the only one of the six runners in the photo to start from a crouch. In all the lanes, each one separated by stakes with knee-high ropes, runners assume a variety of standing positions; one actually grips the stakes holding the ropes. But the race was no contest; off to a clean start, Burke had won easily in 11.8 seconds. Fritz Hofmann of Germany took the day's best second-place time, setting himself up to face the three Americans in Friday's final.

Seated in the Olympic Stadium that first day of competition, Cornell student Eugene Andrews took note. "Greece will not soon forget this frank response from so remote a land," he wrote. "Our boys had little competition except among themselves."

That was a slight exaggeration, but day two of the Games promised more American success with one important difference: The skies had cleared, bringing a truly Olympian day of brilliant sunshine, blue skies, and drier weather that firmed up the track. And the sunny weather helped in drawing another throng to Olympic Stadium, estimated by the *New York Times* at 100,000, with a capacity crowd inside the stadium and another 30,000 or 40,000 dotting the hillside just beyond. King George and the crown prince were there again, as were assorted other royals hoping to cheer a Greek victory.

Day two would also demonstrate the depth of the American team and what the partisan Greek crowd, still stunned from Garrett's upset victory in the discus, was beginning to recognize as a mind-numbing superiority. Right from the outset of the day's opening event, the 110-Meter High Hurdles, as Thomas Curtis, set to run heat two, sized up his competition, the prospect of more American victories became clear. Taking the first heat was the man he had already pegged as his likely competition.

That would be the exquisitely named Englishman, Grantley Goulding, son of a wealthy Gloucester farmer. The two men had actually met Monday, and when Goulding realized Curtis was a hurdler, he insisted in showing him a number of medals pinned to his waist-coat. "You see this medal?" asked the loquacious 21-year-old Englishman, not waiting for a response. "That was for the time I won the championship of South Africa. This one here was from the All-England games." On and on Goulding rattled, enveloped within a massive ego, supremely confident of victory and even consoling Curtis about it. "He was perfectly certain that he would win the Olympic event," Curtis said. "I never met a more confident athlete."

The exchange only added to the insight into the competition that Curtis had been gathering. That process had started back at the hotel on Sunday night when the proprietor, after learning that Curtis was a hurdler, broke into gales of laughter at the news, a curious response to say the least. "It was some time before he could speak," Curtis said, "but when he had calmed down enough, he apologized and explained that it had seemed to him inexpressibly droll that a man should travel 5,000 miles to take part in an event which he had no possible chance to win."

Apparently, the manager had it on good authority that earlier in the afternoon, a Greek hurdler had put forth an absolutely extraordinary, even unbeatable time in the same event. "With a good deal of anxiety," Curtis said, "I asked him what this record was."

The manager glanced about, ensuring no one else could hear his sensational news and directed Curtis to the corner of the lobby. Whispering "like a stage conspirator," the American said, the manager insisted the information was top secret and not to be repeated, but he would tell him anyway. The Greek hurdler's time was 19.8 seconds, a performance that wouldn't win most middle school races then or now. This time Curtis had to work hard to suppress a smile. "I had never heard of anyone running the high hurdles . . . in such amazingly slow time," added Curtis, bemused but relieved. "I decided that I should not take the mental hazard of the 'Great Greek Threat' too seriously."

Goulding was another matter. For all his vanity, the Englishman was a real threat, having torn up competition back home. But Goulding also came with bravado and baggage—principally, a reputation for turning in either spectacular performances or stunning flameouts. For the most part, Goulding either smoked the competition or finished at the bottom with seldom any middle ground. Bursting on the scene in 1895, Goulding had taken impressive second-place finishes at the South Africa and then the British Midland championships. Advancing to the British AAA championship, he never emerged from his heat, taking dead last.

In Athens, Goulding was part of the 10-man team from Great Britain, which included Ireland. Like the Americans, they were an eclectic—and sometimes colorful—group. There was Robertson, the Oxford student who had authored the Olympic ode. There was a 25-year-old Irishman named John Pius Boland, also from Oxford, who went to the Olympic Games as a spectator but became an athlete once he was there. When a friend with the Athens Organizing Committee entered Boland in tennis, the Irishman figured he might as well give it a go—wearing his only pair of shoes, leather-soled with heels. In doing so, Boland took the singles, and teaming with Frederick Traun of Germany, the doubles. Boland would go on to achieve fame as an Irish Nationalist politician and a member of Parliament, but among his greatest achievements was being one of Britain's first—and surprise—Olympic champions.

But no athlete from Great Britain was more striking than the team's first Olympic champion: the 21-year-old Scot, Launceston Elliot. At 6'2" and weighing 224 pounds, Elliot towered above his teammates, most everyone in Athens, and maybe all of Greece. Elliot went to Athens primarily for weight lifting, at which he was Great Britain's champion—but would give rope climbing, wrestling, and track a shot, as well. Running, however, wasn't his specialty; he didn't move beyond his heat in the 100 Meters. A day later, the big man found his stride—winning the Single-Handed Lift and finishing runner-up to Viggo Jensen of Denmark in the Two-Handed Lift.

Other Olympic athletes were swifter, but few were more memorable. Sporting powerful arms, a narrow waist and little body fat, Elliot was often photographed with arms over his head and wearing only a tight pair of shorts—the late-19th-century variation of the pin-up. Heads turned everywhere Elliot went in Athens, onlookers gazing upon his impressive physique. Even Olympic officials were captivated: Contained in the official weight lifting report were all the pertinent facts and figures with a curious editorial amendment about "this young gentleman [who] attracted universal attention by his uncommon type of beauty." Elliot was a man "of imposing stature, tall, well-proportioned, his hair and complexion of surprising fairness," the smitten official wrote. But when another official praised

James Connolly in a photo by Albert Meyer. IOC OLYMPIC MUSEUM COLLECTIONS

Spiridon Louis: Donning native costume, the Olympic Marathon champion is honored at the Games' closing ceremonies. The photo was almost certainly taken by Burton Holmes, who lugged his big camera that day to the infield in capturing highlights of the celebration. IOC OLYMPIC MUSEUM COLLECTIONS

Royal Welcome: A constant of the first modern Olympic Games was the daily entry to the stadium of the Greek Royal Family and their army of helpers. IOC OLYMPIC MUSEUM COLLECTIONS

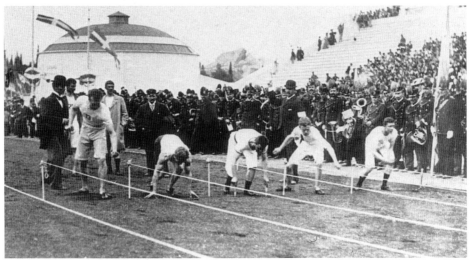

To Your Marks: Albert Meyer's dramatic shot of sprinters in heats of the 100 Meters on the opening morning of the 1896 Games. This appears to be the oldest surviving shot of the competition in Olympic history, though the cameras were not yet equipped to adequately capture "action" shots. Note the variety of starting positions, including (second from left), Thomas Curtis in his crouch start. Curtis would win the heat—and the championship. IOC OLYMPIC MUSEUM COLLECTIONS

Bon Voyage: Greece's newest heroes and America's instant ambassadors, the US Olympic team, push off for home, before a festive crowd at the Athens train station. From left are John Graham, James Connolly, Thomas Curtis, Arthur Blake, and Tom Burke. IOC OLYMPIC MUSEUM COLLECTIONS

BAA—Rah! Rah! Rah!: The Boston Athletic Association contingent poses for Albert Meyer a the Olympic Stadium. There are no IDs, but tha looks like Ellery Clark at the right of the top row and William Hoy, sitting at the right in the first row. IOC OLYMPIC MUSEUM COLLECTIONS

The Closing Ceremonies. IOC OLYMPIC MUSEUM COLLECTIONS

Packed House: A capacity crowd takes in the High Jump on the final day of Olympic track and field competition. IOC OLYMPIC MUSEUM COLLECTIONS

The panorama of the Olympic Stadium in the midst of field competition—possibly the Shot Put. IOC OLYMPIC MUSEUM COLLECTIONS

Man with a Mission and a Mustache: The Founder of the modern Olympics, Baron Pierre de Coubertin. BAIN COLLECTION, LIBRARY OF CONGRESS, PRINTS AND PHOTOGRAPHS DIVISION

Pride of Boston: Back from the Olympic Games and awash with success, several members of the Boston Athletic Association sit for a more formal shot. Standing (from left) are Tom Burke, Tom Curtis, and Ellery Clark; sitting (from left) are William Hoyt, Sumner Paine, John Graham, John Paine, and Arthur Blake. Note the variation on the uniforms, including Blake's adornment of the BAA and Harvard logos. And why exactly did the Paine brothers feel compelled to lug those big pistols to the photo shoot? COURTESY OF THE BOSTON PUBLIC LIBRARY, PRINT DEPARTMENT

Tiger Tradition: Yes, those smart young men from Princeton appear to be well-dressed. And yes, some of them are wrestling as part of the school's traditional cane rush or spree in which freshmen and sophomores grappled for control of several prize canes. This peculiar tradition commemorates a historic freshman uprising against a university tradition that only sophomores and upperclassmen were permitted to carry canes, in which freshman attempted to rob sophomores of their canes in defiance of the rule. The photo has no date, but it is likely take in the early twentieth century. FROM THE BAIN COLLECTION. LIBRARY OF CONGRESS, PRINTS AND PHOTOGRAPHS DIVISION

Basil Gildersleeve. FROM THE BAIN COLLECTION.
LIBRARY OF CONGRESS, PRINTS AND PHOTOGRAPHS
DIVISION

Athens, about the time of the Olympic Games. FROM THE BAIN COL-
LECTION. LIBRARY OF CONGRESS, PRINTS AND PHOTOGRAPHS DIVISION

Classical Athens, circa 1900. FROM THE BAIN COLLECTION. LIBRARY OF
CONGRESS, PRINTS AND PHOTOGRAPHS DIVISION

Albert Meyer.

Burton Holmes. THE BURTON HOLMES HISTORICAL COLLECTION

Ellery Clark (left) and Thomas Curtis, in photos by Albert Meyer. GETTY IMAGES

Old School: Princeton athletes (from left), Francis Lane, Herbert Jamison, Robert Garrett, and Albert Tyler with tools of their trade in a classic shot by Albert Meyer. GETTY IMAGES

B. A. A. TEAM FOR ATHENS.

Records of the Men Who Will Compete in Olympic Games.

Thomas C. Burke, Ellery H. Clark, Arthur Blake, Thomas P. Curtis and Probably W. W. Hoyt and John Graham to Sail Saturday.

T. P. CURTIS, HURDLER.

T. E. BURKE, SPRINTER.

JOHN GRAHAM, MANAGER.

Column 2

Continued from the First Page.

ARTHUR BLAKE, RUNNER

ELLERY H. CLARK.

ARTHUR BLAKE

C. H. CLARK, JUMPER

THOMAS P. CURTIS

Continued on the Third Page.

Column 3

CONNOLLY BACK.

Athlete Who Missed the Train at Paris.

His Prizes, a Cane and an Old Coin Are with Him.

Greeks Will Remember Him for Many a Day.

His Victory Was in One of Their Popular Events.

His Reminiscences of Trip Have an Interest Alone.

W. W. HOYT, POLE VAULTER

J. B. CONNOLLY.

Column 4

QUINTET OF BLUSHING ATHLETES.

Tendered a Public Reception by the City in Faneuil Hall.

Congratulations Heaped Upon Them by Admiring Bostonians Who Shook Their Hands—Sumptuous Banquet Wound Up the Official Welcome Home to B. A. A. Athens Team.

THE RECEPTION AT FANEUIL HALL.

NOT TRAINING TABLE FARE.

Shots from the *Boston Globe*.

Shots from the *Boston Globe.*

The remarkable Charles Waldstein
(Waldston) in a 1913 portrait by Philip de
László. PRIVATE COLLECTION, PERMISSION VIA
THE DE LÁSZLÓ ARCHIVE TRUST

William Milligan Sloane.

Elliot as "the finest man of English birth," the proud Scot bristled. Years later, Elliot's daughter, Nancy, would set the record straight, calling him "Scottish to the bone."

— ◦— —◦ —

Thomas Curtis had a good reason to be concerned about Grantley Goulding. The Englishman looked the part too—he was imposing and seemed to eat up the distance. He had talent, so much so that he was "in fact, a better hurdler than I," Curtis told himself. Goulding's potential in Athens became apparent when running for the first time on cinders. The "good" Goulding had showed up. He swept the field in heat one, winning easily in a time of 18.25 seconds to secure a spot in Friday's final.

Curtis wasn't being overly modest in grading Goulding a better hurdler. For all his speed and the promise of Olympic glory, he was a relative newcomer to track, still unsure of his abilities. It's unclear when Curtis had become a hurdler—the *Boston Globe* reported it had been in January 1896, all of three months before, at the 9th Regiment Games in Boston. But in an event so dependent on technique, it seemed unlikely that he was a relative novice. Chances are that Curtis had started running in his student days at MIT, where he was a big man on campus—studying electrical engineering, running track, and playing football. He was even chief marshal at Class Day. Though Curtis didn't graduate with his class, the 1893-94 MIT yearbook includes him among 28 students who were "intimately connected with the class of 1894 who did not try for degrees."

Perhaps it was his upbringing as a son of the Army's Deputy General, but Curtis had a touch of wanderlust and a healthy appreciation for travel. His parents gave him a camera for the trip to Athens, and the photos he took there are among the first records of the modern Olympics, and were used by the makers of the 1984 film, *The First Olympians*, for help in designing sets. Born in San Francisco, where his father, Herbert, was stationed, Curtis grew up at The Presidio, a next-door neighbor of General John Pershing. At age nine, he and his family set off for St. Paul, as a military career awaited him—or so it seemed.

Appointed to West Point in 1891, Curtis was expelled for kissing a girl. Enrolling at Columbia, he ended up as an MIT engineering student in Boston, where his family had roots. With the military life still beckoning, Curtis joined the Massachusetts Volunteer Militia's 1st Corps of Cadets in 1892 for which he served three years. Somewhere along the line, he turned to sports and became consumed with the idea of competing in the first modern Olympic Games.

Curtis was a wiry 145 pounds, but contact sports, particularly football, came easily. In the Army, Curtis captained a team of officers in a game against the Navy at Governors Island, New York. He captained the Columbia freshmen, and played two years at MIT. In the fall of 1895, Curtis joined the BAA football team and earned a reputation as a breakaway threat—scoring a touchdown against Yale. Against Harvard, he almost did the same thing again—streaking virtually the length of Soldiers Field for an apparent touchdown, which was then called back by a penalty. Just why Curtis wasn't competing *for* Harvard is curious, given his long-running family connection to the university. Curtis's grandfather and father were both graduates, and in later years, his two sons, granddaughter, and great-granddaughter would also graduate from Harvard.

In the mid-1890s, Curtis started applying his football skills to track. Most likely, John Graham suggested he join the BAA team. Or it may have been Fred Lord, his friend from MIT days, then-BAA teammate, and a business partner in the Lord Electric Company.

Success came quickly: At those 9th Regiment Games, Curtis whipped Stephen Chase, the world hurdling champion—to make "a profound impression by his remarkable running," reported the *Boston Globe*. He took the hurdles again a few days later in a meet at Roxbury Latin School and then at MIT, besting Lord both times. Curtis had come a long way in a short time—so much so that on the eve of the Games, the *Globe* called him "the most promising hurdler in America."

Part of Curtis's concern about the Englishman Goulding was that he appeared to be among the few other hurdlers with any semblance of technique. Although the Greek team had hired an English trainer to compensate for their apparent inexperience in most every track event but field events and distance running, there was only so much the overworked man could do. "In the sprints, the middle, and the long-distance runs, he could give them useful hints on form and condition, but the pole vault and the hurdles and the high jump were too difficult for any such athletic 'cramming,'" Curtis said. "Greece, as a nation, knew very little about modern track and field sports." Exhibit A was Lagoudaki, the sprinter-turned-marathoner whom he had met on the boat. Exhibit B was "the Greek Threat," the man Curtis heard about at the hotel. No question the "Threat" had speed, but anyone in the know would have snickered at the man covering the 110 yards of the hurdles by treating each hurdle as a high jump . . . that is, by trotting up to it, leaping and landing on both feet. "Given the method," the American said, "his time [of just under 20 seconds, as the hotel manager had said] was remarkable."

Alas, the Threat didn't move beyond his heat, but Curtis had no trouble, qualifying for Friday's final by taking the second heat in 18.0 seconds. Far from the American's best, mostly due to the soft track, it was the day's fastest time. So Curtis and Goulding were set for a showdown.

There were no preliminaries in the Long Jump. The entire competition was on day two on the rough jumping path of the Olympic Stadium. Each of the eight competitors would get three attempts. The field included Americans Connolly, Garrett, and Ellery Clark; as well as the Greeks, Alexandros Chalkokondilis and Athanasios Scaltsoyannis, both from the National Club of Athens; Alponse Grisel of France; Henrik Sjöberg of Sweden; and the versatile German Karl Schumann, who would earn two Olympic championships in gymnastics. In contrast to Curtis, who was a relative newcomer to his sport, Clark had been a fixture on the East Coast track scene. Though he had just turned 22, the Boston native and Hopkinson School graduate, now a Harvard student, was already a mainstay of New England's track and field circuit. And his specialty wasn't one or even two events; it was several.

At the 1895 championships of the Maritime Provinces in Canada, Clark dominated—taking *five* firsts—high jump (5 feet, 10⅝ inches), shot put (39 feet); long jump (21 feet, 6 inches); the 110-yard hurdles (17:2.5) and hammer throw (99 feet). That season, he achieved personal bests in the hammer (123 feet, 6½ inches) and the long jump (21 feet, 10 inches). At 5'10" and weighing 172 pounds, he was "not an ideal hammer thrower, neither [did] he look like a jumper," the *Boston Globe* wrote. While Clark didn't stand out in any particular event, he excelled in doing many things well. He was never flashy, but rather serene and calm in his demeanor. An almost zen-like peace, even in competition, was Clark's trademark—a quality that made him easy to underestimate. Connolly called it an "even, reliable temperament that does not allow him to waste his power in single great efforts."

Connolly and Clark were the American Olympic team's Mutt and Jeff. Maybe that's why the excitable, high-volume Irishman so admired the even-keeled Clark. In the year they had been classmates and teammates at Harvard and fellow Olympians, Connolly said he never heard Clark "indulge in a solitary exultant whoop of superiority, a thing which one might be disposed to allow a powerful athlete as a natural outburst of strong feeling."

The two differed in another way. Whereas Harvard turned down Connolly's request for a leave to compete in Athens, the university had accepted Clark's application. The precise reasons are lost to the mists of time. Clark was only an average student, but it probably didn't hurt that his father was a pillar of the Boston community and had been a Harvard classmate of President Charles Eliot. Even so, the school's decision to let him go was predictably grudging. Dean LeBaron Briggs conveyed President Eliot's sentiments in his letter to Clark:

My dear Clark,

After consulting various persons, I have decided to let you go to Greece. I understand that the absence will not be more than a month, and will include the spring recess. Of course you take your own risks so far as your courses are concerned.

May I ask you not to emphasize unduly the Harvard side of your athletic competition. I am quite willing that the facts should be known; but I should not like an exaggeration of the facts. You go, as I understand it, in the capacity of a B.A.A. man, and the fact that you are a Harvard man is, so to speak, accidental.

Yours very truly,

L.B.R. Briggs

Even with his university's tepid support, the usually calm Clark was suddenly consumed by the jitters during the final countdown to the Long Jump. It wasn't the 100,000 people eyeing his every move or

115

the quality of the competition. But it was because judges were again prohibiting the jumpers from marking their spot. The same quirky rule that bedeviled Connolly in the Triple Jump was throwing Clark off stride as well. Like Connolly, Clark depended on a mark, usually a sweatshirt or a hat tossed in the grass, to guide him to the point of takeoff. Unlike in Connolly's situation, officials were no longer willing to consider appeals, not this time. Without his trusty mark, Clark said he was "practically lost."

Prince George had returned to his original position in the matter and wasn't budging. He believed that the use of any measurements or mark was an unfair advantage, one smacking of professionalism—and wasn't allowing it now in the Long Jump as he had with Connolly in Monday's Triple Jump. The Americans argued meekly, not wanting to create a stir. But this time, the judges stood firm.

Neither Connolly nor Garrett seemed affected by the judges' decision. Both athletes were already Olympic champions, and got off fair jumps, their first of three. Of the Americans, only Clark was having troubles, exacerbated by the uneven ground of the runway— "utterly unlike the closely rolled cinders to which I had been accustomed" in the United States. In his opening jump, he misjudged the takeoff and stepped over the board, a foul. For his second jump, Clark tried envisioning where he would have placed a marker—and fouled again. In the meantime both Garrett and Connolly continued jumping well, moving into first and second with their efforts. Though well off the two-year-old world mark of 23 feet, 8 inches set by Ireland's J. J. Mooney, Garrett covered 19 feet, 8¼ inches and Connolly 19 feet, 2 inches. Clinging to a distant third with a jump of 18 feet, 10 inches was Chalkokondilis of Greece.

Clark was down to one last try, heading to the foot of the runway for a last shot at Olympic glory. Reaching his starting point, he turned around and pondered his fate before his teammates and 100,000 others: "It was little short of agony," he remembered years later. "Five thousand miles . . . I had come; and was it to end in this? Three fouls, and then 5,000 miles back again, with that for my memory of the Games." Even top athletes like Clark hit slumps at inauspicious moments of big events like the Olympic Games or the World Series. Looking for a spark, anything to jump-start performance, some resort to superstition. Others are more methodical, breaking down a particular task to its essential steps to be performed deliberately, one after another. That way, a slumping baseball player looks not to drive a ball into the outfield gaps, but simply to connect solidly. So it went with Clark in the Long Jump: For him, there was no need for superstition or a rabbit's foot. Instead, he decided to focus on what came first—beginning his stride "as well as I could," as he put it—figuring the rest would follow, just as he had done all those times before in drafty New England armories and gyms.

His mind cleared, Clark barrelled down the runway and hit the takeoff right this time—there was no foul—and sailed into the air, gaining height and distance with each fraction of a second. Stretching, he thrust himself as far forward as possible, and landed 6.35 meters or 20.83 feet from takeoff, surpassing everyone. Clark had done it on his final jump, winning America's third Olympic championship, and heading a US Long Jump sweep with Chalkokondilis taking fourth. For all the drama of his victory, Clark downplayed it, choosing instead to focus on how close the margin of victory had been and what he stood to learn from the experience. "[I] jumped and won," he wrote later with all the emotion of a trip to the grocery store. "My, what a closeness! . . . But there were a few moments before that third trial which I have no wish to repeat."

The American flag again climbed the flagpole, prompting another round of American "war cries." The sight of the Stars and Stripes and the distinctive American cheer were becoming standard fare in Athens. Clark would humbly repeat the story of his dramatic jump in his book, *Reminiscences of an Athlete: Twenty Years on Track and Field*, written in 1911, and occasionally after that in newspaper remembrances, usually before the start of another Summer Olympiad. But curiously, in 1932, more than three decades after Athens, Connolly attacked Clark in the *Boston Transcript* for stealing his story about not being able to mark his run at the '96 Games. By then, Connolly was earning a handsome living as a well-known author and lecturer, but had convinced himself that Clark wasn't giving him his due as the first modern Olympic victor.

Clark was astounded. He defended himself in an interview in the next day's paper, saying that he had in fact given Connolly credit for being the first modern victor, and stating that the same incident about marking his spot in the Long Jump probably had also happened to Connolly in the Triple Jump. He was right—and Garrett would later corroborate Clark's memory.

Several weeks later, Connolly curiously picked up where he had left off, this time accusing Clark of secretly marking his third run, something that would have been exceedingly difficult to pull off in a stadium packed with tens of thousands of people. Garrett again rushed to his old teammate's defense, stating that Connolly, "in modern phraseology [has] gone 'ga-ga.'" The ever-gracious Clark attributed Connolly's accusation to the summer heat "or if not the heat, the humidity." It turns out what had really bothered Connolly all those decades later was Clark's recollection of Burke being the first athlete to be honored with a flag-raising and the National Anthem for winning an Olympic championship. Clark had inadvertently mixed up a minor detail—Connolly was first—which threw the old triple jumper into a tizzy. "The raising of that flag was Connolly's moment of glory, a moment he had often recreated before spellbound audiences, and he thought Clark had deliberately stolen it from him," wrote Jonathan Shaw in a 1996 *Harvard Magazine* article. "The spirit of competition had spilled off the field."

Barely two days into the Olympic Games, the Americans were putting on a masterful show. Not bad for a group of college athletes who had spent most of the last two weeks on a ship. What Thomas Burke and Robert Garrett were about to do in the next two events would put an accent on the US domination at the inaugural Olympic Games.

A lean, efficient stride made Burke's performance look effortless, the picture of fluidity. He and Princeton's Herbert Jamison had qualified easily Monday in the 400 Meters, both winning their heats. Burke's 54.2-second qualifying time wasn't fast enough to win a lot of high school meets, and was far from his personal best. But few events were as adversely affected by the soft, damp track and turns so sharp that runners had to drastically slow down to keep from falling. Nor was Jamison's qualifying time of 56.8 seconds memorable, but the Princeton junior was fortunate to be there. At 5'9" and 165 pounds, he seemed too compact to be a top middle-distance runner. A last-minute substitution, Jamison was Garrett's pick to replace James Colfert, the talented freshman and team's top 400-meter man whose parents had insisted he not make the trip.

Garrett had made a good choice. At twenty, Herbert Brotherson Jamison was unassuming, diligent, and an honor student—with a knack for landing in the right place at the right time. In 1893 when Jamison was the Peoria (Illinois) High School track captain, the

University of Illinois Athletic Association established the first state high school championships to which all state captains were invited. Jamison dominated the sprints—taking state titles at 50, 100, and 220 yards. Three years later, here he was at the Olympic Games in Athens with a legitimate shot at doing something for the ages, in part because Edgar Bredin of Great Britain, the co–world record holder in the 440-yard race at 48.5 seconds, wasn't there, barred for turning professional.

The result of the four-man final of the 400 meters wasn't a big surprise. At the gun, Burke shot into the lead and never let up—winning easily in 54.2 seconds, a 13-meter margin over Jamison, in second; Charles Gmelin of Great Britain third; and Germany's Fritz Hofmann, fourth. An article in *Stars and Stripes* claimed that Burke was so far ahead that he stopped just short of the finish line and walked across, but that story is unsubstantiated anywhere else and not at all in the character of the Boston runner.

Burke's superiority on the track had been expected. The same went for Garrett, newly crowned king of the Discus, in the 16-Pound Shot Put, his specialty. Again, the Greek crowd was energized by the presence of several of their countrymen; of the seven performers, two were Greek, Mitiados Gouskos of the Pan-Hellenic Club and Georgios Papasideris of the National Club, their era's athletic stars, whose efforts, great and small, were greeted with frenzied cheers. Leading the applause were the crown prince and Prince George, still hoping to master the finer points of the American cheer. The royals watched the competition intently from the field—their applause a cue for their countrymen to cheer as well.

Garrett and the 200-pound Gouskos, nicknamed "Hermes," were the class of the field. As in the discus, the Greeks hurled the shot put with impressive theatrics. But they were no match for the Princeton track captain: Garrett reached 36 feet, 9¾ inches—far below George Gray's world record of 47 feet—though three-quarters of an inch ahead of Gouskos to earn his second Olympic title in as many days. Again, the Greeks seemed more interested in imitating antiquity—choosing a mostly stationary posture in which their shot putters looked fabulous but barely moved, hardly incorporating their legs. So again, the American won with superior technique—blending the full force of his whole body, legs *and* arms, into the throw. And he won in another display of coolness under pressure, making on-the-spot mental and physical adjustments. Though he had hoped to use his own lead shot, at the officials' insistence Garrett had to use a European version, smoother and made of iron ore. But instead of protesting, he just shrugged, deciding that it simply didn't matter. Nor did it matter that the athletes were relegated to a significantly smaller circle from which they could launch the shot—a European-style 6.5-foot or 2-meter circle, instead of the more spacious 7-foot area of the US model. Garrett adjusted again—incorporating his rhythm and strength into a faster, more explosive launch. The only likely effect was keeping him from achieving a better first-place throw. "Probably if the seven-foot circle had been allowed instead of a two-meter square, and permission to use his own lead shot been granted," Tyler noted, "Garrett would have made a record worth keeping."

So for the third time on day two of the first modern Olympiad, the American flag shot up the pole to honor a new Olympic champion. "Our boys are now called the 'American invincibles,'" said Holmes, gauging the mood of the crowd. Sitting nearby, Rufus Richardson marveled at the continued good nature of the Greek crowd amidst their mounting frustration that their countrymen had again missed out. "The Americans were . . . evidently great favorites with the audience, partly, perhaps," he ruminated, "because they lived so far away as to take the place occupied in Homer by 'the blameless Ethiopians,' almost beyond the sphere of their jealousies and antipathies."

News of the American success was cabled home. At Princeton, there was great joy at Garrett's continued success and Jamison's good work. Two of its finest had brought glory to their country and the college. Even the *Daily Princetonian* editorialist, just days before out of sorts that the athletes' prolonged departure could affect the Yale and Columbia track meets, conceded that their performances in Athens had been special. The praise, however, was stingy: The success of Garrett and Jamison, he sniffed, is "most gratifying to every Princeton man" and "should give fresh impetus to the members of the track team at home, and arouse renewed interest in a branch of athletics in which we have been so deficient in recent years."

Given the resounding American success, there was relief in some circles that the winners of the program's next stadium events, the Weight Lifting competition, were guaranteed to have a European champion. The US team had no weight lifters, establishing the versatile Danish champion Viggo Jensen and the striking Scot, Launceston Eliot, as favorites. The Weight Lifting competition was one of four sports in which the 21-year-old Jensen competed in Athens. Having just participated in the shot—he finished fourth—Jensen headed several hundred feet to the sanded weight lifting area in the Olympic Stadium infield. Midweek, Jensen would participate in Rope Climbing and two shooting events, Free Pistol and Military Rifle.

Weight lifting was a basic affair at the 1896 Games. There were no weight divisions, just eight lifters in two events—a Two-Hand Lift and the One-Hand Lift or snatch. Judges would add weight to each attempt—awarding additional points for style, a critical factor if the competition was close. That was the script Jensen and Eliot followed after both lifted 11.5 kilograms in the Two-Hand Lift—beating the rest of the field handily, with the Dane awarded the title on points after Eliot moved his feet. Fittingly, Eliot took the next event, the One-Hand Lift, hoisting 71 kilograms, for a convincing victory. Again, Greek athletes came close—but in this case, managed only thirds. They could have used Prince George, who, upon noticing a worker laboring to remove one of the iron weights, gave him a hand. Anxious to stay on schedule, the prince bent down and put the weight aside with apparent ease. The crowd took note, roaring their approval.

So Weight Lifting was done, but the Americans were not. The hearty band of US collegians had one last shot at glory on day two, in the 1,500 Meters. The task would be up to Arthur Blake, the slender, heavily mustached 24-year-old Harvard graduate, now a real estate agent in Boston. And it was Blake's cocky comment, cracked partly in jest, back on February 9 at a track meet at Mechanics Hall, that had triggered the BAA drive to get their athletes to Athens in the first place.

Blake had been one of Boston's top distance runners since his student days at Harvard. There he starred in a sport called hare and hounds or paper chasing, a rowdy ancestor of cross-country. Kicked off in the late 1870s by a group of young, athletic New Yorkers looking to stay fit in the fall and winter, paper chasing became a version of distance running with a party hat. It designated a runner or a hare to take off and drop pieces of paper as a clue to his route—with a pack of pursuers or "hounds" some minutes later in pursuit.

Whole packs could play, but generally, two runners were designated as hares, with the rest hounds. Rules varied but the hares usually got a five-to-ten-minute head-start, and tried passing hounds to a predetermined destination by any course they desired. Their only obligation was to drop bits of paper—"the scent"—as clues along the route. Harvard students took to this new game starting in 1879, giving rise to periodic mad dashes by clusters of the pursued and the pursuers through the streets of Cambridge and often over fences and hedges, and even up the steep Corey Hill in Brookline. "To the young men who inaugurated paper chasing . . . the sport must have seemed as delightfully wicked as streaking would to their counterparts a century later," wrote George Gipe in a *Sports Illustrated* remembrance. "Hot-eyed runners pounding down city streets, leaping hedges, fording brooks and leaving multicolored trails of shredded paper wherever they went constituted the kind of foolishness certain to raise eyebrows among the more sober-sided citizens of the late 1870s and early 1880s."

Blake took to hare and hounds, which prompted more formal success on the track and at cross-country meets at Corey Hill. Joining the BAA after college, Blake blossomed into a talented indoor runner, particularly in the mile, which by the early months of 1896 he had completed in 4:39. That was among the best times in the northeast United States in the era, but far from world-class. For the record, the outdoor best in the mile at the time was out of Blake's league—a blistering 4:12.75, run nearly a decade before by Great Britain's Walter George. But George had set the mark as a professional, so wasn't eligible for the '96 Games, by which time he was 37 years old anyway. Yet no man would run a faster outdoor mile until 1931.

For Blake, outdoor training could be a bit perilous, and it wasn't always the nasty Boston winter or traffic that was at fault. So startling was the sight of a runner on the late-19th-century streets of Brookline that residents periodically took Blake for a madman and sought to have him arrested. Blake usually laughed it off. Slight of frame and distance-runner gaunt, he sported a floppy handlebar mustache that dominated his lower face—giving him a striking resemblance to a distance runner of a later era, the great Steve Prefontaine. Blake and Prefontaine shared other characteristics as well—an outgoing personality, an engaging sense of humor, and supreme self-confidence. But that's where their paths differed. Part of Prefontaine's enduring appeal was his disdain for the stuffed shirts of track's authority figures, and a blue-collar intensity. Blake was nothing like that; he was the son of a prosperous Boston physician and ran purely for the fun of it.

The 1984 film, *First Olympians*, treats Blake badly. Alex Hyde-White is a dead ringer for Blake, but plays a character so supremely arrogant and condescending to the working-class Connolly, played by David Caruso, that the men brawl. If the athletes did have a spat—and there is no evidence of that—they soon got over it. Back in Boston after the Games, the two men would retain a long, abiding friendship.

Even so, Blake's route to Harvard was considerably easier than the one traveled by Connolly, ordained by the legacy of his family. Blake's father, Dr. John Blake, was a graduate of Harvard College and its Medical School, among Boston's most respected figures. He was the personal physician to the Archbishop and would spend more than a half-century working at Boston City Hospital. Blake's mother, Mary, was a noted poet, novelist, and travel writer with a string of admirers from Longfellow to Theodore Roosevelt.

At the BAA's 1896 amateur handicap games in February 1896 at Mechanics Hall, Blake dominated the 1,000, utilizing an efficient, compact stride to win in 2:27. His 20-yard margin of victory electrified the standing-room-only crowd of nearly 4,000, among them a BAA member and wealthy stockbroker named Arthur Burnham. Congratulating Blake just after the race, the two fell into conversation.

"You're the best runner in Boston"—or something to that effect, Burnham told Blake.

"Oh, I'm too good for Boston," Blake said, laughing. "I ought to go over and run the Marathon, at Athens, in the Olympic Games."

The Olympic Games? Burnham had heard of the revival planned for April in Greece. Momentarily lost in thought, the older man gazed at Blake. The runner's seemingly throwaway comment had struck a chord. "Would you really go if you had the chance?" he asked.

"*Would* I!" said Blake, his way of offering an emphatic "yes!" If the humor hadn't registered, the young runner's determination had. Burnham resolved to tap his fellow BAA members for the funds to send Blake and several of his teammates to Athens as members of the American team. He lobbied the BAA's Athletic Committee to initiate a subscription drive among members to raise funds for the athletes, but there was little enthusiasm and after two weeks, less than half the needed amount had been raised. The committee was about to abandon the project when, according to one account, "club pride revolted against such failure [and] the money was guaranteed." Donating the most sizable chunk was Oliver Ames, a former Massachusetts governor and a BAA member. Some six weeks after the meet at Mechanics Hall, the Boston contingent had the funds to get them to and from Athens. (Clark's rendition of the Burnham story appeared in his memoir of track, published in 1912, only 16 years after the Games. That story gets the nod over another version, appearing in the July 27, 1932, issue of the *Boston Transcript*, some 36 years after the Games. In that version, Blake says Burnham told him to "win the 1,000-yard run at our indoor games and we'll send a team to Athens.")

Also set to run the 1,500 Meters at the Olympic Games was the Australian Edwin Flack. He and Arthur Blake were from different backgrounds, but shared a bona fide love affair with distance running. Born in London, the wiry, 6-foot, 22-year-old emigrated as a boy to Melbourne, where he excelled in his studies and at sports. A hare and hounds enthusiast himself, Flack used a distinctively long stride and exceptional stamina to make his mark in 1894 by winning the State of Victoria mile and half-mile championships.

Moving to London in 1895 to work as an accountant for Price Waterhouse, his father's old company, Flack kept running. He joined three athletic clubs, including the London Athletic Club, which nominated him for Athens. In November 1895 at about the time Flack won the Thames Hare and Hounds Club 4.75-mile Challenge Cup, he began saving money with the intention of taking a month-long Olympic break—at his own expense. But Flack was unsure whether to go as a spectator or an athlete, even after his employer granted him leave. Only when his father gave his blessing that he could compete, provided he spend no more than 30 pounds, did Flack book passage to Athens.

The trip was difficult. Seasick on the voyage, Flack arrived in Athens weak and in seemingly no condition for running. Sharing a house with the Englishman, George Robertson, he soon recovered, and on Monday, April 6, served notice that he would be the man to beat in the 1,500 Meters. That afternoon, Flack captured the first heat of the 800 Meters, in which no Americans were entered, in a pedestrian time of 2:16 on the confounding mushy track with the sharp turns. He would be in the final Wednesday, facing among others, France's Albin Lermusiaux, winner of the second heat.

So there were Flack and the speedy Lermusiaux, who Blake quickly sized up as his chief rivals among the eight men in Tuesday's

1,500-Meter final; there were no heats. At the start, Lermusiaux and Flack went out fast. Utilizing their experience from those sharp turns in Monday's 800-Meter heats, they accelerated on the straightaways, and forced the pace. Blake gave chase—and the field, including two Greeks, quickly dwindled to a threesome in the race of roughly 3¾ laps. Flack clung to a slight lead, and only on the backstretch of the final lap were Blake and Lermusiaux able to pull even with the Australian.

The finish line loomed. Lermusiaux fell off and it became a two-man race. Blake and Flack exchanged the lead—Blake led Flack, then Flack led Blake. One of them was about to become an Olympic champion. There were 100 meters to go, then 60, 50, 40—and now they were dead even, striding mostly side-by-side. Then Blake fell a stride behind and caught up again. He felt strong—all those long, hard hare and hounds chases through Cambridge were paying off. But just when he sensed he had the advantage—30 meters remained—Flack turned his way . . . *to chat.* "Ah, it's you, is it?" Flack asked as if he was on a Sunday stroll in the park, before shifting into overdrive. Using his long legs to lengthen his stride six or eight inches, Flack held on to win by two meters. His time of 4:33.2 bettered Blake by four-tenths of a second, with Lermusiaux a distant third in 4:36. Four decades later, Blake remained deeply impressed at the performance of his Australian rival. "I almost broke my stride trying to hold him," he said. "He was a great runner, Flack."

Flack's in-the-moment comment, of course, was not as casual as it appeared. It was tactical, designed to throw off the American at a critical time, demonstrating that he had plenty of energy left. "As soon as I got into the final straight, I went for all I was worth," Flack wrote in his diary. "[Blake] almost caught me in the first 30 yards, and we raced together for about the same distance, when to my relief, I felt that he was falling back and that I had him beaten. I finished up strong and fresh but he was quite done up."

Flack's greeting would pass into Olympic lore. More than a half-century later, at the 1952 Olympic Games in Helsinki, the great Czechoslovakian runner, Emil Zátopek, would do something similar. Already the winner of the 5,000- and 10,000-meter races at the Games, Zátopek was in a twosome leading the marathon at the 16-mile mark when he turned to his co-leader and race favorite, Great Britain's Jim Peters, and said, "We go a little faster, yes?" Peters went faster but there was Zátopek, trotting alongside and then asking with a grin, "Don't we go faster?" The psychological effect was shattering. Peters did not even finish the race and Zátopek went on to win in an Olympic record.

Flack's victory in the 1,500 Meters was the first by a non-American in any track and field event at the modern Olympic Games. Looking on from the stands, several neighborly Greek spectators turned to photographer Burton Holmes and congratulated him on yet another victory by a countryman. No, not this time, Holmes corrected them: Flack was an Australian, not an American. "Oh well," said one, "that is about the same thing; we congratulate you [anyway]." Those Greek spectators weren't the only ones who were a tad confused. Olympic officials were, as well. In the awards ceremony honoring Flack, an Austrian flag shot up the mast. Realizing their mistake, officials quickly replaced it with the British flag and played "God Save the Queen," because Flack lived in London, represented the London Athletic Club, and competed for a British colony. It would take 40 years for Flack to be credited as an Australian in the Olympic record books. Meantime, Flack remained a busy man in Athens. On Wednesday at the Temple of Olympeion (or Olympian), he borrowed a tennis racket to play singles, and partnering with

George Robertson, doubles; though he never made it out of preliminaries in either event. After tennis, Flack returned to the Olympic stadium, and easily won the 800-Meter final in 2:11, thanks in part to the absence of Lermusiaux, who had withdrawn to focus on the Marathon on Friday, April 10.

Flack had one event left—the Marathon—but his legacy as a two-time Olympic champion was already secured. By mid-week, Flack could no longer walk the streets of Athens without being followed by admirers. "They tell me I have become the 'Lion of Athens,'" he wrote to his family. "I could hear people talk Greek and have my name mentioned."

For the Americans, the lionizing had already happened. In three days, they had become the dignitaries of Athens, unable to enter a clothing store without offers of free neckties. And in the cafes, coffee was on the house. On Tuesday evening, giant spotlights streaked light across the Acropolis with multicolored flares bouncing off the Sacred Rock and the ancient ruins. It fed the celebratory mood: Spotting Garrett, Connolly, and Clark as they made their way back to their hotel, admirers and shopkeepers shouted "Niké!"—the Greek word for "victory." "I think it was on the third or fourth day of the Games that the Americanization of Europe began," said Curtis. "The Greek people, from high to low, treated us with great courtesy and friendliness. Sometimes their kindness was embarrassing. . . . But the whole thing was so simple, so naïve, that in spite of our amusement we were touched and pleased."

On Wednesday, April 8, Americans back home woke up to the news of continued US success in Athens. Only a few days before, the Olympic revival was barely a story at all, relegated to the back pages of newspapers. No longer. THE AMERICANS STILL LEAD, blazed a headline in the *New York Tribune*. THE AMERICANS AHEAD, countered the

New York Times. Even the *New York Evening Post*, having missed the story entirely the day before, starting reporting the news everyone was talking about. Continued Success of the American Athletes, trumpeted the headline, the first of several it would run the rest of the week. What had started as a journey of two US track teams, each wearing a variation of their club or university logos, had transformed into a celebration of American nationalism.

Back in Princeton, Professor William Milligan Sloane followed the news from Athens through telegrams, and most likely by reading the New York papers. Unfortunately, his reaction was never recorded, but you can only imagine him practically busting his buttons with pride. The film, *The First Olympians*, includes several scenes of Sloane tearing open telegrams with the good news, and crowing to anyone in earshot about his "boys" making their mark. Could you have blamed him? Against considerable odds, Sloane's dogged determination to create an American Olympic team was paying off handsomely.

CHAPTER 7

"Man of Many Parts"

It was Thanksgiving weekend 1893, and William Milligan Sloane was frustrated. Hosting his friend Pierre de Coubertin, he wondered why few other influential academics were able to grasp, as he put it, "the conception of international sport." But Sloane and Coubertin certainly "got" it; they were fast friends from the time they first met several years before in Paris, bonding from common interests in scholarship, education, and athletics, all of it—they were hoping—to come together in 1896 in Athens. Yet Sloane had achieved little progress in establishing meaningful American interest in the Frenchman's efforts to build an Olympic revival.

It had been nearly four years since the baron's first visit to North America, and a year since Coubertin had stood at a lectern at the Sorbonne University amphitheater in Paris and called on European delegates to support his dream for an Olympic Games for the people and athletes of all nations. Many applauded his lofty calling—sports *did* have benefits—but the mixture of diplomats, representatives of sports clubs, and noblemen had no clue how to actually go about organizing an Olympic Games. "Total, absolute incomprehension," the baron called the inaction. He was right; the attendees had enthusiasm but no ideas about how to build anything. The irony was the baron himself wasn't much better in his technical know-how—"always

Coubertin's weakness," wrote Olympic historian John Lucas. Nor could anyone agree on the exact meaning of "athletic amateurism." The result was inertia, occasional nationalistic hissy fits, and massive misunderstanding.

To some delegates, the Olympic concept was an idealized pageant—"theatrical reconstructions," as one called it. Another asked if the athletes would be nude, as in ancient times. (No.) Another wanted to know if women would be allowed to participate? (Not yet.) When a delegate asked if competition was open to the French only, Coubertin replied magnanimously that the French were most welcome, as would athletes worldwide. "Oh then," the delegate shot back, "we will see Indians, Negroes, and Chinese." The baron, forever putting his own spin on things, was stunned. "I was prepared for irony and protest, but not indifference," he said. "People applauded, wished me well, but failed to understand that I was serious."

Remaining passionate as ever about the Olympic concept, Coubertin plowed ahead anyway. He organized another Sorbonne conference, in June 1894, the so-called Second Congress, in which he toned down the rhetoric—"pitch[ing] his tune in a lower key," he said—and made dogged progress in quelling the bickering of the delegates. Another shrewd move was turning to an influential friend—another baron, the French diplomat, Baron de Courcel—to preside at the Second Congress. De Courcel quickly made his mark by defusing what would become an Olympic tradition, a threat by several members of French athletic clubs to boycott if a German team was allowed to compete. Getting the malcontents in line, Baron de Courcel then won support for the Games from a parade of European leaders, including the King of Belgium, the Crown Prince of Sweden, the Prince of Wales, and even Sir Arthur Balfour, the 1st Earl of Balfour and leader of the British Conservative Party. Then, when Charles

Waldstein delivered one of the baron's biggest prizes—convincing the royal family of Greece to be honorary members of the Congress—an Olympic revival in Athens was beginning to look like a reality.

But Coubertin wanted more than Europeans; he wanted Americans, whom he felt would turn the Games into a truly global event. So in 1893, he had gone to America, his second trip there—looking to secure the support of key North American sportsmen heading to the Second Congress. The baron had a number of strategies up his sleeve—first and foremost, hoping to lean on the connections of his influential friend, Professor Sloane. In the meantime, he would expand his own connections by traveling the United States under the pretext of launching a nationwide program to dispense medals among university debating clubs for initiating French political themes. The baron moved briskly—awarding the first medal in 1894 to one J. S. Campbell of Princeton for his lecture on the political structure of the 3rd French Republic, and then making stops at debating societies at Princeton, Tulane, Stanford, Harvard, Johns Hopkins, Cornell, and the University of California at Berkeley. It was all rather grand, filled with ceremony, but a bit disconnected to his ultimate goal of building support for the Olympic Games.

Arriving in the fall of 1893 in New York, Coubertin headed directly to Chicago's Columbian Exposition, though he regretted missing that summer's International Congress of Education. Like his compatriot of an earlier generation, de Tocqueville, the baron had taken to America—and its refreshing optimism, liberal political views, and boundless thirst for material progress. Of Chicago, he said, "I felt myself filled with admiration at the sudden rising of this vigorous city." The baron was especially taken with its Roman Catholic convocation and the liberalism of Chicago clergymen, James Cardinal Gibbons, later the president of Catholic University, and

Monsignor Keane, and their advocacy for a nontraditional amnesty between Catholic theology and modern science.

From Chicago, Coubertin took a train to Denver and then California, anxious to experience the country's wide-open spaces and beauty. He marveled at California's lushness, writing that "the very abundance of this land gives rise to a sense of its unreality." In San Francisco, he stayed at the swanky Olympic Club and toured the picturesque campus of the University of California at Berkeley. But for all the universities he visited, the baron left no record of whom he met or of any progress or contacts he made on his travels through the midwestern and western United States. He headed back east through Texas, Louisiana, then north to Washington, DC, and wound up back where he had started, in New York. But he didn't linger, anxious to head across New Jersey for a three-week visit to his old comrade, Sloane, at Princeton.

The eminent professor was not only a good friend and a mentor of sorts; he was the man the baron perceived as his ticket to American participation in the Games. They had met in either 1888 or 1889 in Paris. Years later, Coubertin claimed their first meeting was in 1889 at the home of French historian Hippolyte Taine, though the baron may have mixed up the exact year; at the time, he was looking back four decades. More likely, the two men first met in 1888, according to several Austrian newspaper articles unearthed by historian Stephen Wassong. That date seems to be backed up by Sloane's correspondence, which put him in Paris in January 1888, and a citation in the *New York Times*, which claims he was there that May.

The two men hit it off. They were intellectuals. Sloane was fluent in French and could converse in half a dozen other languages. Coubertin spoke passable English but felt more comfortable chatting with Sloane in French. They shared a passion for education and for each other's native country; Sloane would write several books about French history. And most of all, they shared a passion for education and their belief that amateur athletics was a critical tool in building strength and character in young men. In the 1880s, Coubertin's Olympic dreams were still several years away, but he was already heavily invested in advocating English-style games in French schools. Sloane had served as chairman of Princeton's Committee on Outdoor Sports since its inception in 1885, proving himself a skillful infighter as the university champion in many of the controversies that raged about college athletics. Sloane aptly demonstrated his worldview in a March 1890 *Harper's Weekly* article, arguing that athletics teaches young men the values of discipline and commitment—critical qualities, he stated, in securing America's economic and political future. "As patriots we want our educated men to be ready for great undertakings, fearless before the most portentous obstacles, versed in human nature, and adroit in politics," the professor wrote. "There is no better school for the nurture of such qualities than the management of intercollegiate athletics."

Just how William Milligan Sloane found the time and the energy to plunge into amateur sports and contribute influential opinion pieces is remarkable. For all his many accomplishments, it's even more interesting that Sloane's significant Olympic role was rarely mentioned— and not at all in the many laudatory remembrances of him after his death in 1928. For one reason, Sloane never talked much about his Olympic involvement. For another, he simply had too many other things happening in his long life of scholarship. "A man of many parts," the *Princeton Alumni Weekly* called Sloane. A friend and colleague, Princeton Dean Andrew Fleming West, referred, appropriately, to the Greek ideal in describing Sloane. "The Greeks had a saying that 'the workman is greater than his work,'" West said. "It was so with him. He had a strong and far-reaching mind, and [an] extraordinary range of knowledge."

Sloane's moral code and his aspirations formed early. The son of a Presbyterian pastor, he was destined for a life of the mind. When he was four years old, his family relocated from Ohio to New York, where his father, James, took a position as a professor of systematic theology at Allegheny Theological Seminary. Less than a decade later—*at 13*—Sloane entered Columbia College, graduating in 1868 at 18. Then he taught classics for three years in Pittsburgh and returned to Columbia for a year, before deciding to pursue graduate work in Germany. At the University of Leipzig, Sloane cultivated his gift for foreign languages and a prolific range of scholarly interests, and earned a doctorate in Asian history.

In Leipzig, Sloane met the man who would have a profound influence on his career. It was George Bancroft, among the era's most important historians, and President Ulysses Grant's ambassador to Germany. Sloane became Bancroft's secretary, helping research the historian's 10th volume of his hefty *History of the United States*, and developing a hankering for history himself. Sloane spent three immensely important years in Germany, and after earning his PhD, returned to the United States to accept a position at Princeton teaching metaphysics, Latin, Hebrew, and Arabic.

Bancroft's influence on Sloane went well beyond the classroom. Prior to living in Germany, Sloane had never shown the slightest interest in anything athletic. But in his 1890 article in *Harper's Weekly*, Sloane gave credit to Bancroft for developing his recognition and growing interest in the power of exercise. Bancroft, wrote Sloane, had a proven routine for staying sharp mentally: Two hours a day in the open air, rain or shine, with "exercise if possible on horseback or in some other pleasant way, but out-of-doors whatever you do."

At Princeton, Sloane's star rose quickly. He became one of the best-known faculty members, so well rounded that he was destined to play a critical role throughout the 1880s in helping President McCosh reform the university curriculum. In 1883, McCosh created Princeton's School of Philosophy, and elevated Sloane, then 33, to a full professorship. Given his reputation and relatively newfound belief in the benefits of exercise and fresh air, Sloane was a natural to assume another post, as chair of the university's new Committee on Outdoor Sports and its faculty athletic committee.

Sloane tackled his sports duties with gusto. At a time when Princeton, Yale, and Harvard, or the so-called "Big Three," ruled the roost in American college athletics, defending his university was a contact sport in itself. With Yale dominating sports through the 1880s, especially in football, the competition between Princeton and Harvard was particularly intense, prompting a stream of bickering between the two. Accusing one another of harboring professional players was perhaps the most common charge, as happened in 1889, when before their annual football clash, Harvard said Princeton's All-America quarterback William George was getting paid to play. Sloane saw right through the ploy, telling the *New York Times* that Harvard was looking to "weaken Princeton's 11" at a vulnerable time. Princeton, however, wasn't a bit weakened—drubbing the Crimson 41–15, and a week later, upsetting Yale to win the Intercollegiate Football Association championship.

More than a fierce and skillful infighter and capable of wielding a sharp elbow or two in defense of his school, Sloane became a trusted mentor to scores of Princeton athletes, ever willing to serve their interests among the university administrators. In 1889, the faculty approved Sloane's request to move morning chapel 15 minutes later to ensure football players could make it from practice in time. As for the accusation that Walter George, the quarterback, was a pro,

Sloane quickly set the record straight: George was only supervising school sports at nearby Lawrenceville Academy, he told the *New York Times*. The controversy was as good as done.

The Princeton Olympic foursome weren't the only ones to benefit from Sloane's attentions. So would the American impressionist painter, Mary Cassatt, a second cousin of Mary (Mimi) Johnston, Sloane's wife. The Sloanes were among the few with whom Cassatt shared her works-in-progress, usually during the summers in France where Sloane based himself while researching his monumental biography of Napoleon. It was only fitting that the Sloanes and their four children lived on Bayard Lane in Princeton, in a house with a rich past and a whiff of mystery. Named "Stanworth," the house was built on grounds granted by the British government to William Penn. According to legend, British and Hessian soldiers killed in the Revolutionary War at the Battle of Princeton are buried in the yard. In November 1896, the family would welcome a new neighbor, the retiring US president Grover Cleveland.

Napoleon Bonaparte, A History, was published in 1901 in four volumes, and became Sloane's best-known book. Hailed by critics, it became a centerpiece of the era's Napoleonic revival. But it was just one of Sloane's many books in a prolific writing career that had started with a biography of his father, in 1888, and included histories of the French Revolution and the Balkans, a biography of James McCosh, and studies of US government, Western democracy, and France's role in Morocco. It was said that Sloane's complete works would fill a shelf at least five feet long.

<hr>

Ensconced at Stanworth for three weeks in late 1893, the baron indulged in the Sloanes' hospitality. Four days after celebrating

Thanksgiving together, Sloane and the baron got down to the business of building an American Olympic movement. On November 27
at Sloane's request, they met at the University Club in New York with
officials from Harvard, Yale, and Columbia. But the Frenchman got
nowhere—finding no enthusiasm among the academics who considered the Olympic Games as a costly European junket. Besides, argues
Olympic historian Robert Barney, "they had enough troubles of their
own trying to administer athletic affairs in [a] domestic context." The
only sliver of hope that Coubertin took from the meeting was Columbia president Gustavus Town Kirby's advice that he was targeting the
wrong crowd. The key contract in organizing an American Olympic
team, Kirby said, was James E. Sullivan, president of the Amateur Athletic Union. "Sullivan," he told Coubertin, "is your man."

That was logical. Best known today as the namesake of the annual
award presented to America's outstanding amateur athlete, Sullivan
in 1896 was a 34-year-old sports magnate on the rise. Among the
founders back in 1888 of the AAU and its secretary since 1889, Sullivan was a hard-bargaining New York Irishman who had found his
calling in sports as a teenage track star with the Pastime Athletic
Club. Becoming a sportswriter, Sullivan soon headed the sports
department at the *New York Morning Journal* and then the *Sporting
Times*, both temporary stops on the way to greater things.

In 1892, Sullivan hit the jackpot, hired by Albert Spalding to
head the Spalding Company's newly organized subsidiary, the American Sports Publishing Company. Spalding *himself* was a dynamo—
an early big-league baseball star pitcher who won 253 games, going
an astounding 54-5 in 1875, before retiring *at 27*. Spalding never
looked back, soon launching a career as a sports magnate and official. Assisted by his brother, a loan from their mother, and the same
ruthless efficiency and drive that he used to dispatch batters in his

baseball days, Spalding opened a sporting goods store in Chicago and set about building his empire. Spalding published baseball's first official rules guide—making sure that only Spalding balls were used in big-league games. He founded the annual *Base Ball Guide and Official League Book*, a kind of *Sporting News* meets *Sports Illustrated*, which became the country's must-read in baseball circles and featured a blend of statistics, analysis, and lots of ads for innovative Spalding equipment from sliding pads to mitts and catchers' masks.

Along the way, Spalding became baseball's greatest ambassador. As the owner of the Chicago White Stockings, he led a group of major leaguers on a world tour after the 1888 season. They meandered across the western United States to Hawaii, New Zealand, Australia, Ceylon, and Egypt, where the group posed by the Pyramids. Heading to Europe, they visited Italy, France, and England, where they played before the royal family. Back home, Spalding expanded his sports world—selling equipment and creating rules not just for baseball, but for track, archery, polo, skating, and wrestling, too. Spalding's sprawling enterprise was national, commanding a list of suppliers in stores across the country and based at flagship stores in Chicago and in New York at 241 Broadway, where Sullivan kept his office.

It was likely that Coubertin and Sullivan met at Spalding headquarters at 241 Broadway in downtown Manhattan across from City Hall Park. There is no transcript or record of their conversation. Suffice it to say that the two men sized one another up quickly and did not take to one another. "Their personas clashed immediately," Barney wrote. "Sullivan's background and innate character were as different from that of Coubertin as [end-of-the-century] France was from America." Sullivan didn't recognize the value of committing an American team to the Olympic Games. He considered Coubertin an outsider to the inner fiefdom of sports administration and thought him a snob—a visceral response of the streetwise New Yorker to the French aristocrat. Similar to the college presidents, Sullivan said "no" and emphatically so on the idea of sending a US team to Athens. The trip would be prohibitively expensive. It would mean the college athletes would have to miss weeks of classes and a good chunk of the spring track season. Sullivan had too many irons in the fire anyway—more interested in his duties with Albert Spalding and his desire to become the American amateur sports czar than anything Olympic.

Sullivan would became a convert to the Olympics, but that would happen well after the 1896 Games, and most likely after he and Spalding recognized they could exploit attention to the Games to sell more sporting goods. And with the US success in 1896, it was likely that the Games fed Spalding's role as an often-quoted national spokesman for the superiority of all things American at a time when the country was flexing its muscles and becoming a global super-power. In 1905 after Henry Chadwick declared that baseball grew from the British sports of cricket and rounders, Spalding felt com-pelled to object. Of course baseball had British origins, but Spalding wasn't listening, and organized a commission to study the origins of the game. "Our good old American game of baseball must have an American Dad," Spalding argued, and few dared to disagree. Three years later, after reviewing some dubious information, the commis-sion declared that baseball was the invention of Civil War general Abner Doubleday, who it said had organized the first game decades earlier in Cooperstown, New York. It was a nice story, but a complete myth. The theory was almost immediately proved false in a 1909 article in *Collier's* magazine.

Sullivan and Coubertin, and by extension, Sloane, would never move beyond their early antipathy toward one another. For years, they bickered in correspondence, using Coubertin as a sounding board. In a

letter to Coubertin, Sullivan described just what he thought of Sloane—
"a lovely gentleman [who] knows nothing about athletics . . . [and is]
certainly unknown in the athletic legislative halls of [America]." Firing
back in a letter to the baron, Sloane comes off as a snob, calling Sullivan, "a ghetto-poor Irish-American" and "a man whose great faults
are those of his birth and breeding." Sloane wasn't done: "[Sullivan],"
he wrote, "is unfortunately a representative man and holds the organized athletes of the clubs in the hollow of his hand." Not surprisingly,
the baron sided with his friend, the professor, and even after Sullivan
became an Olympic convert, turned down his request to join the International Olympic Committee. That riled up Sullivan all over again: "An
inept leader," he wrote of Coubertin, "a powerless and pathetic figure."

With his meetings in the United States going nowhere, the baron
was fortunate to join Sloane in heading into New York for some
much-needed leisure time. On Saturday, November 30, they joined
the multitudes squeezing into the Polo Grounds, then Manhattan
Field, in northern Manhattan, to watch Princeton's underdog football
team drub defending national champion Yale 6–0.

The victory ensured Princeton of its first national championship in
four years, its first victory against Yale in a decade. "The lads from New
Jersey were clearly superior in team work, tackling, interference play and
other points," gushed the *New York Times* in front-page coverage of the
game. "It was ideal and historic football." It hardly mattered that Coubertin couldn't tell a football from a hockey puck: He found the game
and the ensuing hoopla madly exciting, and an atmosphere he hoped
to replicate at the Olympic Games. A four-hour parade preceded the
game and the excitement of the stadium's biggest crowd to date—some
25,000 of them inside the stadium, and another 20,000 or so watching

from nearby Coogan's Bluff—was magic to the baron. Back at Princeton after the big game there were all-night fireworks in celebration—accompanied by a "tidal wave of howling and immature manhood," as the *New York Tribune* put it. Here was sports at its best, a combination of young, healthy scholars competing before the charged-up multitudes. "The game was a gloriously confusing experience for Coubertin," wrote Lucas. And "what will become of the $20,000 profit?" in ticket prices, Coubertin wondered in drilling down to details. "Shall it be used as an indemnity fund and be divided among the different participants?"

That was only one of the many questions consuming Coubertin as he headed back to Europe, ever more convinced of the righteousness of his Olympic ideal. US apathy aside, the Baron plunged ahead in planning the Second Olympic Congress set for June 1894. In doing so, he described the Congress as a debate on amateurism. On the agenda of the so-called International Congress at Paris for the Study and Extension of the Principles of Amateurism were eight items, the first seven dealing with issues related to amateurism. Slipped in under the radar was an eighth item—actually, a two-part proposal about the "possibility . . . [to] restor[e] the Olympic games" and discuss "under what circumstances [they] could be restored?"

As the baron's American commissioner for the Congress, Sloane did what he could to build interest in the United States. But it remained minimal. The professor distributed invitations to anyone of influence who had a chance of attending, some of them people Coubertin had been writing for years. He invited Johns Hopkins president Daniel Coit Gilman to address the conference in Paris. Gilman turned him down, as did everybody else, though George Adee, the former president of the New York Athletic Club and William Torrey Harris, the US commissioner of education, signed on as honorary members. But the support was token at best: The only American to attend the Second Congress was Sloane himself.

The mighty NYAC was the most obvious source of athletes to fill the American team. But mimicking Sullivan, its leaders weren't interested. Mainstream America had little interest in an impending Olympic revival, perceived as a European-centric event. Newspapers ignored any news about the organization of the Games, with the the *New York Times* including only a single piece, a March 1, 1894 brief under the headline, Minor Sporting Matters. Looking for a spark Coubertin in May amended the schedule for the Congress to include Olympic matters in half the agenda items.

Coubertin set an ambitious agenda in Paris. He asked the 79 delegates from 13 countries and more than 50 athletic organizations to make a clear Olympic commitment. And he wanted the delegates to designate Athens as home for the first Games. To make it happen, the baron promised a fine show intended to dazzle. Opening June 16, the Second Congress mixed in some work with a lot of grand dinners, poetic orations, and classical references guaranteed to win the hearts of the most hardened critics.

Setting the tone was a dazzling opening session in the amphitheater of the Sorbonne—"to show," as the baron said, "that [this was] something more important than an ordinary sporting conference." Some 2,000 people, including elegantly dressed women, got not just a speech by Baron de Courcel and an oration from the poet Jean Aicade, but a choir singing the Hymn of Apollo. "Hellenism filtered through the vast enclosure, producing a harmony that transcended the ages," Coubertin said of the opening. "I knew from that moment, no one would vote against the reestablishment of the Olympic Games."

All week, the Baron treated his guests to the splendors of Paris. Coubertin wasn't just head of the Congress; he was its social and travel director, too. Delegates played tennis at the elegant Luxembourg Gardens. They fenced. And they wined and dined, each dinner seemingly more lavish than the one before. Hosted by the Racing Club of Paris at Bois de Boulogne, delegates enjoyed dinner in a meadow lit by torches amidst mock battles on horseback—now, *there* was a way of using racehorses on a day the track was dark—set to live music from an orchestra of trumpets. After all of that, who would dare partake of the baron's largess—and turn down his plan for the Olympic Games? To remove any last doubts, Coubertin on day six of the Congress delivered a whopper when he read a timely telegram from Greece's King George I thanking him "with deep feeling toward [his] courteous petition"... and "my best wishes for the revival of the Olympic Games."

In between the festivities, the baron ensured some serious work got done. He designated two committees, which hammered out a definition of amateurism and set a basic outline of the inaugural Games. The vote in favor of reviving the Games was unanimous—setting the inaugural Games for Athens in 1896, to be followed by Paris in 1900 and St. Louis in 1904, which would coincide with the World's Fair. Delegates also entrusted the administration and organization of the Games to an International Olympic Committee, comprised of 14 members, handpicked by the baron and including Sloane. Though it would take Coubertin far more work to nail down the endorsement of the more cost-conscious Greek government officials, the baron had won his prize. The man who James Sullivan of the AAU had derided as knowing "nothing about athletics" had maneuvered stealthily to fulfill the dream of a lifetime.

To no one's surprise, the classical orations were flowing again, this time on Saturday, June 23, 1894, at the farewell dinner of the Sorbonne Congress at the Jardin d'Acclimation. Dimitrios Bikelas, Coubertin's hand-chosen delegate from Athens, addressed the assembly, as did several others. Presiding over the ceremonies like a proud family patriarch, Coubertin could barely contain himself—reaching for new levels of lofty prose by "lift[ing] my glass to the Olympic idea, which has traversed the mists of the ages like an all-powerful ray of sunlight and returned to illuminate the threshold of the 20th Century with a gleam of joyous hope."

After that, it was a wonder that the baron still had a breath. But he wouldn't forget his friend, Sloane, who had stuck with him through thick and thin. So at dinner, Coubertin bestowed Sloane with the Ordre des Palmes Académiques or Order of Academic Palms—an Order of Chivalry of France for educators. Created by Napoleon for eminent members of the University of Paris, the award had been expanded to include major contributions to French national education from anyone, even foreigners. For the professor, it was among many honors during a distinguished career, but perhaps the only one to acknowledge his significant contribution as the father of the American Olympic movement.

The Princeton professor still had a lot more work to do in his quest to put together an American Olympic team—and more than a century later, his Olympic contributions still float well under the radar. The baron's ego may have something to do with that; for all his graciousness at the end of the conference, Coubertin would eventually morph into an ego-driven, one-man Olympic public relations machine, puffed up by his own importance and convincing everyone that he and he alone was responsible for creating the modern Olympics. "As for myself," the baron would say, "I hereby assert my claims for being sole author of the whole project." Sole author? Princeton's '96 Olympians, whom Sloane mentored, would disagree.

CHAPTER 8

Smoking Guns

STRIDING THROUGH THE DOOR OF HIS PARIS APARTMENT FOR LUNCH on the last day of March 1896, 27-year-old Sumner Paine was in for a shock.

A visitor was waiting, unexpected and unannounced. It was Paine's younger brother, John, having just arrived from the United States. After a quick exchange of pleasantries, he got right to the point.

"When does the next train start for Athens?" the 25-year-old John asked.

"I don't know," Sumner responded.

"Well, find out, and get your revolvers and we will go there," said John, "for the Boston Athletic Association has sent a team over, and as there are two revolver matches we may be able to help out the Americans."

Sumner never hesitated. Just like that, the brothers Paine, both expert marksmen and members of the BAA, decided to head to Athens, where they would become the most dominant part of the 1896 US Olympic team outside of track and field. They would make history—and long be remembered after firing their last shots as two of the more dashing members of America's first Olympic team.

John must have known he wouldn't need a hard sell to recruit his older brother for Athens. Of course, Sumner Paine would go. The

Olympic Games sounded fun. The brothers, members of one of the richest and most prominent families in Massachusetts, could afford it. Entry into the Games' shooting competition was mostly a matter of owning the appropriate weaponry and showing up. And the Paine brothers were hands-down the best marksmen in the world, practically guaranteed to win their events. The only pressing questions revolved around details and conditions and the specific rules of European competition.

They would find out in Athens. That afternoon in Paris, the Paine brothers lunched and repaired to the Gastine-Rennette Galleries and firearms shop, a few steps south of the Champs-Elysées at 39 Avenue Victor Emmanuel III (now Avenue Franklin Roosevelt), where Sumner worked as a gunsmith. Unsure of the quantity or the accessories they would need in Athens, the brothers settled on 21 centigrams of nitro powder and rounded bullets cast by the well-known firm of George R. Russell & Co. of Boston. "I did not care to trust the French bullets, with their long screw tails, in such an important match," said Sumner.

Not sure of the weaponry required and the number of rounds allowed in the matches, the brothers, accompanied by Sumner's wife, Salome, arrived in Athens with enough firearms to start a revolution. Thanks to their wealth, neither cost nor quantity were issues in building a collection: With them were eight weapons—two Colt army revolvers, two Smith & Wesson Russian model revolvers, a Stevens .22-caliber pistol and a Wurfflein, two pocket weapons—and fearing multiple rounds of competition, 3,500 rounds of ammunition. The Paine brothers would be ready for just about any challenge thrown their way.

They were entitled to own all the weaponry they wanted. They were *Paines*. Direct descendants of Robert Treat Paine, the

Massachusetts representative who signed the Declaration of Independence, John and Sumner Paine were the sons of General Charles J. Paine, a Civil War hero turned business tycoon and yachtsman. Like many male members of the family, Charles was born in Boston, attended Harvard, and turned to business—in his case, earning a fortune in railroads. In 1861 just after the outbreak of the Civil War, Charles entered military service as a captain in the 22nd Massachusetts, working his way to a generalship and command of a division of the Union Army's African-American troops in Virginia.

Charles Paine's youngest brother was Sumner, his future son's namesake, and said to be the finest scholar of his class at Harvard. But in May 1863 when Sumner was suspended for some trifling offense, he headed straight to the governor for a commission as an Army lieutenant. Motivated by patriotism and perhaps a dose of peer pressure, Paine joined the celebrated 20th Massachusetts, known as the Harvard Regiment for the number of its officers who were recent Harvard graduates, including future Supreme Court justice Oliver Wendell Holmes Jr. and Paul Revere Jr. But the regiment drew its fame from its members' unwavering heroism at some of the Civil War's biggest and bloodiest battles, including the savagery of the Peninsula Campaign, Antietam, Fredericksburg, and in young Paine's case, the vortex of the Battle of Gettysburg.

On July 3, 1863, at Gettysburg, the 20th Massachusetts formed a crucial part of the line of defense against the Confederate Army's last infantry attack, Pickett's Charge, considered one of the turning points of the war. And in the midst of it all was young Lieutenant Paine, with less than two months in service—and bravely encouraging his men to rush forward to meet the enemy. "Isn't this glorious?" he shouted above the mayhem to a fellow officer. A moment later, a shell burst knocked him down, breaking his ankle. Quickly bounding to his feet, Paine kept waving his sword and leading his men until a bullet ripped through his chest, killing him instantly. He was 18.

Massachusetts mourned the loss. So distraught was fellow lieutenant, L. E. Hubbard, that he apologized to Paine's father for not stopping in the heat of battle to see after his son. "Unnatural as it may seem, a soldier and an officer especially cannot stop during his engagement even if his own brother [goes down]." Three years later, in 1868, Charles named his first son in honor of his heroic younger brother.

John Paine was born less than two years later, in 1870, and by all accounts, the boys had an upbringing typical of New England's richest families. Growing up on Beacon Hill in Boston, they summered at their family estates, and attended the Hopkinson School and Harvard. But the Paines' upbringing differed from the norm in two crucial respects: Like their father and uncle, both Sumner and John were destined to enter the military. And in doing so, they learned how to shoot as well or better than anyone else on the planet.

John enlisted first. Graduating from Harvard in 1891, he gave the university's law school a brief shot, then opted for business. Steered by his railroad chief of a father, John took positions at the Mexican Central and Boston Elevated railways. Returning in 1894 to Boston, Paine joined the 1st Massachusetts Regiment Infantry and soon distinguished himself by superior marksmanship. Commissioned within weeks as 1st lieutenant, he was soon inspecting the regiment's rifle practice.

Sumner's path was more circuitous, filled with stops and starts in which the dots rarely connected. Entering Harvard's class of '90, he never graduated. Deciding to study medicine, he ventured west to Denver and enrolled in Gross Medical College, later the Colorado University School of Medicine. Along the way, he stayed active in sports, mostly as a shooter and as an official. On October 24, 1894, in a drenching rainstorm in New Haven, Sumner refereed the Yale football team's 23–0 defeat of the BAA. Married in 1892 to Salome Brigham, he and his wife adopted a daughter, Julia, in 1894.

Just why he and Salome moved to Paris is a bit of a mystery—*The Secretary's Report* of Paine's Harvard class of '90, published in 1909, claims it was part of his course work to "study in the hospitals" there. But why in 1896 was he working as a Paris gunsmith? And how in the world did a medical student–turned-gunsmith find the time to suddenly drop everything to spend two weeks in Athens, presumably in the middle of his spring semester? Though Sumner Paine never really answered those questions, he and John headed to Athens for the challenge, a bit of adventure, and an opportunity to give a clinic in marksmanship.

The Paines cut it close, arriving in Athens on Tuesday, April 7, a day prior to the start of the shooting competition. After registering at their hotel, the brothers headed to the American Consulate and obtained certificates of amateur status. Then on Wednesday morning—day three of the Games—John, Sumner, and Salome Paine headed to the shooting range, the "Skopeftirion" in Kallithea, about three kilometers south of the City Center. A handsome marble building with distinctive columns, the Skopeftirion took the shape of the long, rectangular shooting range within its walls. Salome Brigham's photo of the venue would accompany Sumner's lengthy report of the competition in the May 1896 issue of *Shooting and Fishing* magazine.

With some exceptions, the particulars of Olympic competition didn't faze the Paines. The Greeks infused the proceedings with a touch of hoopla by sending the Queen of Greece to preside at the opening. Baron de Coubertin, said to be a competent shot who had created a sizable program reflective of his interest, was there as well, most likely to keep the queen company. There would be five events—300-Meter Rifle, 200-Meter Army Rifle, 25-Meter Dueling or Rapid-Fire Pistol, 25-Meter Army Pistol, and 30-Meter Target Pistol. Among the 61 shooters from seven countries was their countryman and the baron's good friend, Charles Waldstein.

Still unfamiliar with the rules and conditions of competition, the Paines submitted their weaponry for inspection. Olympic rules limited shooters to use "any weapon of usual caliber" with a trigger of up to 4.5 pounds. So out the door went the Paine brothers' heavy .22 pistols, bouncing them from rapid-fire pistol competition. Posing a further challenge were the European-style targets, marginally smaller in Athens than the standardized American model. Still another complication, as Sumner would explain in exquisite technical detail in *Shooting and Fishing*, was the sunlight—the glistening Athenian sunlight, which bounced off the polished steel of their weapons, making it difficult to clearly detect the white background of the center zone. To reduce the glare, the brothers cooked up a homegrown solution by passing burning matches over the lock, stock, and barrel of their guns.

The sheer number of last-minute complications would be enough to cause fits for many in the exacting and precise world of competitive shooting. But it barely troubled the Paine brothers, who quickly adjusted, fortified by frequent nips of whiskey from their pocket flasks. Deciding to enter the remaining two pistol events, John ended up in only one—the 25-Meter Military Revolver competition on Saturday, April 11—and won easily, scoring 442 on 25 hits out of 30 shots. Completing the family—and US—domination in the event was Sumner, who took second with 380 points on 23 hits. No one else was close; in third, far behind the two Americans, was Nikolas Dorakis of Greece, compiling 205 points, less than half of John's score.

Helping the Paines was their superior weaponry—Colt revolvers, far superior in quality to the arms of their opponents. But so lopsided was the margin of victory that the brothers would have won using cap guns.

So John Paine of Boston was an Olympic champion. So why not withdraw in order to let his brother share the glory with a title of his own? His victory had seemed so effortless that John figured it would be unsporting *not* to bow out and leave Sumner with a shot at first place in the 30-Meter Target Pistol event. A somewhat leisurely affair next to the other more compressed shooting events, the free pistol gave competitors 2½ hours to fire 60 shots at a target 50 meters away. The 10-ring or bull's-eye of the target was all of two inches in diameter. In the final, competitors took 10 shots with 75 seconds in between each.

John's sportsmanship paid off. Using an S&W Russian model, Sumner Paine on Saturday, April 11, obliterated his four opponents, totaling 442 points, miles ahead of the second-place finisher, Holger Nielsen of Denmark, who accumulated 285 points. That Nielsen, a 29-year-old native of Copenhagen, should even score that well was still a feat; like his countryman Viggo Jensen, he was among the Athens Games' most versatile athletes. In addition to shooting, he fenced, taking third in sabre competition, and even threw the discus. Nielsen's versatility would continue long after his competitive career; he would develop an early set of handball rules, as well as a technique of external cardiopulmonary resuscitation.

Sumner Paine's victory near the end of competition at the Athens Games was the 11th championship earned by the 14 American Olympians. In becoming the first brothers to place one-two in a single event and the first to win Olympic titles, the Paines had made history—and a compelling morsel of trivia. They had done so with exquisite style and a dash of sportsmanship and irreverence—Sumner's report of the competition in *Shooting and Fishing* magazine would be complemented by detailed descriptions of the many parties and receptions the Paines attended throughout their time in Athens. Both men would leave Greece with heavier baggage, thanks to gifts from admiring Athenians that included a case of local wine and a dozen silk ties from an Athens department store. Of the 3,500 rounds of ammunition they carted to Athens, the Paines blasted through all of 96, making barely a dent in their arsenal.

So impressed by the Paines were their Greek competitors that they took to imitating them, thinking perhaps their quirks and technique would rub off. Watching them dip frequently from their pocket flasks of whiskey, the Greeks made a run on the Athenian supply of flasks and nipped away. By day two of competition, "not a Greek contestant sighted a gun, without first applying a black bottle to his lips," reported a bemused Holmes. Watching the brothers apply burning matches to their weaponry to blunt the glare, Greek competitors smoked their guns too—"almost reducing them to ashes in their desire to do the proper thing," Holmes said. It didn't matter that they really need not have done so since day two was so overcast. "Thus the flattery of imitation," added Holmes, "was carried to ludicrous extremes."

But Greek marksmen weren't as helpless as they seemed. On the final day of competition in shooting at the 1896 Olympic Games, Ioannis Phrangoudis took the Rapid-Fire Pistol; Pantelis Karasevdas, the Free Rifle; and Georgios Orphanidis the Free Rifle, Three Positions. So did the versatile Viggo Jensen smoke his weapons and help himself to nips of whiskey? He wasn't saying, but the remarkable Dane had quite a time in the shooting competition himself—taking a third in the Free Rifle, Three Positions competition and sixth in the Free Rifle. But overall, marksmanship in Athens belonged to the Americans.

CHAPTER 9

"A Foreigner Should Not Win This Race!"

TAKING HIS PLACE IN A CARRIAGE DRAWN BY THREE HORSES LATE IN the afternoon of Thursday, April 9, outside the Hotel D'Angleterre, Arthur Blake was confident that he could handle the hefty task that awaited him the following day. From Athens, the carriage would carry him north into the countryside along curvy, rutted and mostly unpaved roads to the start of one of the most eagerly anticipated events of the first modern Olympic Games.

Blake was headed to the little town of Marathon from which according to legend, a Greek soldier named Pheidippides was dispatched in the year 490 BC to Athens to announce that his army had miraculously defeated the Persians in battle. It is said the gallant Pheidippides ran the entire distance of more than 20 miles without stopping, but moments after proclaiming his message, "*Nenikekamen*" ("We were Victorious!"), collapsed dead from exhaustion.

Blake's event was the Marathon, simply and elegantly named after the town. On Friday afternoon, he and 16 other hearty athletes would leave town, head south to Athens, and close with a lap or so around the track at Olympic Stadium before the multitudes, just as the final day's track events were finishing. Would a Greek runner finally break through to win an Olympic championship? The hopes of the entire country were high. By the time the marathon was finished, the drama of the event would more than live up to its billing. Two roads led from the battlefield of Marathon south to Athens, one covering a distance of about 34.5 kilometers (21.4 miles) and mountainous, with the other flatter and a bit longer at 40.8 kilometers (25.4 miles). The legend says Pheidippides took the mountainous but shorter route in order to avoid a buildup of Persian soldiers south of town.

So was there really a messenger named Pheidippides, and if so, did he really run that far? It's a dubious tale at best: The fifth-century BC historian Herodotis, who was noted for his affinity for gossip, never mentioned Pheidippides's journey in his summary of the Battle of Marathon. The story of the messenger wouldn't appear in print for 600 years after it was said to happen. Nor did the ancient Olympians ever run anything even close to marathon distance; for the record, their longest race was 4,800 meters—about three miles—according to Olympic historian David Wallechinsky.

But the legend mattered. The tale of Pheidippides fed pride among Greeks in their glorious past, particularly after winning their independence from the Turks. For Olympic organizers, it was a link to what would become one of the Games' storied events. Though Greek athletes had by the start of the Marathon earned two Olympic titles in gymnastics—Ioannis Mitropoulos in rings followed by Nikolaos Andriakopoulos in rope climbing—those events were traditionally European competitions dominated by Germans. The Greeks were desperate for a victory against the Americans, who hadn't fielded any gymnasts. There was a lot at stake: Without a victory against the world, a new Greek tragedy was in the making. Many Greeks prayed openly that one of their runners would prevail in what organizers had deemed would be the longer 25.4-mile or 40.8-kilometer route.

Should a Greek runner be victorious, he could take advantage of the many incentives already offered by merchants in Athens—a year's worth of free clothes from a tailor, shaves from a barber, and restaurant meals. Throw in another few prizes, a lifetime guarantee of shoes, and even an offer of marriage.

The baron's friend, a French linguist named Michel Bréal, was the father of the Marathon. Traveling with Coubertin on the 1894 trip to Greece, the two men peddled the idea of the ultra-long event for the Olympics, linking it to the glory days of the ancient land. It wasn't a hard sell: There was a lot to like about a race that commemorated the exploits of a Greek runner dispatched to report the news of victory in battle. Averoff, the businessman, got firmly behind the event and other Olympic officials consequently fell in line. Bréal insisted on presenting the victor with an exquisite silver cup, with Ionnos Lambros, a noted collector of Greek antiquities, set to present yet another award, an antique vase. They were handsome gifts to be sure, but not as practical as the shoes.

As the Games neared, the Marathon attracted both excitement and alarm. Blake looked forward to the challenge, though he had never run a competitive race remotely close to marathon distance. Others considered the concept of a 25-mile run over the hills of the Greek countryside as nothing short of outrageous, and medical experts warned it could be dangerous. But as novel as the Marathon was to many, it had some precedent since people had been covering long distances for years. In the 1700s, a 60-year-old Englishman named Foster Powell ran 402 miles around England. Six-day races became the rage in the 1870s and 1880s in both the UK and the United States, with runners covering endless laps on a track with periodic breaks. It was around the same time that pedestrianism or long-distance walking soared in popularity, thanks to big-time speed walkers like Edward Payson Weston, who in the winter of 1861 on a bet and a prayer walked 478 miles from Boston to Washington, DC, in 10 days.

At the Athens Games, the Marathon was the event that gave the Greeks the greatest home-field advantage. Several months before the Games, Greek organizers announced that a team would be chosen from the top finishers of two time trials, and there were reports that as many as three Greek runners died in training. In February, two Greeks ran the course on their own with one G. Grigorou—his first name lost to history—leading the way in 3 hours, 45 minutes. On March 10, 1896, in possibly the first Olympic trial ever staged, 12 members of various Greek sports clubs vied for the opportunity to run a month later at the Games. Charilaos Vasilakos was the fastest to cover the distance, in 3:18, trailed by Spiridon Belokas and Demetrious Deliyannis. At the second trial, held Saturday, April 4, just days before the start of the Games, 38 runners took off from Marathon with Ioannis Lavrentis winning in 3:11. Overlooked but ultimately chosen for the Greek team was the race's fifth-place finisher, Spiridon Louis, a 24-year-old water-carrier from the north Athens suburb of Marousi.

Organizers directed some of the day's athletes to run 25 miles twice within a few days, demonstrating how little anyone knew in those days about effective distance training. That went for the American team, for whom Blake exuded an easygoing confidence, but as BAA trainer John Graham would admit later, was a runner better prepared for a mile on the track. Graham would do what he could, accompanying Blake's Marathon-bound carriage on his bicycle, joined by Howard Alexander, the 14-year-old son of the American ambassador. The two planned to shadow Blake during Friday's trek back to Athens, hoping to coach and encourage him along the way.

The journey to Marathon gave the Americans their first real sense of the long, arduous course that awaited Blake. For starters, the route was hilly—"half a dozen rises higher than [Boston's 635-foot] Blue Hill," he reported. And it was winding, dusty, filled with ruts and roots, and downright desolate in places—all of which added up to a "killing" course, Graham said. All in all, it was a considerable change from the charms and crowds of cosmopolitan Athens that the Americans had been enjoying most of the week.

If the runners had little sense of how to train for the Marathon, they knew next to nothing about the proper nutrition. Arriving Thursday evening at a Marathon inn secured by Ambassador Alexander for all the runners, Blake happily tore into Graham's idea of a pre-race training meal—not pasta, but an oversized steak accompanied by eggs and milk. Cooking the steak in a mammoth fireplace, the Americans relaxed and soaked in the atmosphere of the Greek countryside.

They certainly weren't in Athens anymore. At dinner, a big-boned man wearing a goat's-skin hat and a six-foot gun slung over his shoulder came lumbering into the inn. He was a hunter—a man who "shot game [and] wild animals," as the innkeepers informed his American guests. That evening, Blake, Graham, and young Howard Alexander strolled about Marathon and called on the village priest, before heading back to the inn. By then, the other runners had arrived from Athens, also in wagons. All were given quarters in a big room covered with mattresses for the evening.

But they weren't quite done meeting the locals. In the pitch-black dead of night, another new acquaintance—this one a man with a knife between his teeth—crept into the room. Several stirred, light went on, and full-scale panic ensued at the sight of the intruder. Just as surprised was the knife-wielding man, who wasn't looking for mischief, only a mattress for himself and his knife. Things calmed down relatively quickly.

Blake still got a fitful night's rest. On Friday morning, he, Graham, and young Howard Alexander killed the hours before race time at 2:00 p.m. by visiting the plains where the legendary Battle of Marathon had taken place. Sauntering back to the inn, they joined a contingent of Greek soldiers who had arrived to accompany the runners on the course, but for now, were intent on practicing the BAA cheer. That took care of any pre-race jitters as Blake and Graham offered a bellowing tutorial on the finer points of the cheer. Giving it a few tries, the appreciative soldiers retired to toast US president Grover Cleveland and various branches of the US military, adding another notch to the ever-improving state of Greek-American foreign relations. "We responded in like manner," Graham reported.

Meanwhile, the American trainer coordinated his race strategy. Graham directed the carriage driver to go to a house halfway through the course and wait should Blake decide to drop out. Having ridden the course, he recognized the perils of what could be an endeavor more difficult than anything Blake had ever attempted. So Graham leveled with his charge, telling him his Olympic performance had already been a success—and that there was no dishonor in stopping. Should he feel unable to continue, Blake should just bow out.

The Greek runners followed a different pre-race regimen. Most went to church, where prayers were offered for a home-team victory. Then Louis and the other runners from the village of Marousi set off on a short trot about town to loosen up and break in the new race shoes donated by people in their community. Back at the inn, a Greek doctor holding a little hammer waited to give them a short pre-race exam. Proceeding to give each man several raps on the knee, the doctor laughed when Louis's knee shot up. The little examination baffled Louis and the other Greek runners, but satisfied the good doctor: "He came back to me after he was finished with all the others and gave my knee a fourth knock," Louis said. "'He might make it,' I heard him saying to a man from the committee."

The weather gods had cooperated, delivering what accounts report was a cool, dry day—hardly good conditions for swimmers, but ideal for the marathoners. (There are very few descriptions of the weather during the last afternoon of track competition. The only concrete description is from the Official Report on the 1896 Games, filed months later, that stated in the late afternoon during the pole vault— referred to as "pole jumping"—the athletes were getting leg massages to fortify them against the increasing cold.) The organizers had done their work as well, clearing most of the roads along the route of traffic with mounted cavalrymen ready to make sure that not a single cart or errant goat, sheep, donkey, or pedestrian even think of crossing the road anywhere near the runners. Several medical wagons would follow the pack as would the horseback-bound soldiers—two to a runner. Of the 17 starters, 13 were Greek, all of whom had presumably completed one of the trials. They were joined by Blake; Gyula Kellner of Hungary; the great Edwin Flack of Australia; and France's Albin Lermusiaux. Though the field included the top three finishers of the 1,500 Meters, Kellner was the only non-Greek to have run the equivalent of a marathon. Meanwhile, Italy's Carlo Airoldi had traveled nearly 1,000 miles on foot to reach Athens, but was kept from the race on grounds that he was a professional. How history could have changed had he been let in; Airoldi was by far the most experienced ultra-distance runner in the field, having competed in several 50-kilometer (or 31-mile) races. But the Games were for amateurs only, and Airoldi was out.

Lining up for the start at Marathon bridge, the collection of runners had a ragamuffin look. Variety ruled with some wearing singlets, others in white undershirts, some bare-headed and others in caps. Children watched from rooftops as runners spread across the road, three to a line and six rows deep. Securing spots in the first row were Lermusiaux, perhaps looking to bolt from the gun as he had in the 1,500 Meters, and Blake. Louis was in the back, near another runner who started grumbling about his position so vociferously that Blake, who was up front, offered to switch positions. "Take my place," Blake called. "I was spotting him nine yards in 25 miles, and he thought I was a great sport." With that, Major General Papadiamantopoulos mounted his horse and described the course, in Greek and then French. Then the general fired his pistol and the inaugural Olympic Marathon field was off, headed to Athens and into legend.

—

Why all of Greece was so desperate for a victory in the Marathon by a countryman was becoming crystal clear back at Olympic Stadium: They were nearly out of time. In front of another throng, many of whom had arrived after watching the swimming event at the Bay of Zea, and untold thousands of non–ticket holders who took their customary spots on the big mountain overlooking the stadium, the Coogan's Bluff of Athens, the Americans were dominating the competition of the final day in track and field. Greek journalists had grown ever more exasperated at the inability of Greeks to beat any Americans on the track. Their theories were all over the map, from one who traced the American success to inheriting the training techniques of Native Americans to another attributing the American edge to their piety, thinking Garrett was praying when he blew on his hands to moisten them while preparing for the discus. Another actually wrote that the Americans got their endurance from chewing gum—yes, gum chewing, which he said, strengthened the lungs.

Taking great delight in all the theories were the American spectators; Burton Holmes would list a few of them in his Olympic lectures.

Gymnastics had launched the final afternoon of Olympic competition, and quickly ended. Attention then shifted to the track, and the Americans went to work, methodically aceing one final event after another—"a repetition of the same story," as Richardson put it in *Scribner's*. In the day's first final, Burke, as expected, aced the field in the 100 Meters—matching his qualifying time in 12.0 seconds and beating Fritz Hofmann of Germany by two meters (12.2) to become a two-time Olympic champion. Three others, including Francis Lane, were bunched four meters behind. Notably absent was Thomas Curtis, who had decided to save his strength for the 110-Meter Hurdles and what he perceived would be a tough race against the pompous Englishman, Grantley Goulding.

So Curtis skipped the 100 to give his full attention to Goulding and the hurdles—"the race I had come especially to run." That done, he could "look at the other final contests with much greater pleasure," as he put it. In doing so, Curtis seemed to have triggered a minor trend: Another American hurdler, Bill Hoyt, decided to skip the hurdles as well to better focus on *his* specialty, the pole vault. When another finalist, Frantz Reichel of France, dropped out, Curtis and the boastful Goulding were left to duel in a two-man Olympic final.

With the gun, Curtis caught a break. Goulding stumbled, giving the American a short lead. Curtis took full advantage—fighting to maintain the lead, even as Goulding started to close the gap. Races of any length are seldom decided at the start, but the Englishman's mishap had cost him dearly. Running smoothly, Curtis doggedly held on as the two men steamed toward the finish—or so it seemed. Both men crossed the line in 17.6 seconds, but officials declared Curtis the winner by a scant five centimeters—"the most exciting finish of the

Games," Clark declared in his memoirs. That set the American athletes off, launching into another round of BAA cheers. Not taking the result so favorably was the pouting Goulding, who Curtis said "stopped neither to linger or say farewell, but went straight from the stadium to the station and took the first train out of Athens." And with that, Goulding's excellent adventure at the Olympic Games was done.

Around the same time, Ellery Clark became a two-time Olympic champion, leading an American sweep in the High Jump. Clark won with a jump of 5 feet, 11¼ inches, with Connolly second and Garrett third—each man cleared 5 feet, 5 inches—in competition that the *New York Times* called "a fine exhibition of scientific jumping." Right in character with his understated demeanor, Clark would say next to nothing about his victory in his memoirs. "I won the high jump," he wrote blandly. If Greek spectators were still frustrated that a countryman had yet to take a championship in track and field, Clark had given them another reason to bond with the Americans—having sewn the arms of the Greek royal family above the American flag on his jersey.

Lost in the blizzard of American success was the tale of Clark's Harvard, BAA, and US teammate, Bill Hoyt. Like Clark and Connolly, he had been a Harvard student in good standing and member of the university's track team with a fierce desire to get to Athens. But then Hoyt's path suddenly changed direction; whereas Clark was granted permission to attend the Games and Connolly was denied and withdrew from school, Hoyt's status was somewhere in between. School officials didn't inform him one way or another if he could go to Athens, but the 21-year-old Harvard sophomore was determined to go anyway.

Hoyt had burst into prominence at Roxbury Latin School, where he hurdled and pole vaulted his way to several Massachusetts outdoor and indoor championships, including his top vault of 11 feet, 2¾ inches at the 1895 Mott Haven Games. Still, the details of how William Welles Hoyt actually made the US Olympic team remain murky; he never applied to Dean Briggs to make the trip nor was he a member of the original BAA team selected for Athens.

"Not a strong character," a former teacher wrote of Hoyt. "Lacks purpose and will, probably from rather weak health. Vaults with a pole about eleven feet six inches, and has great love of music. Music may undue him." That may have been so, but Hoyt would demonstrate a creative touch in stating his case for going to Athens: By feigning weak health, hard to fathom for a top athlete, Hoyt was able to convince two doctors that "a foreign trip would benefit me greatly." So he became a BAA stand-in—and only after a member contributed $200 at the last minute, an American Olympian. Hoyt withdrew from Harvard on March 20, 1896, but unlike Connolly, would eventually return to the school and earn a medical degree.

How appropriate that Hoyt should take to vaulting—both he and the origins of his sport were a tad quirky. Just where pole vaulting got its start is unknown, but by most accounts, it developed from a variety of cultures as a practical way for the presumably physically fit ancients to surmount physical obstacles from canals and streams to irrigation ditches. Indeed, Egyptian relief sculptures, circa 2500 BC, depict warriors using poles to scale enemy walls. The first known pole vault competitions date to 1829 BC at the Irish Tailteann Games. By the 1850, "running pole leaping" was a part of track and field, with vaulters using rigid poles made of ash to launch themselves into the air, and using their hands in climbing the pole for additional height.

Americans banned pole climbing in 1889, clearing the way for a more athletic technique in which vaulters led with their legs upward, and then reversed their bodies in an attempt to curl around the crossbar. The technique is still in use, though pole vaulting would not become widespread in college athletics until the turn of the 20th century. Though Hoyt and Princeton's Albert Tyler had moved beyond ash to a slightly more flexible bamboo pole, pole vaulting in Athens was still a fairly primitive exercise. Vaulters didn't have a runway, a hole for the pole, or even a pit for a comfortable landing, instead having to hit the hard ground with a thud. Compare those hardships to today's vaulting, with its fiberglass poles, deep pits, and comfortable, inflated landing pits and arguably, no other event in track and field has been transformed as radically by equipment and technology.

Hoyt and Tyler were among the five Olympic vaulters; the other three were Greek and really hadn't yet gotten the hang of the sport. Nor had the judges, who started the bar so low that it wasn't much above the height set for high jump, somewhere in the mid-7-foot range. So Hoyt and Tyler elected to pass on the early jumps. Meanwhile, vaulters had three tries at each height, and the Americans watched all three of their opponents knock themselves out before they had even started. Watching from the grandstand, Eugene Andrews of Cornell said the competition "was almost comic"— both for the mismatch and because "the bar was so set ridiculously low at first. . . . (and) was raised by only 1 centimeter between tries."

Andrews was probably right about that, but he appeared to stretch the truth when he wrote that the American vaulters drew "a clamor of protest" from their Greek opponents in passing on the low heights. Passing on the low heights was common practice for an injured or top vaulter or high-jumper to preserve his strength. Nor was a protest likely to mean much in light of the great sportsmanship the Greek vaulters would show their American competitors in the latter stages of the competition. So with all three Greeks gone with the bar still set at only 7 feet, 7 inches, the inaugural Olympic

Pole Vault championship had come down to a competition between two Americans, neither of whom had even started. Only after getting the judges to raise the bar another 1½ feet to 2.80 meters (9 feet, 2 inches) would they begin. Not bad for a couple of vaulters better known for other things—Hoyt as a hurdler, and if that teacher was to be believed, a lover of music, and the other, Tyler, a cog on Princeton's powerful football team.

At 24, Tyler was older than most of his teammates. He combined the strength, speed, and coordination essential for a top vaulter, all of which had come in handy as starting right tackle the previous fall for Princeton's 10-1-1 football team for which he served as an able replacement for the graduating captain and All-American Langdon Lea. Ruggedly handsome and humble, Tyler formed half of a team within a team as Lane's classmate, cousin, and fellow native of Franklin, Ohio. That a railroad town 40 miles north of Cincinnati—population 2,700—should contribute two members of America's inaugural Olympic team was uncanny, prompting a considerable burst of pride among the residents of southwestern Ohio. "A splendid specimen of manhood," the *Cincinnati Enquirer* gushed of Tyler in one of several articles detailing the accomplishments of its suddenly prominent native sons. "He not only stands high at Princeton as an athlete, but has distinguished himself in his classes."

That was certainly true. A two-time victor of the pole vault in meets against Columbia—his best jump was 10 feet, 9 inches—Tyler excelled in the classroom, especially in mathematics. Back home during the summers in Franklin, he often saw Lane, vaulted in local track meets that he usually won, and lived with his grandmother, who, "it is unnecessary to say, is justly proud of her grandson," the *Enquirer* reminded readers. Others were as well. "When the news was received [in Franklin] that two of our boys were to take part in the Olympic

Games," the paper continued, "Albert Tyler and Francis Lane were the subject of conversation among all classes."

The Americans started vaulting at 2.80 meters or 9 feet, 2 inches—both clearing the bar with ease. The height went to 10 feet. Tyler got over the bar right away, but not Hoyt, who missed once and then again. Just as Clark had faced a moment of truth several days before in the Long Jump—having to jump cleanly on his third and final try after two fouls—Hoyt was up against it. "I can remember now the anxiety with which I saw him come running down the path on his last trial," remembered Clark. "[But] his nerve held; he caught things right." When it was do or die, Hoyt was up and over the bar.

The two men moved on, methodically and coolly matching heights, which rose as the late-afternoon temperatures dropped. In the growing chill, the Greek vaulters kept company with the Americans—massaging their arms and legs, and fetching them hot drinks. The bar moved to 3.30 meters (10.9 feet), which Hoyt cleared. Tyler, however, had reached his limit, failing once . . . twice . . . and then a third time . . . in an effort to surpass his career high. As the bar fell, Bill Hoyt, the last-minute substitution, had become an Olympic champion, the 11th title for the Americans in Athens. Captivated by the drama—and perhaps to keep events on the track until the first marathoner arrived—King George asked Hoyt whether he would continue vaulting. Of course he would. Keeping at it, the Harvard vaulter added several more inches to his height before bowing out at 3.40 meters (11 feet).

Perhaps the busiest man in the stadium that afternoon wasn't a vaulter or a runner. He was the flag man saddled with the task of having to quickly raise the flag of the winning athlete's country. Hoyt's victory meant the Stars and Stripes had shot up the pole four times in a single afternoon—and an astounding nine times during the track competition. American track officials would later criticize the US team for slower-than-usual times and setting no world records in Athens, but their comments missed the point: Hoyt's victory was another notch in the Americans' astounding dominance of the Athens Games, another peg in building the US Olympic movement from scratch. Atop "Coogan's Bluff," the crew of the USS *San Francisco* let loose with another dutiful cheer. Watching the American flag rise yet again, Greek premier Theodore Delyannis turned to Ambassador Alexander and in mocking exasperation asked, "Why did Columbus ever discover your unconquerable country?" Holmes put it another way: "Invincibility," he wrote with a dose of jingoism, "is still with the Americans."

But the premier wouldn't have long to despair. Messengers on horseback and bicycles had sent word through the streets that the marathoners were drawing close—and that miraculously, a Greek was ahead. Though accounts differ on when exactly the leader reached the outskirts of Athens—Holmes said it was after the flag ceremony for the Pole Vault whereas Richardson wrote it was just before—the eyes of 60,000 spectators at the stadium, and another 30,000 or so lining the road, were suddenly absorbed with the likelihood that a Greek runner would soon be heading into the stadium with a real chance of becoming an Olympic champion. If events held up, the prayers of many thousands would soon be answered.

Whether Spiridon Louis was thinking about all those free haircuts and shoes promised to a Greek marathon champion, he wasn't letting on. The 24-year-old water-carrier wasn't one for chatting. A man of simple tastes, he worked at his business, spent time with his fiancée— and ran long distances. That we still know so little about him more than a century later—he has been described variously as a farmer, a soldier, and a goat-herder—feeds the legend.

Though Louis had run the route only six days before, the effort had been worthwhile. He knew the dangers of the terrain in the latter stages of the race. Louis had used the trial to learn how to pace himself. Perhaps most important of all, he had learned quickly to respect the distance—and determined that the real race would likely be decided in the final few miles. In contrast, the foreigners had little sense of the marathon—and were treating it as if they were on the track racing the mile. Take the Frenchman, Lermusiaux, who took off "like a shot," recalled Blake, fortified by the knowledge that the first 10 kilometers of the route were relatively gentle—and slightly downhill. Soon, Lermusiaux was far ahead of a tandem of Flack and Blake, and, not far behind them, Kellner and a smattering of Greeks who included Vasilakos, winner of the trial, and Louis. Though Flack had never run anywhere close to marathon distance, he had both a pragmatic strategy and the confidence of a two-time Olympic champion—that is "not to force the pace but run with the Greeks . . . until about four kilometers from home when I hoped I would be able to make the running as I had more pace than any of them."

Lermusiaux stretched his lead. Reaching the village of Pikermi, more than halfway into the race, in 55 minutes—a blistering pace even by today's standards—the Frenchman had built an enormous lead of nearly two miles. John Graham arrived in Pikermi himself about 10 minutes later, and learning about the gap, quickly called Blake and Flack aside, convincing them to take a short break and talk strategy. Yes, there was still a long way to go, Graham counseled, but the next few miles might be the time to make up some distance, particularly with the terrain turning hilly. So Flack decided to speed it up. Blake and Kellner would follow, Graham trailing on the bike.

A minute or so later, the Greek runners started arriving in Pikermi. Feeling relaxed, Louis thought it might be time to pick up the pace a notch as well. Moving up on Georgios Gregoriou, he paid his respects. "Hello, fellow countryman," he said. "How goes it? It's me, Louis from Marousi."

But Gregoriou was struggling and in no mood for conversation. "Don't talk!" he snapped. "Talking is bad!" Louis was taken aback. "What's this blockhead grumbling about?" he thought to himself. So Louis took several long strides and easily overtook the other Greek runner. "When I turned round after a while to look for him," Louis would remember, "he had fallen far behind."

Louis was feeling strong and gaining confidence. Finding his stepfather waiting on the road with a beaker of wine and a red Easter egg, he paused. "Here Spyros, eat and drink," his stepfather told him. "That will do you good." It did. Polishing off the snack, Louis felt refreshed, got going again, and eyed the leaders.

The marathon course was getting more difficult. From Pikermi, the route turned into a series of hills, climbing nearly 150 meters over the next 10 kilometers. Fortified by his snack perhaps, Louis soon passed another countryman, Dimitrios Christopoulos, who told him that a group of Greeks immediately ahead of him had dropped out.

Soon, Blake was out as well, his sore and blistered feet ending his Olympic dream at the 18.5-mile mark. One minute the American was running and "the next thing I knew, I was jolting along in the bottom of a wagon," he recalled. "I had passed out of the picture.... All my training around Corey Hill had been in vain." So it goes in the fickleness of the marathon, where so many things can go wrong. Graham was disappointed, but philosophical: "Had we had better opportunity to put Blake in shape for this run, I am confident he could have won it handily," he said. "He has done marvelous work on this side of the water."

Lermusiaux clung gamely to the lead, but was laboring in hills. Still ahead as he approached the 20-mile mark at the village of Harvati, the Frenchman got a quick burst of confidence when a group of peasants crowned him with a victor's wreath as he passed under a makeshift model of arches. But Flack was steadily gaining—cutting a gap that only minutes ago had been three minutes down to a minute. Vasilakos and Louis, six minutes off the lead, were gaining as well. Just past Harvati, Lermusiaux was accidentally bumped by a fellow Frenchman on a bicycle. Knocked down, the runner got up, made it a few more feet and stopped—his Olympics done in by a blazing start, the heat, the hills, the distance, and the coup de grace—his bicycle-pedaling compatriot. Flack took the lead.

With 10 kilometers to go, Flack seemed in command. Running smoothly, a third Olympic title was starting to look inevitable, so much so that the first messenger cycled off toward the stadium to report that the Australian was looking good. But behind him, things were turning in favor of the Greeks. Louis was feeling strong himself and drawing strength from partisans now lining the road. "Courage Louis," a Greek infantry sergeant yelled as he sped past. "You've got only foreigners in front of you now." Within minutes, Louis picked off fading teammates and foreigners alike—Vasilakos and Kellner. Perhaps the bicycle messenger had left a tad too soon because just like that, the Olympic Marathon had become a two-man race: Louis, fortified by the hopes of his countrymen, against the Australian.

"For the first time, I was full of ambition," Louis thought. "A foreigner should not win this race!" But Flack was a worthy opponent—"a damned tough guy," Louis recalled. The Australian was feeling

173

both the pressure of the fast-closing Greek and the overwhelming difficulty of the longest and most brutal race he had ever run. "I then began to feel rather done in myself," he would say, "and . . . had the feeling that I should not be able to finish."

With five miles to go, Louis pulled even with Flack. Running side by side, the two runners sized one another up, playing mind games. "I don't know whether it was 100 meters, 200 meters or 500 meters that the Australian and I were fighting each other," Louis said later. "I looked at him perpetually out of the corner of an eye. And I didn't let him gain one meter's ground on me. When he wanted to take the lead and shake me off, I stayed with him." Then Louis put on a burst of speed and eased into the lead, breaking the spirit of Flack, who was quite suddenly done in—completely spent in his bid for a third Olympic title. The Australian kept on for another 100 yards, and then stopped, worn out "as if I should have fallen if I had gone any further," he said. Unable to continue, Flack was herded into an ambulance and dispatched to the dressing room at Olympic Stadium, where Prince Nicholas himself treated him with a drink of brandy with an egg.

The site of Louis leading the pack—and Greeks' Charilaos Vasilakos and Spiridon Belokas, now running second and third—sent the steadily thickening crowd of natives lining the route along the streets of outer Athens into a frenzy. The sudden turn of events prompted another messenger, this time Major General Papadiamantopoulos atop his horse, to take off for the stadium to deliver the latest news to King George, who with the other 70,000 spectators knew nothing of the sudden turn of events. Striding through the big gate and into the stadium, the general cut quite a figure. But there was no time to preen; heading directly to the royal box, he reported the promising news. A Greek was leading the Marathon! The royal box broke into exuberant cheers, the meaning of which quickly spread through the stadium. The crowd roared. There were no BAA imitations this time; "Hellene! Hellene" ("A Greek! A Greek!") they yelled.

Just as the first wave of cheers subsided, a cannon went off in the distance. It was a signal that the leader of the Marathon was approaching the stadium, and people knew what that meant. The big boom sent the stadium crowd into a new wave of delirium at the prospect of a Greek victory in this most Greek of events. By now, a cheering gauntlet of adoring citizens lined the streets—surrounding Louis with a rolling cascade of noise and leaving him with barely the width in spots to pass through. From the panorama of "Coogan's Bluff," people could be seen pointing with excitement in the direction of the runners.

Everyone in the stadium rose, their eyes riveted on the tunnel. "The excitement is intense," remembered Holmes, a spectator. "The suspense is almost painful." Minutes passed, and several spectators reported that even with the noise building outside the stadium, a kind of nervous quiet settled on the crowd inside, broken only by the sudden appearance of a runner bursting through the marble entrance and onto the track. It was Louis! So the news was true, and the sight of the dusty, sweat-covered athlete starting to head the last 600 meters or so around the track unleashed a wave of noise so great that the stadium seemed to vibrate. "It was the sound of a nation's pent-up desire for victory being released," wrote Olympic journalist David Randall. People yelled themselves hoarse and waved handkerchiefs and tiny Greek flags. A flock of white doves was released. And up on the bluff, the thick cluster of people jumping up and down in feverish excitement seemed to get the whole hillside throbbing. Forgetting his royal bearing, the king waved his military cap with such vigor that the visor broke off. Breaking from the royal box, Crown Princes Nicholas and George ran alongside Louis the last several hundred feet to the finish line and then carried him to the box.

Louis finished in 2:58:50, a considerable improvement over his performance at the trials. Seven minutes later, Vasilakos crossed the line to be followed in short order by another Greek, Spiridon Belokas, and then Kellner, the Hungarian. Watching their countrymen sweep the first three spots sent the crowd into more paroxysms of joy, though Kellner accused Belokas of traveling part of the way in a carriage. Belokas admitted his deception and the Hungarian was named the third-place finisher.

But the pure relief and joy of a Greek victory dwarfed the controversy—and handed all of Greece an emotional release it would long remember, arguably the country's greatest moment since independence. At last, one of their own had bested one of theirs—an American. In doing so, Louis gave the Games a gigantic shot in the arm that endured for a generation—branding the Olympic movement and securing its future. "Had an American or Frenchman won the coveted marathon, the disappointment of the crowd might have doomed the Olympic movement," Randall wrote. "As it was, the hysterical celebration of Greeks and visitors alike propelled the modern Olympic movement into the 20th century."

CHAPTER 10

"Jesu Christo! I'm Freezing!"

EMERGING FROM THE FRIGID WATERS OF THE BAY OF ZEA AT PHALERON, near Piraeus, on the morning of Saturday, April 11, Alfréd Hajós of Hungary should have been basking in the enormity of the moment.

Before 40,000 spectators, many still crowing about Spiridon Louis's dramatic win the previous day in the Marathon, the 18-year-old Hungarian had just captured his second championship of the modern Olympic Games. But he wasn't quite ready to celebrate. After all, he said, "My will to live completely overcame my desire to win." Hajós wasn't being flip; he was responding to the bone-chilling, possibly hypothermia-inducing temperature of the water. The weather in Athens had turned sharply cold for the only day of the Olympic swimming competition; though it was sunny, the temperature had dropped to a blustery 55 degrees Fahrenheit with 12-foot waves and turned the competition into a grim slog of attrition. So why on Earth had the Olympic organizers put together an elaborate shooting hall, but hadn't even bothered to build an indoor pool?

For all the discomfort endured by the 13 swimmers who gathered for the first of the three Olympic swimming events, the 100 Meters, Hajós had a critical advantage: a steely will to succeed fortified by tragedy. At 13, he resolved to become a good swimmer after his father drowned in the Danube River. By 1896, the Budapest native had become the European champion at 100 meters with a burning desire to prove himself at the Olympic Games. Along the way, Arnold Guttmann, like other prominent Jewish athletes of the era—took a new name, becoming the more Hungarian-sounding Hajós, short for "sailor" in Hungarian.

But just as American college officials threw roadblocks in the path of their athletes, Hajós got no support from his academic and athletic officials, namely the dean at Polytechnical University where he was studying architecture. The dean allowed Hajós to compete, but reluctantly. Back at school after the Games as Hungary's newest national hero, Hajós was promptly dragged back to Earth. "Your medals are of no interest to me," the dean told him, "but I am eager to hear your replies in the next examination." Apparently, Hajós rose to the challenge, passing his examinations.

In reality, the Bay of Zea was a choice spot for competition. It was relatively compact for a harbor and usually calm. Perhaps best of all, it had great natural beauty with a steep embankment that doubled as an amphitheater from which the multitudes could comfortably view the events, all of them before lunch. King George and Crown Prince Constantine were spectators, as were several American athletes, including Thomas Curtis. Thousands were making a day of it, bringing picnics and planning to head from swimming to the stadium for the afternoon's final competition.

If competitive swimming in open waters seems unusual these days, it wasn't so at the time of the first modern Olympic Games. For every US city with a public pool—the first municipal pool in the United States opened in 1887 in Brookline, Massachusetts—there seemed to be just as many rivers or oceans hosting competitive swimming events. There had been organized swimming events in the great outdoors for probably as long as there was water, but the Maidstone

(UK) Swim Club in 1844 was thought to have been the first organization to have daily training sessions from a river raft. By 1873, a silk dress was the prize for a mile swim down the Harlem River in New York City in which 10 women competed. And what sports lover of the era could not help but admire the exploits of British captain Matthew Webb? In 1873, Webb read of an account of a failed attempt of another Englishman, J. B. Johnson, to swim the English Channel, resolved to give it a go himself, and would become one of the greatest athletes of his time.

Leaving his job, Webb trained at a pool in the London borough of Lambeth, then in the Thames, and finally in the Channel itself. On August 12, 1875, the 27-year-old former sea captain made his first attempt to cross the Channel, but had to abandon the effort because of strong winds and choppy waters. Twelve days later—on August 24— he tried again, diving into the Channel from Admiralty Pier in Dover. Slathered in porpoise oil to retain body heat and trailed by three boats, Webb headed toward Cap Gris Nez, France. Stung by jellyfish, he plowed toward his dream, and emerged from the waters after 21 hours, and because of the strong currents, closer to Calais. His challenging journey wasn't the 22 miles he had envisioned but a shade under 40.

Webb became an international sensation, the world's first swimming superstar. He turned professional—swimming exhibition races and once spending 128 hours floating in a tank. Webb licensed his name for matchboxes and commemorative pottery, and wrote a "how-to" book, *The Art of Swimming*. But his daring would also be his undoing: In 1883 for a $12,000 prize, Webb decided to swim across Niagara River—and directly into the foaming, roaring rapids at the foot of the famous Falls. Many said it was impossible, and they were right. Within 10 minutes of starting his daring swim, Webb was dragged under the roaring surf. His battered, decomposed body was found four days later, though his reputation lives on. So would swimming's outdoor tradition; not until the 1912 Games in Stockholm would the Olympic swimmers move to a manmade pool.

～

Details of swimming's lone day at the 1896 Olympic Games are sketchy. A boat ferried the swimmers out into the bay to a float serving as a starting point for the first event, the 100 Meters, from which they would head back to shore. At the gun, they dove into the frigid, icy waters, which as Hajós recounted, "cut into our stomachs." Swimming for 70 meters neck-and-neck with Otto Herschmann of Austria, Hajós then reached deep for his second wind and pulled away. He won in 1:22.2, slow for him, to edge Herschmann by six-tenths of a second. Beyond Hajós's recollections and the results of the two finishers, there are no records of the Olympic Games' first swimming race. Were there other swimmers? Probably. Did everyone finish? Considering the cold temperatures and what would happen in other races, it was unlikely. Meanwhile, Herschmann, another of the outstanding Jewish swimmers of the era, would swim and fence in future Olympiads, earning a silver medal in 1912 as a member of the Austrian fencing team. In later years, Herschmann served as president of the Austrian Olympic Committee; he would perish in the Holocaust.

Getting a handle on other events during that uncomfortable morning for swimmers is an even more difficult task. Ioannis Malokinis took the Greek Navy's exhibition 100-Meter Freestyle in 2:20.4. Hajós had intended to swim all three of the open events—there were no relays—but withdrew from the second event, the 500-Meter Freestyle, to save his strength for the last event, the grueling 1,200 Meters. That gave Austrian Paul Neumann a window, and he promptly cruised to victory in 8:12.6. Another multitasking dynamo,

Neumann would emigrate to the United States in 1897, play water polo for the University of Pennsylvania, and become a physician. Of the 29 competitors in the 1,200 Meters, 26 came to their senses and refused to even commit themselves to the frigid waters. That left all of two other finishers—Ioannis Andreou and Efstathios (sometimes spelled "Eustathiois") Choraphas, both from Greece. Chorophas, meanwhile, would earn the day's iron-man honors as the only swimmer to compete in all three Olympic events.

Just where the lone American swimmer fit into the day's events is lost to history. Boston native Gardner Williams was 18, the American team's youngest competitor, and a BAA member. Used to competing in swimming pools, and not the chill and choppiness of the open sea, he was also a tad lackadaisical about conditioning. "A very pleasant companion," the *Boston Morning Journal* special correspondent—most likely John Graham—wrote of Williams in a dispatch describing the boat trip to Athens. "He ate and slept with the best of them, but he did not show up with amazing regularity at exercising time." Unlike his BAA teammates, Williams was funded for his trip to Athens by his wealthy family, not other club members. The young swimmer's father, Jeremiah Williams, was among Boston's most admired businessmen. A self-made man who never attended college, the elder Williams built the city's leading wool company and served as the first president of the city's Wool Trade Association. Like his wealthy teammate, Robert Garrett, Gardner Williams would one day join his family business.

P. H. Mullen, the author of *Gold in the Water: The True Story of Ordinary Men and Their Extraordinary Dream of Olympic Glory*, writes that Williams took fifth place in back of Hajós in the 100 Meters. Thomas Curtis spun a slightly different tale, writing that Williams never completed the event. Williams had "won many races in warm

American swimming pools," Curtis recalled in a 1932 memoir of the Games. "He journeyed to the Piraeus on the day of the first swimming competition blissfully ignorant that even the Mediterranean is bitterly cold in the month of April."

"[Williams] had traveled 5,000 miles for this event, and as he posed with the others on the edge of the float, waiting for the gun, his spirit thrilled with patriotism and determination," Curtis wrote. "At the crack of the pistol, the contestants dived headfirst into the icy water. In a split second his head reappeared. 'Jesu Christo! I'm freezing!' With that shriek of astonished frenzy he lashed back to the float. For him the Olympics were quite suddenly over."

So what's the real story? Common sense points to Mullen's 2001 heavily researched and comprehensive book, since Curtis was recalling the race from memory 40 years later by which time some of the details may have grown murky. But whether Gardner Williams finished or not, his few seconds in the water secured his enduring place in the record books: He was America's first Olympic swimmer, the pioneer of competitions the United States would soon dominate. Eight years later, at the 1904 Games in St. Louis, the United States would win its first Olympic championship, inaugurating its championship aquatic legacy.

Hajós's strength-saving strategy worked. He took his second Olympic title, the 1,200 Meters, though not easily. Again, the arctic conditions made it almost unbearable for the swimmers. And again, Hajós's oral history is about the only detailed account of what happened. This time, Hajós prepared as best he could, smearing his body with a half-inch layer of grease. "I was more cunning after the 100-meters event," he said, "and tried to protect myself against the cold."

As in earlier events, boats hauled competitors to the starting float from which they dove into the water and swam toward shore. "I must say that I shivered from the thought of what would happen if I got a cramp from the cold water," Hajós said. But he soon grabbed the lead and "cut through the water with a powerful determination"—largely motivated to reach the finish line as quickly as possible just to end his misery. Heading into the mouth of the bay, he became aware of boats humming about and fishing out those swimmers too numb by cold to push on. Near the finish, "the roar of the crowd increased," Hajós wrote. "I won ahead of the others with a big lead."

His time was 18:22.2, a commanding 1:41 ahead of his nearest competitor, Ioannis Andreou of Greece, with the dogged Efstathios Choraphas, third. Hajós's matter-of-fact analysis wasn't brashness: A blunt-speaking man who may have been a tad uneasy speaking English, he would respond to the crown prince's question about where he learned to swim so well. "In the water," Hajós said. The youngest winner in Athens, Hajós would later play forward for Hungary's national soccer team and capture national track championships in the 100- and 400-Meter Hurdles and the Discus. As a prominent architect, he would specialize in sports facilities and design the Budapest swimming arena used for the 1958 and 2006 European championships.

Little more was heard from Gardner Williams. Presumably, he went back to the hotel and had a hot bath and, true to form, a hearty meal. After the Games in Boston, he joined his Olympic and BAA teammates at celebratory banquets for the returning heroes. But to some degree, Williams's brief time in the water—like the Greek domination of Friday's Marathon—was a blessing in disguise for the Olympic movement. It helped break the extraordinary string of American success in Athens—giving athletes from other countries their turn at Olympic glory.

The work of the American team in Athens was done. It was time to celebrate.

"Rah! Rah! Rah! Ellas, Ellas, Ellas, Zito!"

BASEBALL? YES, THE CROWN PRINCES OF GREECE *WERE* UP FOR learning the fundamentals of America's national pastime. It was Tuesday, April 14—four days since the last US athlete had competed in the Games—and most of the country's first Olympic team were dressed formally and gathered at a celebratory picnic as guests of Madame Schliemann, widow of the noted German archaeologist, Heinrich Schliemann, among the lead excavators of Troy. The green expanse of the madame's country home at Daphni Monastery outside Athens provided all the space needed for good times and an impromptu game of baseball with their Royal Highnesses.

The Americans had become the world's newest diplomats, basking in the continued good cheer of their Greek hosts with whom a genuine warmth had arisen. They would linger another week or so in Athens—kicking back and taking in a steady round of picnics, receptions, and dinners in their honor. On Saturday, April 11, they dined with Rear Admiral Thomas Selfridge Jr. aboard the USS *San Francisco*, decorated for the occasion with thousands of colored lights. There they met more than a few of the sailors who had cheered them lustily all week from the steep hillside high above the Olympic stadium. On Sunday, April 12, at the Royal Palace, the American Olympians attended King George's banquet for foreign athletes, dignitaries, and foreign press—260 people in total—and prompted another round of special attention when the king himself dispatched his chamberlain to the American table with a request that "our boys," as Holmes explained, "kindly repeat their strange 'war cries'"—or what Greek journalists had taken to calling "onomatopoeia."

Everyone knew what that meant. The King wanted a last round of "BAA! Rah! Rah! Rah!" and its quickly assembled variation, "Rah! Rah! Rah! Ellas, Ellas, Ellas, Zito!" ("Hurrah for Greece!"). From all reports, the Americans delivered a command performance replete with gusto and a touch of irreverence, thanks in large part to the anonymous Yank who turned heads by answering the call for "Informal Dress" by donning gym shorts. The cheer completed, his Majesty shook hands with his newest group of friends, pronouncing himself delighted. The feel-good atmosphere had proven to be quite enduring; preserved from Madame Schliemann's reception is a memorable photograph taken by an unknown photographer. Most of the American team stands or sits in a group photo of 22: Connolly, at the left, leans toward another of the Greek princes who attended, 14-year-old Andrew, future father of Prince Philip of Great Britain, with Spiridon Louis posed cross-legged in the front row and the stadium's head architect reclining with his cane and bowler hat.

On Monday, April 13, Ambassador Alexander threw a reception for the American athletes. Meanwhile, the Games steamed toward its conclusion. Though stormy conditions had canceled the sailing contests at Phaleron, no one gave it much thought with the country continuing to bask in Greece's uplifting Marathon triumph. Louis was still the man of the hour, prompting Greek journalists to speculate on what exactly he did for a living. Some called Louis a water-carrier, others a shepherd, and still others everything from a post office messenger to an army officer and even a well-to-do farmer. The focus eclipsed another couple of Greek victories—starting with Georgios Orphanidis taking 300-Meter Free Rifle (with the versatile Viggo Jensen, third). Then, on Tuesday afternoon in cycling's version of the marathon, the 87-kilometer cycling race from Athens to Marathon and back again, Aristis Konstantinidis captured a rousing Olympic race. Leading at the halfway point in Marathon, Konstantinidis broke down shortly after turning back to Athens. So borrowing a bicycle, he was passed by the Englishman, Edward Battel, caught up, and again broke down. Grabbing another bike, Konstantinidis doggedly clawed back, and the two traded the lead several more times before Battel crashed this time. So it was the plucky, mud-splattered Konstantinidis after all pedaling into the hearts of his countrymen and Olympic lore in crossing the Velodrome finish line ahead of the pack at Nea Phaleron. It was another feather in the cap of a triumphant Olympic Games.

That evening at the Royal Palace reception, the king joined the cheers as Louis entered the Great Hall, accompanied by his stepfather. Addressing the throng in French, the king said the Greek people had "rejoiced" in hosting the athletes, coaches, and officials. "Soon, you will return to your homes," he said. "I will not say 'adieu' to you, but 'au revoir.' Keep a good souvenir of us, and do not forget the enthusiastic welcome we have given you." Everyone seemed to agree—with the exception of Baron de Coubertin, to whom the king had delivered a coded barb or two.

The baron was upset for several reasons. In his remarks, King George graciously acknowledged several people by name, but failed to mention Coubertin, the International Olympic Committee, or the 1894 Paris Congress. Coming from a practiced, polished monarch, the oversight was curious and probably deliberate. "George perhaps purposely avoided those topics this time because of another item," figured Olympic historian David Young of the University of Florida. The other reason, suggested Young, was the king's reference in his speech to "our land . . . a permanent site of the Olympic Games," which cut right to the heart of the baron's plan to rotate the Games every four years among the "great capitals of the world." Eventually, Coubertin's wish came true—it would take 108 years for the Games to return to Athens—but the king's remarks exposed a bone of contention. For the moment at least, the baron played it cool—deciding "to play the simpleton, the man who did not understand," as he later said. That was an issue for another day.

—◦—

At Tuesday's picnic, Ellery Clark was the baseball ringleader. Asking the 27-year-old crown prince, later King Constantine, if he had an interest in learning the rudiments of America's national pastime, he found the prince and two of his brothers, 26-year-old Prince George and 24-year-old Prince Nicholas, pleasantly receptive. "Ellery, my boy," the crown prince said, "I never heard of it, but [here] it goes." It was as if they had been mates for years—the comfort of their exchange revealing the prince's colloquial command of English, and just how close the royal family and the American athletes had grown in all of two weeks. Even the king himself provided some needling: "You may win this time," he teased Burke, "but we will beat you in 1900 if I have to run myself!" Taking in the exchange, Holmes was delighted: "Rather democratic, is it not," he said with a whiff of elitism, "to see Prince Constantine, Prince George, and Prince Nicholas of Greece, grouped there with the peasant Louis, and our young Bostonians and Princeton men?"

Had the Greek royals really never heard of baseball? Granted, there was no baseball in Greece, but it's hard to believe the princes really had no idea what it was in light of the enormous attention generated by Albert Spalding's celebrated round-the-world tour of baseball all-stars in 1888 and 1889. Then again, the grand tour of Spalding's Chicago White Stockings and a group of big-league all-stars hadn't gone to Greece. Though baseball is a sport of nuance and not easily described in brief, the Americans did their best without so much as a ball, a bat, or a glove.

First, they explained the functions of the pitcher and catcher, the infielders and the outfielders, and how to run the bases. "Nothing would do, however, except a demonstration," recalled Curtis. Thinking quickly, the Americans turned a walking stick into a bat and an orange became a ball. Chosen to pitch was Blake with the crown prince first up to bat; Prince George was the catcher. Needing space, the ringleaders gently prodded the guests to move back, creating a "playing field" ringed with a hefty part of the crowd looking on. The crown prince, by all accounts, was a quick study—nailing Blake's delivery and sending several large, juicy slices to the chest of his formal court uniform and elsewhere in the vicinity. The prince was "a good sport" about it, said Curtis, and joined the gentle laughter that accompanied the demonstration. But perhaps the impromptu game of baseball and messy remnants of the orange were just a tad too frivolous for royalty. "I think the Americanization of Greece ended right there," Curtis said.

For all the easy informality at Madame Schliemann's reception, one American faced a crisis of etiquette. It was James Connolly, who found himself in a pickle after showing his lucky rabbit's foot to

Hadji Petros, the chief marshal of Prince George's court. Thinking it was a gift and facing a gaping language barrier, Petros pocketed the item with thanks, leaving Connolly to wonder just how to get back the charm that he had carried to victory in the Triple Jump. Poor Connolly felt powerless to ask for his rabbit's foot back and decided to drop it, but became so distracted by the loss of his trusty good-luck charm that he left his overcoat on the grounds of Daphne. That evening at a café in Athens, a still-distracted Connolly mislaid his handsome walking cane. Borrowing a cane from Tom Barry, his friend, he lost that one too, as well as an overcoat, one he had borrowed from Hoyt. But that was Connolly, who had lost his wallet in Italy, as well—and had already earned a reputation among his teammates as a bit of a flake.

At least everyone was lucky to be outdoors—managing to squeeze in the picnic after it had been steadily raining for nearly two days. So intense had the rain been on Tuesday morning that organizers decided to postpone the Games' real finale, the one for which everyone was eagerly awaiting: the grand awards ceremony at the stadium. With the festivities reset for Wednesday, Athenians awoke that morning to a radiant sun, which helped to dry the soggy streets and put everyone in an upbeat mood. What a wonderful setting it would be after all for the closing ceremony that Greek Olympic historian Charalambos Anninos promised would be "dignified and fine . . . reminding [spectators of] its majesty of the splendor of ancient days." So with the gates of the stadium thrown open to all, it was packed for a final bit of pomp, to be topped by the royal family's medal presentation to the victors.

Anninos was spot on. By 10:00 a.m. Wednesday, the stadium was filled to its rafters, as Anninos wrote, with "about as many as on the day of the Marathon." All had been admitted first-come, first-serve—there were no tickets—with everyone anxious to cap the glorious two weeks in Athens with something special. Setting the tone, George Robertson, the Oxford scholar and discus competitor, stepped forward and facing the royal box, recited his Pindaric Olympic ode in flawless ancient Greek. Recited in Pindarian meter, the address gave reverence to the glories of ancient Greece, and hit all the right chords.

Spellbound, the crowd exploded in cheers as Robertson finished. Practically busting his buttons with pride, King George stepped from the royal box on to a platform erected for the medal ceremony and congratulated the Englishman. Vigorously pumping Robertson's hand, the king reached back to a small table filled with olive branches for the victors, and gave him one. Coubertin was moved, viewing the moment as a perfect bookend to the ceremony that had launched the Games back on April 6. "Music had opened [the Games] and poetry was present at their close," the baron said, savoring the moment in which his vision of athletics, education, and antiquity aligning in perfect symmetry seemed to come true.

Next the victorious athletes gathered on the stadium infield near the royal box, prompting Hadji Petros, the chief marshal of Prince George's court and fortified perhaps with luck from Connolly's rabbit's foot, kicked off the ceremony that everyone had come to see: the announcement of each victor's name, country, and event. On hearing their names, athletes, most of them dressed formally, ascended the five-step platform to the royal box. There they bowed to the king, who offered a formal salute, prizes, and congratulations in their native tongue.

To the victors went quite a stash. There was the silver medal—gold would come in later Games—not presented as today on a ribbon and hung on the winner's neck, but in a handsome case, lined in blue velvet. Also, they received an oversized, rather exquisite diploma, on either white or blue paper, and trimmed with gold paper; and an olive branch, plucked from the sacred grove of Olympia in Delphi. Double winners like Tom Burke, Alfred Hajós, Robert Garrett, and Edwin Flack got two of everything. Positioned with his camera near the royal box, Burton Holmes snapped photos of the occasion, and imagined what it might feel like to be an Olympic champion. "It must have been a thrilling moment for him," he wrote of Burke, "as he stood there face to face with the King, the Crown Prince and a host of royal personages, while on every side there arose tier on tier of eager faces, a cloud of witnesses which seemed to touch the sky—that same blue sky of Greece which has looked down upon so many heroes." Holmes's portrait of Burke shows the young Bostonian facing the lens, dressed formally, and in desperate need of a shopping cart: In addition to his two sets of awards for winning the 100 and the 400 Meters, he is clutching an American flag.

Medals for the winners had been expected. What happened next was a pleasant surprise—second-place finishers were summoned to the royal platform where the king presented them with laurel branches. Still later, at the king's reception, the runners-up would get something else—bronze medals cast from the same die as the silver one.

Stadium cheers greeted the award winners—particularly the Americans and the loudest of all for Greece's man of the Games, Louis, again wearing native costume. The Marathon champion also picked up a few additional prizes beyond the promised free haircuts: the silver cup from the Frenchman Michel Bréal and Ionnos Lambros's exquisite vase. Afterwards, a flock of pigeons were released far above the stadium—and Louis, waving the Greek flag, led a procession of the victors around the track to another round of thunderous applause. As the parade ended, King George stood up and announced, "I declare the end of the First International Olympic Games."

— ⁓ —

So the first modern Olympic Games were dramatically finished, leaving the pundits to determine their significance. Armed with all the photographs of the event and impressions for his travelogue back home, Holmes marveled at the enormity of the crowds and the setting. "Almost the entire population [of Athens] was present at the Games," he wrote. "[And] the festival itself was purely Hellenic, although so many of the victors were 'barbarians.'" For Charalambos Anninos, the primary author of the official report of the 1896 Games, the Olympics were a resounding success, amounting to more, much more than a sporting event. For him, the Olympic Games had accomplished a real intangible: giving foreign visitors "impressions of affection and admiration for Greece, and with firm conviction, that, according to the Royal sentence that Greece was destined to be the peaceful meeting ground of the Nations, the permanent and continual field of the Olympic Games."

No other group however had influenced the first Olympiad more than the Americans. They had dominated the competition—winning all but three of the 12 athletic events in which they had competed. Of the 14 Americans, 12 returned to the United States with medals. Their 11 championships prevailed, outdoing Greece with 10 first-place finishes, Germany (seven), France (five), and Great Britain (three). In the cases of Burke and the Paine brothers, their margins of victory were so vast that it seemed unfair. And Garrett's improbable victory the first time he had ever thrown a discus in competition was a case of sheer athleticism at its best. In its many accomplishments, this ad hoc team, thrown together at the last minute, earned front-page headlines. In doing so they essentially created the American Olympic movement from scratch—setting a precedent for more than a century of continued success by future generations.

But not everyone in the United States was impressed by the '96ers. No world records had been set at Athens. Overall, the performances were mediocre for international events because of uneven competition, the poor quality of the track, and the cool, often wet weather. "Judging from the times returned, the entries must have been few, and certainly the quality of athletes below the average of winners usually seen at important Anglo-Saxon track games," penned the columnist Casper Whitney with a touch of crustiness mixed with elitism. "There seems to have been no English entries of the first class; and outside of Burke, Hoyt and Clark, there was no one of the Americans who could be expected to win in open games in the United States." Whitney's "only remarkable performance" of the Games was Louis's in the marathon. "How exceptional this time is may be appreciated by saying that the best amateur time for 26 miles is 2 hours 47 minutes and 14 seconds, and that was run on a cinder track," he wrote.

Whitney may have been right, but his comments missed the essence of the first American Olympic team's contribution to history. Trainer John Graham had seen many athletes record better times or longer, higher distances at track and field events, but he understood and appreciated the significance of what the Americans accomplished in Athens. "These Games, I believe, will create a great international interest in athletic sport," Graham said. "We showed the Grecians the great difference between modern and ancient sports. We excelled in jumping, both high and otherwise; pole vaulting; putting the shot; and hurdles. . . . We knew that we could win."

Olympic historian Bob Fulton thought so, as well: "These intrepid pioneers who weathered adversity en route to Greece and surpassed every expectation once they got there," he wrote, "could celebrate not only victories but a pre-eminent role in a momentous event—the rebirth of the Olympic Games."

CHAPTER 12

"A Set of Men That the Nation May Well Feel Proud Of"

BOUNDING OFF THE OCEAN LINER *LAHN* ON MAY 6 IN HOBOKEN, Arthur Blake retained a considerable spring in his step. First in the party of returning Boston-based Olympians to disembark their big boat at about 6:15 p.m., Blake had a considerably shorter distance to cover than the marathon. At the bottom of the steep stairway, he ran smack dab into the arms of his brother, Fred. "Their reunion," an observer noted, "was most fraternal."

It had been more than seven weeks since the spirited but small group of family and friends had seen the Americans off at the same Hoboken dock. Overjoyed to be home, the team had only a vague sense of the excitement their performances in Athens had created in the United States—and of the prolonged series of celebrations that awaited them, especially in Boston. For now, the official welcoming party was small; only Fred Burke and Billy Cuntz from the BAA, Nelson Innis from the Suffolk Athletic Club (SAC), and Harry Cornish of the New York's New Manhattan AC were there. A number of other prominent New York and Boston civic leaders with an eye to a good photo op had intended to greet the team, but the *Lahn* had taken advantage of clear skies and calm waters and reached Hoboken three hours ahead of schedule. Anxious to get back on their native soil, the team had appealed to Collector of Ports James Kilbreth, and been passed ahead to the front of the line for customs, quickly cleared and free to head into the night.

Tom Burke was next down the plank. He would have been the first US Olympian to emerge from the ocean liner, but the two-time Olympic champion was weighted down with "so many diplomas and presentation canes that [Blake had] beaten [him] out," a reporter said. Reunited with family and friends, Burke, Blake, and the other Bostonian athletes exchanged spirited BAA cheers, shook hands, slapped backs in triumph, and kicked off the celebration. Actually, Burke and Blake had already started to display their wares; as customs inspectors pulled out the top drawer of his trunk, Burke reached in and grabbed his olive branch, anxious to protect his most perishable souvenir.

"Is *that* the olive wreath?" asked an admirer.

"It's not a wreath but a collection of twigs," Burke explained. "[But] I wouldn't part with it for the world."

In addition to his medals and diplomas, Burke had acquired some other items on his travels—a $13 suit bought in London en route home; a handful of neckties from a Greek admirer; a small plaster bust; and three canes, one with an opera glass, one that squirted water with the touch of a button, and another made from—guess what?—an olive tree.

Not all the Americans had dawdled to party in Athens after the Games. Anxious to resume their studies and rejoin the college track team, the Princeton contingent had departed Greece on April 16, right after the closing ceremony. Garrett, Jamison, Tyler, and Lane headed first to Italy, squeezing in a tour of Pompeii, then stopped briefly in Paris and London before catching the North German

Lloyd liner, *Spree*, on April 21 for the voyage to New York. In contrast to their Atlantic crossing six weeks earlier, the foursome spent a good portion of their trip in deckchairs and did no training. They had earned the right.

On the afternoon of Friday, May 1, 1,000 or so Princeton revelers gathered to welcome home the team that the *Trenton Evening News* called "truthfully . . . the most successful athletic team that Princeton University has turned out in recent years." After traveling more than 4,900 miles from Athens to New York by ship, and 52 more miles across New Jersey by train, the team's final leg of their journey had been wonderfully familiar—the 2.7 miles aboard the Princeton local or "Dingy" from Princeton Junction station to the little station in the shadow of Blair Hall. Among the mostly student crowd of merrymakers on hand to meet them were several of Tyler's burly comrades—fellow footballers prepared to escort their returning classmates back to campus. First out of the train, by design, was Garrett, clutching his leather box with the laurel wreath, and followed in short order by Jamison, Tyler, and Lane. True to their word, the footballers hoisted all four of the Princeton track men to their shoulders, and amidst the scrum of noisy congrats, celebration, and excitement, ensured the men from Athens got a hero's welcome.

Princeton's Olympians were back and the town was buzzing—with church bells clanging to herald their arrival with a cascade of cheers going out for "Old Nassau," the college's answer to the BAA yell. At the Princeton Inn, the four heroes took in a late lunch amidst more hearty congratulations. Overjoyed at their reception, they were probably relieved, as well, with exams for Princeton juniors set to kick off on May 14—less than two weeks away. The *Daily Princetonian* editorial staff was pleased as punch that the athletes had made it back in time for the next day's Caledonian Games and the track meets in subsequent weeks against Columbia and Yale. That evening, the foursome went to the gym for a workout—their first in several weeks—as fellow students lit a giant bonfire outside in their honor. "The enthusiasm displayed was in vivid contrast to that manifested on their departure six weeks ago," the *Daily Princetonian* opined. "It is safe to say that never before has such a recognition been given by the college to track athletes, and we trust it indicates that their department is being rapidly raised to the same plane in the estimation of the college as football and baseball."

Not one for speeches, Garrett echoed the team's appreciation for their Greek hosts. "We met everywhere with the most hearty reception," he said of their Olympic experience to friends at the Princeton Inn. "The Greeks' treatment of us was fairness itself, although they were greatly disappointed at the defeat of their champions." Meanwhile, Garrett was matter of fact about the lackluster time and distances achieved in Athens by the winning athletes. "Many of the records made were poor," he acknowledged, "and it is probably not fair to draw from these Games any inferences as to the strength of the athletes . . . members of the many teams complained that the best men had been left at home." Garrett would live a long life filled with achievement, but those were among the few public remarks he would ever give about the 1896 Olympic Games. True to form, he and his fellow Princeton Olympians just got on with things, piling up the victories that Saturday against their classmates at the Caledonian Games: Garrett took both the shot put and long jump and tied for third at high jump, Tyler won the pole vault, and Lane and Jamison placed second and third in the 100. Their performances underscored just how inferior the track and the conditions had been in Athens: Garrett sent the shot 36 feet, 11½ inches, nearly 2 feet beyond his Olympic distance. Another two-time Caledonian Games winner that day was James Colfert, the freshman whose parents had prevented him at the last minute from going to Athens. In taking the 440 and the 220, the young Baltimorian may have sent more than a few spectators to wonder what might have been in Athens.

Back among the Bostonians, only Clark had classes to attend, making his and his comrades' departure from Athens a lot more leisurely. They left Athens on Friday April 17—seen off at the train station by a group of 100 university students who, inspired by the BAA cheer, had composed their own original cheer in Greek that Curtis said resembled "Brek-ek-kek, co-ax, co-ax." Wending their way across Greece to Patros, the Americans were showered with plaudits at each way-station thanks to a savvy telegraph man who had sent ahead word of the team's itinerary. Bands thundered and crowds applauded as if it were the president of the United States on a whistle-stop campaign. In Patros, there was more ceremony—bands and torch-bearing boys, who escorted the Americans, procession-like, from the station to their hotel. From Patros, the heroes sailed north via the Adriatic to Corfu and then to Brindisi.

Heading northwest toward Southampton, England, where they would catch a US-bound ship, the traveling party paused in Rome and then Paris, where they got their first inkling that they were big news back home. In Paris, John Graham called on Sumner Paine, already back at his French apartment, and got a chance to see a few of the early-April issues of the *Boston Globe*, just then trickling into the Paines' mailbox. Excited by the *Globe*'s extensive Olympic coverage, he shared the news with Burke, Curtis, Blake, Connolly, Clark, and Tom Barry, sending the whole group to the Paines, anxious to see the papers for themselves. Treated by Salome Paine to a Boston "Sunday breakfast" of baked beans, brown bread, and fish eggs, with "all the trimmings," as the *Globe* reported, the group had a grand time.

Sumner Paine wouldn't be returning to the United States quite yet. Nor would John, opting to tour Italy with his parents. But the Paine brothers would forever cherish the Olympic experience and particularly their American teammates: In their honor, John soon made a $1,000 donation to the BAA.

James Connolly would also take his time getting home. Enjoying the splendors of Paris, he lingered and decided to go his own way, saying he would meet up with his teammates in Southampton. But Connolly missed a connection at Dieppe, or so he said, and arrived too late—again—to catch the boat. So armed with two suitcases stuffed with his Olympic spoils—the diploma, protected by the cylindrical cardboard box; a silver and gold cup, a gift of Prince George; the olive wreath; three souvenir canes together with string; 20 yards of silk for his mother to make a dress; and Hoyt's overcoat—he decided to stick around in London and be a tourist. Connolly wouldn't get to Boston until May 14, missing most of the celebratory parties. "I looked at my cases and my bundles and had to laugh," he said, arriving home with his Olympic medals stuffed into his hip pocket. "I was thinking what a hero I had been in Greece and what a tramp I looked like here."

For his teammates, Bostonians extended the red carpet. Their returning Olympians had bested the world, drawing glory and attention to their hometown. Greeting them with enthusiastic front-page headlines, reporters were ready to record their arrival, every movement, and tales of triumph. Victors Return, Champions Come Home and City's Tribute of Pride trumpeted the *Herald*. Triumphant Entry into Boston and Quintet of Blushing Athletes countered the *Globe*. What wasn't to like from these accomplished and modest group of athletes? From the dock in Hoboken, Harry

Cornish had chaperoned the group to the New Manhattan AC club-house, where they spent the night. Those civic leaders and politicians who had meant to meet them at the dock showed up the next morning to pay their respects. That alone would have been quite enough fuss, said Clark. "To be met in New York by special cars, bearing our city fathers come to welcome us, it was sublime."

That wasn't the half of it. Leaving Grand Central Station (now Terminal) in New York aboard the Boston Express for the final leg of the journey, the athletes were handed miniature American flags for the reception in Boston. Seated in the parlor car, adorned with the American flags and a big Greek flag that Graham had tacked to the wall, they held forth on the Olympic experience. The voluble Blake praised his Australian rival Edwin Flack, "a very fast man [with] plenty of endurance as well as speed." He chuckled at the tale of Connolly's lost rabbit's foot, and how hard his new friend had taken it: Apparently, the Greeks were as interested in the power of the rabbit's foot as he was, and when a military attaché to the king asked him for it, Connolly turned him down flat. "If I give that to you," he had said, "there is nothing to prevent you being king inside of two years." Ah the royals, of whom enough good things couldn't be said! "We sized the [Crown] Prince up and went in and had a good time with him, and that is just what he wanted," Burke said. "After our men saw that the Prince wanted to throw off his official trappings, everybody joined in the fun. The people like Americans in Greece."

In Providence, the train paused briefly as relatives and friends of the athletes piled aboard, prompting a fresh round of hugs, hand-shakes, and hearty shouts of congratulations. Tom Burke's sisters joined the rolling party. So did Curtis's mother, Clark's father, Blake's parents, and Arthur Burnham of the BAA. Blake told the appreciative audience how the BAA cheer had charmed the Greeks and belted out a quick version of the "Ellas, Zito" cheer that the Americans had developed in tribute to the Greek hosts. For effect, the boys then belted out a London concert hall tune called "Tim Tolan," substituting a few of their own words, explaining that it was a tune favored by their fast friends, the crown princes.

At 9:00 p.m., May 7, the train bearing the Olympians pulled into Boston. Finally, they were home, prompting pandemonium. Some 3,000 people engulfed the train, many of them wild with enthusiasm and waving flags as the team pulled in. Some were BAA members who had spent an hour waiting for the train by reciting, over and over, the "BAA! Rah! Rah! Rah" cheer. A delegation from Boston University, anxious to welcome their classmate, Burke, was there too. So was a group from Boston College, more city officials, and a lot of proud locals. "The scene will long be remembered by those who witnessed it," the *Herald* reported. "In proportion to the number present, the cheering far outclassed that of a Harvard-Yale football game, and every man yelled until hoarse."

This time, Burke was first to the platform, and before he even had a chance to say a word, he was hoisted onto the shoulders of his Boston University classmates. The surge of the crowd was so strong that a local judge took to protecting John Graham's wife, there to greet her husband. Blake took a ride atop the shoulders of admirers, as well, but not Clark, Curtis, or Hoyt, who slipped off to taxis. The men of the hour then sped to the BAA clubhouse on Exeter Street to enjoy the first of several "welcome-home" receptions.

Two days later, the BAA threw a formal dinner for Boston's newest heroes. Seated at long tables in the BAA gymnasium, the guests included Massachusetts governor Roger Wolcott and Boston mayor Josiah Quincy. The gathering dined on filet of beef with fresh mushrooms, littleneck clams, frozen pudding, and assorted cheeses—with newspaper reporters on hand to record every detail, as if the pope were visiting. The BAA roar was in full throttle—some members only now realizing that it had become a popular cry on two sides of the Atlantic—as were more stories. Blake showered praise on the team's Greek hosts, and detailed to a hushed crowd the story of Spiridon Louis's stirring Marathon triumph. Graham complimented Sumner and Salome Paine for the marvelous hospitality and helping of Boston baked beans in Paris. Curtis marveled about the Greek royal family's impromptu game of baseball and their hospitality, moving the BAA members to grant honorary club memberships to Princes Constantine and George, which, everyone agreed, was altogether fitting. Then Governor Roger Wolcott hit the key note of the evening, calling the athletes "not only a credit to the city and the commonwealth, but a set of men that the nation may well feel proud of."

Boston wasn't quite finished, directing the BAA athletes to one last set of official doings—a public reception on the afternoon of Tuesday, May 12, at Faneuil Hall—and another banquet that evening at the Hotel Vendome. So for two hours at the flag-draped Faneuil Hall, Mayor Josiah Quincy followed by Burke, Alderman David Barry, and then Curtis, Hoyt, Clark, and Graham, gathered in a receiving line and met anyone who cared to show up. In the days before autograph collecting was the rage, most were content to just shake hands, including one man, a native of Greece, who had bicycled all the way from Lowell, to present Burke with a yellow rose—"a bit wilted," the *Herald* duly reported, "but . . . fresh with . . . sincere appreciation." Adorning the reception area was an oversized vase of roses, grouped with silk flags of the United States and Greece. The mayor spoke and so did his assistant Thomas Mullen, who read an ode from one Henry O'Meara, composed especially for the occasion. The ode, "To Our Laureled Sons," was modeled after another popular song in Boston, "Fair Harvard."

Then Graham spoke, heaping more compliments not just upon their hosts but also the entire country of Greece from King George "down to the lowest peasant," as the *Herald* put it, for their extraordinary hospitality. There were shouts of approval and applause when Graham mentioned that the popularity of the Americans had triggered a run on the supply of US flags in Athens. And there was laughter all around when he told the story of how Sumner Paine had scoured Athens for a souvenir American flag, and ended up with an enormous 18-footer. It was the only one left in the city.

With another round of pithy remarks, the US trainer had emerged as the smooth-talking and engaging voice of the US Olympic team. But now that he was back in Boston, Graham was already looking ahead. He said he wanted nothing more than to get back to the banks of the Charles River to do what he did best: training athletes. That prompted more hurrahs—and a call for Burke, the man who had earned the biggest ovation, for another speech. But Burke ever so politely declined. What more was there to say? The first modern Olympic Games were history—with the members of America's first Olympic team home and showered with honors. For the most part, they would spend the rest of their lives just getting on with things—families, jobs, and life—and seldom looking back at those two glorious weeks in April 1896 when as the greatest pick-up team in history, they had startled the world.

"Good Feeling and Fellowship Predominated"

At 3:00 p.m. on May 14, two days after the Faneuil Hall reception, James Connolly slipped quietly into Boston. The self-described "tramp" had arrived in the United States that morning, docked aboard the German Lloyd steamer in Hoboken, and quickly hopped a train for Boston. A sizable group of his friends amassed at Park Square Station, where they expected him to arrive on the 1:30 p.m. train. But to no one's surprise, Connolly was late, and by the time he finally arrived 90 minutes later, only his brother, Francis, and Tom Barry, the best friend who had accompanied him to Athens, were there to welcome him home.

Connolly didn't care. He took a streetcar home to South Boston and joined his mother for tea and apple pie. That evening, Connolly dined with friends at Clark's Hotel and spoke of his admiration for the Greeks and of the experience of a lifetime. "Greece is the place for an athlete to live, and the place of all others where the [Olympic] Games should be held," he said. "The people love athletics, and the support given the Games there by the people gives the promoters the power to conduct them on as nearly ideal lines as possible."

A few weeks later, South Boston honored Connolly, hosting a parade for their resident Olympic champion, filled with carriages and a double-line of police to keep it all orderly. Peering at the assembled multitudes as he rumbled down Broadway, Connolly took particular delight when he recognized a policeman in line as the very one who had chased him many times years before while playing ball in the streets—"a grave crime in his code," Connolly said.

The policeman had never caught the younger Connolly, "but I heard him many a time shouting after me that he would get me," the athlete said. Now the tables had turned, as the cop looked up at Connolly and recognized him as the one-time troublemaker. The man of the hour was delighted. "I got a great kick out of the look he gave me when he recognized me," Connolly said.

Indeed, America's first Olympic champion would forever get a charge from life. Joining the 9th Massachusetts Infantry, he fought in the Spanish-American War at the famous siege of Santiago. By 1900, he was earning $25 a week as physical director and football coach at the Gloucester (Mass.) Athletic Club when he decided to give the Olympic Games another shot. Connolly and a friend, marathoner Dick Grant, paid their own way, in steerage, to the 1900 Games in Baron de Coubertin's hometown of Paris. There, they lived on the cheap—rooming on the top floor of the tallest apartment house on the Rue de Rome, dining on 15-cent lunches in Montmartre restaurants, and walking miles to the track in the Bois de Boulogne.

Connolly's itinerant experience in Paris that year reflected the somewhat ramshackle doings of the second modern Olympiad. Staged as an appendage to the 1900 World Exhibition, the Paris Games started in May and lumbered on for nearly six months all the way to the end of October. Organization was poor and attendance spotty, and there were no opening or closing ceremonies. Competing in a bewildering array of sanctioned and nonsanctioned sports—19 in all—were more than 1,300 athletes, including 11 women, from 22 countries. There was a smorgasbord of events in Paris with everything from angling to cannon shooting—yes, cannon shooting!—as well as kite flying and pigeon racing. Things were so disorganized that some athletes didn't even realize until later they had been a part of the Olympic Games.

Track and field at the 1900 Games took place at the Bois de Boulogne, the same tree-lined grass racetrack where members of the Olympic Committee had dined in extravagance six years before. Presumably avoiding the trees, the Americans again dominated—taking 16 of the 23 events. A big chunk of the US medals were earned by University of Pennsylvania roommates Alvin Kraenzlein, Irving Baxter, and John Tewksbury, and a field-events man from Purdue, the remarkable Ray Ewry. Kraenzlein won four championships; Ewry, three; and Baxter and Tewksbury, two each. Ewry would end up winning eight championships in three Olympiads, in the Standing Long, Triple, and High Jumps; all events are now defunct.

With his trademark resilience and a flair for coming up big when it counted, Connolly did well—taking second to Meyer Prinstein in the Running Triple Jump, reaching 45 feet, 10 inches, nearly a foot beyond his winning jump in Athens. Giving it another go, as well, was Robert Garrett, the only other member of the '96 US team to compete at the Paris Games: The 1897 graduate of Princeton, by then a Baltimore banker, took third in Shot Put and Standing Triple Jump. His seventh-place performance of 108 feet, 5 inches was well off the winning toss of 118 feet, 3 inches by Rezsö Bauer of Hungary, but more than *12 feet* beyond his performance in Athens.

～～

Connolly skipped the 1904 Games in St. Louis, and gave it one more shot at the unsanctioned Athens Games of '06. But he was 37, and failed to make a valid jump in either the long or triple jump. Two years later, at the '08 Games in London, Connolly was there but this time as a correspondent for *Collier's*. By then, he had turned his lifelong love for water and affinity for rambling into an adventurous career as a writer of sea stories. Connolly would do just about everything and anything on water—serving in the US Navy, sailing with Gloucester fishermen, working his way across the Atlantic on a cattle boat, whaling in the Arctic, racing yachts, and living aboard every conceivable kind of craft from warships to submarines. He would cover U-boat warfare in World War I and become America's foremost expert on saltwater sailing. Connolly would even dabble in politics—running in 1912 for a congressional seat in Massachusetts, but losing to James Curley.

The author of many novels and short stories and a frequent lecturer, Connolly penned his life story in an entertaining 1944 autobiography, *Sea-Borne: Thirty Years Avoyaging*, which, as the titles implies, focuses on sea stories. That left precious little to his track career—all of a single, 10-page chapter—though he was always happy to discuss his Olympic career in lectures.

Connolly settled in the Chestnut Hill section of Boston, and became both an elder statesmen of his sport and a beloved and feisty guardian of amateur athletes. In newspaper and magazine pieces, he warned of the perils of the specialization of athletics and of excessive alcohol consumption. Railing against what he called the unchecked egos and heavy-handedness of top American amateur sports officials, Connolly saved his most blistering attacks for Joseph Sullivan, the AAU president. Like Coubertin, Connolly loathed Sullivan, calling him more focused on his wallet and being a stooge for the Spalding

Sporting Goods Company than serving the needs of amateur athletes. "Every young man who registers as an AAU athlete today is simply another advertising agent for [Spalding]," he wrote in 1910. An exception, he added, was the BAA, "which always held out for clean athletics."

But Connolly wasn't above peddling his own name. He endorsed Tuxedo tobacco—"a delightful combination of splendid flavor and genuine mildness . . . that suits me perfectly." As a lecturer, Connolly flashed periodic bouts of hard-headedness and a propensity for keeping grudges, particularly in his longstanding resentment of Harvard. But the tale of how Connolly had left the school in the early spring of 1896 depended on the audience. At times, Connolly insisted he had been "tossed out." Other times, Connolly said he had withdrawn on his own—and that Harvard administrators had offered him an honorary degree, and that he refused. The stories had elements of truth here and there, but none were completely accurate. In reality, Harvard never offered Connolly an honorary degree, though the Harvard athletic committee did confer on him a major honorary "H" or a varsity letter, which he icily accepted in 1948, at his 50th class reunion.

That was Connolly being Connolly. There was the little spat in 1932 with Ellery Clark over who had been the first to be recognized with a flag raising in Athens, but the dust-up was quickly forgotten and the friendship resumed. Critics compared Connolly's prose to Melville and Kipling, and Joseph Conrad called him "America's best writer of sea stories." In 1948, about the time Connolly finally earned his Harvard "H," the Eire Society of Boston awarded him a gold medal, its version of the "H." Connolly would also earn honorary degrees from the University of Dublin, Boston College, Colby College in Maine, and Fordham University in New York. The Special Collections at Colby houses a collection of Connolly's books and medals, including his 1896 medal for the Triple Jump. A gift of Connolly's daughter, Brenda, and a friend, James Healy, the collection helped to establish the Maine college's highly regarded collection of Irish literature. America's first Olympic champion died in 1957 at the age of 88.

———

Ellery Clark got over Connolly's spat. After all, it was he and Arthur Blake who had arranged for Harvard to give a letter to their old friend. How typical of Clark, who approached post-Olympic life as he did track and field—modestly. As much as Clark had enjoyed the Games and the reception back in Boston—"verily wonder succeeded wonder" he would write of the lavish attention from his hometown—"it was almost with the feeling that we had been living in a land of shadowy romance that we settled down again to the quiet routine of every day."

So Clark returned to college and pursued routine. On May 16, 1896, the same day Yale drubbed Princeton, Harvard's two-time Olympic champion contributed to the Crimson's easy defeat of the University of Pennsylvania with a second in the long jump and a second-place tie in the high jump. If the performances seemed considerably less than Olympian, Clark's real talents emerged June 22 when he easily took the New England "All Around Championship" against his only competitor, the overmatched E. L. Hopkins of South Boston's Peninsular Athletic Association. Competition in the one-day, nine-event competition, the decathlon of its era, ended abruptly in event number six—the pole vault—when Hopkins hurt his leg and withdrew. But Clark was already comfortably ahead—having taken the first events, the 100-yard dash, shot put, high jump, 880-yard walk, and the hammer throw. "All Round Man," trumpeted the headline in the *Globe*. Clark would capture the national all-around championship twice more, in 1897 and 1903. He remains the only athlete to earn Olympic titles in the long jump and high jump.

Like Connolly, Clark kept a hand in sports. At Harvard, he earned undergraduate and law degrees while serving as physical director of the Browne & Nichols School in Cambridge. And like Connolly, Clark would lead a varied, productive life, in his case, practicing law, coaching, and penning a memoir of his track and field career along with a score of other books, one of which was made into the 1952 film, *Caribbean*. A well-known civic figure in Boston, Clark was a member of the Boston School Committee and the Board of Aldermen. His son, Ellery Jr., would achieve prominence on his own as a race walker and a devotee of the Boston Red Sox and author of several critically acclaimed books about the team. Clark, the elder, died in 1949 at the age of 75.

◆━◆

Like his comrades, Tom Burke continued racing after Athens, racking up awards and records. In July 1896, at the AAU championships in New York, he ran 48.45 seconds in the 440-yard run, a world record that would last a quarter of a century. That September, he set a world mark in the 600-yard run, and the following year, another in the 500-yard run. Along the way, he became the intercollegiate quarter-mile champion at Boston University and later Harvard, where he attended graduate school. In later years, Burke turned to law, coaching, and writing. He then became a staffer with the *Boston Journal* and the *Post*, and in World War I enlisted in the Army. At 43, he earned his aviator's wings, the oldest pilot in the US service to do so. During the war, Lieutenant Burke served as physical director at aviation fields. The father of one, he died in 1929, at 54.

With one notable exception, the other BAA Olympians of '96 followed similar paths—raising families, pursuing careers, and becoming community pillars. When they died, the Boston newspapers ran laudatory obituaries, never forgetting what they had accomplished in Athens. Every so often, usually before an Olympic Games, one or a couple members of the first American team were interviewed about their experience as Olympic heroes, though the details in those statistically challenged days could get a bit muddled. In a 1932 interview in the *Boston Evening Transcript* before the Los Angeles Games, Blake recalled that on the team's arrival in Athens, Ambassador Eben Alexander passed out Colt .45s for their protection. None of his teammates disputed the claim, however preposterous the tale. Blake probably just forgot, and there was no film footage or ESPN documentarians to set the record straight. By then a prosperous insurance executive and the father of five, Blake had settled in Dedham and turned to less strenuous pursuits like golf and sailing. He died in 1944 at the age of 72.

Blake's Olympic experience would also connect him to the start of another enduring institution: the Boston Marathon. So inspired was John Graham by the spirit of the Olympic marathon that back in Boston after the Games, he undertook to start a similar race in the Boston area. Working with Boston businessman Herbert Holton, Graham and company considered several distances before selecting a 24.5-mile route from Ashland, west of Boston, to Irvington Oval for their marathon. And so on April 19, 1897—the date chosen to commemorate Paul Revere's famous ride, now called Patriots' Day—one John J. McDermott of New York City secured an everlasting place in the trivia encyclopedia by breaking free of the 15-man field and overcoming a near collision with a Massachusetts Avenue funeral procession to capture the first Boston Marathon in 2:55:10. Little is known about McDermott, who apparently had won an earlier marathon, in September 1896 from Stamford, Connecticut, to New York City, referred to by the (US) National Track & Field Hall of Fame Museum in New York as the "very 'first' New York marathon."

In 1924, the BAA moved the starting line several miles southwest of Ashland to Hopkinton, where it remains. Three years later, the route was lengthened to its standard 26.2 miles. The current distance was created at the 1908 Games in London when King Edward VII and Queen Alexandra requested that the Olympic Marathon start at Windsor Castle so the royal family could watch. Organizers then added the final two-tenths of a mile or 385 yards at the end of the race so the runners could finish in front of the royal box.

Those extra two-tenths of a mile added at the London Games would result in perhaps the most dramatic Marathon finish in history, cementing the event as one of the Olympic Games' most captivating dramas. With a capacity crowd including the queen looking on, Dorando Pietri of Italy entered the Shepherd's Bush Stadium ahead of the pack but was clearly in distress. Circling the track, Pietri staggered several times like a man on a bender. Each time, the officials scraped him up and guided him in the right direction so that Pietri was practically thrust across the finish line. Almost unnoticed in the excitement was the performance of the American, 24-year-old Johnny Hayes of New York City, who crossed the tape next, but unaided. Pietri was disqualified, giving the gold to Hayes, an assistant to the manager of the sporting goods department at Bloomingdale Brothers, where he trained on a cinder track laid out on the roof of the store. So moved was the queen by Pietri's ordeal that she presented him with a silver-gilt cup. Writing home, an American spectator told his family that he had "just seen the greatest race of the century."

Returning to the United States from Athens, William Hoyt was at a crossroads. Having withdrawn from Harvard for "health" reasons, he asked the College to let him resume his hygiene course "as my health is now restored." An Olympic title presumably works wonders for one's overall well-being. Although Hoyt withdrew the request a few days later, he was admitted that autumn to Harvard Medical School. Earning an MD degree in 1901, Hoyt practiced in Chicago, and with the Army in France during World War I. In later years, he moved back to Chicago and then returned to France as a surgeon with the foreign branch of the US Public Health Service. Returning finally to the United States, he settled in tiny Berlin, New York, pursuing his medical practice. Hoyt died in 1954 at 79.

Thomas Curtis was also touched by war. He commanded the Massachusetts National Guard Ambulance corps and served as an aide during World War I to Massachusetts governor and future president Calvin Coolidge. Otherwise, he lived a quiet life: He and his wife, Frances, raised four children, and back at Lord Electric, Curtis helped lead the company in development of the toaster and food blender. Long active in the BAA as well as a number of other Boston-area community and sports organizations, Curtis died in 1944, at 72.

The post-Olympic career of Gardner Williams, the BAA swimmer, was practically set from birth. Williams worked in his family's wool business. He died in 1933, at age 56. John Paine stuck to his family business as well; after serving in the Spanish-American War, he turned to investment banking and philanthropy and managed his family's fortune. In 1925, Paine donated a 10-acre island off the Massachusetts coast as a bird sanctuary to the Federation of Bird Clubs. His family patriarch, Paine died in 1951, at 81.

But for Sumner Paine, life took a hard turn. Like John, Sumner fought in the Spanish-American War, where according to one report, he was seriously wounded in the head. Earning a medical degree in Colorado, Paine would return with his wife, Salome, and their daughter, Margaret or "Betty," now nine, to a handsome town house on Chestnut Hill in Boston where things quickly unraveled. Early in 1901, Paine filed for bankruptcy, a sad and curious turn of events for the 33-year-old Olympic revolver champion and son of privilege. Then, on the evening of May 29, 1901, Paine, a lieutenant in Company A of the 1st Massachusetts Heavy Artillery, returned home unexpectedly early from the armory to find Salome and Betty's violin teacher, one Peter Damn of East Lexington, Massachusetts, in "a compromising position," as the *Globe* delicately explained. Damn fled through the back door and into the night—"without stopping for his coat or hat," the newspaper reported—and Sumner Paine, his .32-caliber pistol conveniently in hand, fired four shots in the direction of the fleeing violin teacher. No bullet ever reached its mark; Paine later explained that he was just trying to frighten the man. He was fined $500 anyway. Less than two months later, Paine filed for divorce, citing the alleged adultery of Salome, and calling her an opium addict. The drama seemed to portend more dire developments: Less than three years later, on April 18, 1904, Sumner Paine died of pneumonia, too soon at the age of 35 and the first from the team of '96 to pass away. The family kept things quiet—making the announcement in a single paragraph on the inside pages of the Boston papers.

━◂▸━

Back at Cambridge University, Charles Waldstein resumed his life of scholarship, his brief career as an Olympic organizer and athlete rarely attracting attention. So went the busy life of an accomplished academician more focused on teaching and writing about archaeology and a broad array of subjects beyond athletics. Waldstein wrote books on psychology, Jewish issues, eugenics and ethics, and even a biography of the English art critic and poet John Ruskin. The *Times of London* called Waldstein's 1916 book, *Aristodemocracy*, which linked the rise of moral anarchy in Germany to World War I, "by far, the most valuable contribution he made to the thought of the time."

Married in 1909 to Florence, the widow of Theodore Seligman, Waldstein was knighted in 1912 and earned many doctorates and foreign orders during his long and distinguished career. As World War I raged, Waldstein changed his name to Walston, most likely to distance himself from his family's German heritage. The end came in 1927 from pneumonia while on a Mediterranean cruise, not far from many of the archaeological sites that he had discovered. Sir Charles Walston was 70.

~

How appropriate that after their boisterous lunch at the Princeton Inn, the four Princetonian Olympians went to the gym. Amidst lingering cheers of "Tiger! Sis! Boom! Bah!" they worked off the staleness of another long ocean voyage to prepare for the next afternoon's interclass games. Integrating quickly back to the college life, they just got on with things, seldom talking about their brief, triumphant careers as Olympic pioneers.

Albert Tyler was an exception. His article, "The Olympic Games at Athens," in the July 1896 issue of the Canadian magazine, *Massey's*, is one of the few descriptions of the event by a participant. The Games "well deserve to be chronicled among the greatest and grandest issue of the 19th century," Tyler wrote. "Never before in the history of the world has there been an assemblage of races where such good feeling and fellowship predominated, while vying for international supremacy."

Back on Princeton's football team for the 1896 season, Tyler started at guard—playing an integral role for the undefeated team that shut out Harvard 12–0, knocked off Yale 24–6, and marred an otherwise perfect record with a scoreless tie against Lafayette. Graduating in 1897, Tyler taught math, and coached and officiated football. He taught at the prep schools Lawrenceville and Exeter, and became headmaster at Providence Country Day School. While teaching math at Rutgers University in 1945, Tyler died during a camping trip. He was 73.

Tyler's cousin, Francis Lane, became a physician, graduating from Washington University Medical School and eventually heading the ophthalmology departments at several Chicago hospitals. He died in 1927, at 52. Herbert Jamison, meantime, headed home after Princeton to Peoria, Illinois, where he followed his father into the family manufacturing business and eventually started an insurance agency. Married in 1901 to Caroline King Grier, he and his wife had two children. Jamison died in 1938 at 62.

Robert Garrett's star continued to shine—and particularly at his alma mater. At graduation, his Class of 1897 elected him president, a position he held for the next 64 years. In 1906 at the request of university president Woodrow Wilson, Garrett became a Princeton trustee and served until his death. Ever the collector, Garrett in 1942 donated to the university's library his collection of Arabic manuscripts, the largest privately owned collection of its type in the world. A decade later, Robert's brother John established the university's Garrett Chair in Near Eastern Studies.

In his hometown of Baltimore, Garrett turned to investment banking and became a civic and church leader and a patron of the arts. As a proponent of physical fitness, Garrett helped bring the Boy Scouts of America to Baltimore and financed a playground that became the model of the city's Playground Athletic League. Constructing a building for his company, he included an employee gymnasium—breakthrough thinking for the era. Married in 1907 to Katharine Johnson, he and his wife had four daughters and two sons. Like their fathers, both sons went to Princeton where they majored in classics and earned varsity letters in sports.

Garrett remained committed to Princeton's athletic programs, dashing off periodic letters to administrators that reflected his high ideals with a tone of crustiness. "Garrett was an upholder of traditional standards who would no doubt find aspects of the modern world disturbing," the historian Michael Llewellyn Smith wrote. In a 1931 letter to university president John Grier Hibben, the old Olympian complained of the "abbreviated costume" of tennis and soccer players on campus. "This practice is extremely unfortunate," Garrett wrote. "It is bad enough to see the tendency towards nudity at the seashore and other places in the summer. . . . I trust we are not heading rapidly towards such extreme practices in this country and particularly among the college elements."

The longest surviving of America's first Olympic team, Garrett died in 1961 at 85. Of his teammates in those inaugural Games, Garrett perhaps came closest to capturing the ideal set forth by the classical poet Pindar, a Greek of course, who wrote, "He who overcometh hath because of the games a sweet tranquility throughout his life forevermore."

Continuing the legacy of their family's Olympic hero was very much on the minds of Garrett's descendants. Before the 1996 Olympic Games in Atlanta, the family was approached with several commercial prospects, one from Kodak with a request to use Robert Garrett's image on television and another from Champion Sportswear to put his face on a T-shirt. "My concern was that the memory of a man who dedicated his life to amateur sports would not be well-served by tying him to commercialism and corporate publicity," Robert Garrett, the athlete's grandson and namesake, told the *New York Times*. Though the endorsements totaled $20,000, not much by today's standards, the Garretts took the money—and donated the entire amount in memory of Robert Garrett, the Olympian, to help with the costs of Princeton's new outdoor track. Today, the battered discus Garrett used to beat the Greeks in Athens occupies an honored spot on the Princeton campus.

Call it another way that US Olympic organizers have maintained an enduring link to Princeton athletics. The Olympic torch passed through Princeton en route to Lake Placid for the 1980 Winter Games; it was carried by rower Alison Carlson, class of '77, who ran a lap around the Garrett Memorial Track. The torch again wended through the town in 1996—100 years after Athens—on its way to the Summer Games in Atlanta, passing by the cemetery where Professor Sloane and trainer George Goldie are buried. As of 2008, 86 Princeton students had participated in the Olympic Games, more than any other school in the Ivy League.

So how best to measure the contributions of America's first and most unlikely Olympic team? For starters, their success ensured that America would never again have trouble fielding a team. It would be years before US sports authorities put together any kind of organized trials, meaning athletes or their schools had to continue to find their own ways to get to the Games. But thanks to its first team, America would forever field a group of athletes with a thirst to get there, often at considerable sacrifice or expense.

There was no official US track and field team at the 1900 Olympic Games, but eight colleges and the New York Athletic Club sent athletes to the Games in Paris. The majority of the nearly 700 athletes from 12 nations at the 1904 Games in St. Louis were Americans, though the Games there were almost as poorly organized as the '00 Games. Coubertin had wanted the Games in Chicago, a city he admired, but when St. Louis officials insisted on fielding the Games as part of the Louisiana Purchase Exhibition, President Roosevelt sided with them, so the Games went there. It hardly mattered to Americans that most European countries didn't send teams—Coubertin didn't attend either—or that the Games dragged on for more than five months, most of it during the intense summer heat of Missouri. Americans were hooked on the Games.

In track and field, US trials launched in 1908, though for years, American athletes were relegated to a complex and often bewildering series of regional competitions and ever-changing qualifying rules. Four different trials—in the West at Stanford, Central in Chicago, and separate Collegiate and Eastern meets in Philadelphia—started the complex process of selecting the '08 team. The US Olympic Committee and the AAU then selected an official team for whom expenses were covered—and a supplementary group, who had to find their own way to London. The rules continued to change all the way to 1976 with adoption of the current Olympic Trials format in which men and women now compete in many sports as part of a single competition.

With each passing Olympic Games emerge new American heroes whose shoe deals and appearances on cereal boxes push the pioneering accomplishments of the first team of 14 farther into the shadows. The 1962 film, *It Happened in Athens*, could have helped revive their accomplishments, but it didn't. The 20th Century Fox production was essentially a vehicle for bombshell Jayne Mansfield, who becomes the love interest of Spiridon Louis, played by newcomer Trax Colton. Labeled by film critic Leonard Maltin as a "silly, juvenile charade made somewhat watchable by Mansfield in a variety of revealing costumes," the film also stars US Olympic decathlon star Bob Mathias as John Graham, of all people. The film not only takes liberties with the story of Louis—Mansfield's character agrees to marry the Marathon winner and Graham arranges Louis's entry in the race—but it also ignores the real story of the Americans. Another film, *The First Olympians*, from 1984, spun similar tales with the truth, but at least created a rash of attention for the '96ers, as did the Centennial Games of 1996, which sent magazine writers scurrying to uncover the stories and legends of America's first team a century before. Meanwhile, in 1987 Boston showed its gratitude to its native son Connolly with the dedication of a bronze sculpture of him finishing a jump. Thomas Haxo's dynamic statue shows Connolly planting his heels and thrusting his torso forward in an effort to keep his balance; a product of the Boston Art Commission, the sculpture is in Joe Moakley Park off Old Colony Avenue in "Southie," close to where America's first Olympic champion became an athlete.

But many historians still choose to overlook the contributions of this influential team—most likely because their times and distances were forgettable, owing chiefly to the poor track and wet, cool conditions. So goes the extra challenge faced by Olympians, who not only have to win but set a world record to be remembered. The National Track & Field Hall of Fame Museum at the Armory in New York features a generous display of information on America's first Olympic team: Ellery Clark's 1897 BAA All-Around Championship medal, a photo of him in his Harvard uniform, and another photo of the BAA team members. But why is Clark the only team member enshrined in the National Track & Field Hall of Fame? Certainly Robert Garrett, Tom Burke, and James Connolly deserve election as well. Since 1974, the Hall of Fame has elected 234 athletes, coaches, and officials, many of whom never got close to winning an Olympic gold medal, let alone the two each earned by Garrett and Burke.

Would the '96ers even have cared? Chances are it wouldn't have fazed Garrett and Burke. Connolly, however, would have likely burned at the lack of recognition and raised a fuss, which would have morphed into a grudge. He was entitled. After all, he and other members of the first US Olympic team were rightfully proud of their accomplishments. Their success created a legacy, setting the stage for more than a century of American Olympic superiority. These unheralded collegians were gentlemen, athletes, and scholars. And for two weeks in April 1896, they thrilled the world.

APPENDIX

1896 Olympic Results

TRACK AND FIELD

In times given below "e" stands for estimate.

100 Meters

1. Thomas Burke (United States) 12.0
2. Fritz Hofmann (Germany) 12.2
3. Alajos Szokolyi (Hungary) 12.6e
4. Francis Lane (United States) 12.6e
5. Alexandros Chalkokondilis (Greece) 12.6e

400 Meters

1. Thomas Burke (United States) 54.2
2. Herbert Jamison (United States) -- (not recorded)
3. Charles Gmelin (Great Britain) --
4. Fritz Hofmann (Germany) --

800 Meters

1. Edwin Flack (Australia) 2.11.0
2. Nándor Dáni (Hungary) 2.11.8e
3. Demitrios Golemis (Greece) --

1,500 Meters

1. Edwin Flack (Australia) 4:33.2
2. Arthur Blake (United States) 4:33.6e
3. Albin Lermusiaux (France) 4:36.0e
4. Karl Galie (Germany) 4:39.0e
5. Angelos Phetsis (Greece) --
6. Demitrious Golemis (Greece) --

Marathon

1. Spiridon Louis (Greece) 2:58:50
2. Charilaos Vasilakos (Greece) 3:06:03
3. Gyula Kellner (Hungary) 3:06:35
4. Ioannis Vrettos (Greece) --
5. Elevtherios Papasimeon (Greece) --
6. Demetrios Deligannis (Greece) --
7. Evangelos Gerakakis (Greece) --
8. Stamatios Massouris (Greece) --

110-Meter Hurdles

1. Thomas Curtis (United States) 17.6
2. Grantley Goulding (Great Britain) 17.6e

High Jump

1. Ellery Clark (United States) 1.81 meters/5 feet, 11¼ inches
2. James Connolly (United States) 1.65/5-5
3. Robert Garrett (United States) 1.65/5-5
4. Henrik Sjöberg (Sweden) 1.60/5-3
5. Fritz Hofmann (Germany) 1.55/5-1

Pole Vault

1. William Hoyt (United States) 3.30 meters/10 feet, 10 inches
2. Albert Tyler (United States) 3.20/10-6
3. Evangelos Damaskos (Greece) 2.60/8-6¼
4. Ioannis Theodoropoulos (Greece) 2.60/8-6¼
5. Vasilios Xydas (Greece) 2.60/8-6¼

Long Jump

1. Ellery Clark (United States) 6.35 meters/20 feet, 10 inches
2. Robert Garrett (United States) 6.00/19-8¼
3. James Connolly (United States) 5.84/19-2
4. Alexandros Chalkokondilis (Greece) 5.74/18-10
5. Alphonse Grisel (France) --
6. Karl Schumann (Germany) --
7. Henrik Sjöberg (Sweden) --
8. Athanasios Skaltsogiannis (Greece) --
9. Alexandre Tuffère (France) --

Triple Jump

1. James Connolly (United States) 13.71 meters/44 feet, 11¾ inches
2. Alexandre Tuffère (France) 12.70/41-8
3. Ioannis Persakis (Greece) 12.565/41-3
4. Alajos Szobolyi (Hungary) 11.26/36-11½
5. Karl Schumann (Germany) --

Shot Put

1. Robert Garrett (United States) 11.22 meters/36 feet, 9¾ inches
2. Miltiades Gouskos (Greece) 11.20/36-9
3. Georgios Papasideris (Greece) 10.36/34-0
4. Karl Schumann (Germany) --

Discus

1. Robert Garrett (United States) 29.15 meters/95 feet, 7½ inches
2. Panagiotis Paraskevopoulos (Greece) 28.955/95-0
3. Sotirios Versis (Greece) 27.78/91-1¾

SHOOTING

25-Meter Rapid-Fire Pistol

1. Ioannis Phrangoudis (Greece) 344 points
2. Georgios Orphanidis (Greece) 249
3. Holger Nielsen (Denmark) --

Free Pistol

1. Sumner Paine (United States) 442 points
2. Holger Nielsen (Denmark) 285
3. Ioannis Phrangoudis (Greece) --
4. Leonidas Morakis (Greece) --
5. Georgios Orphanidis (Greece) --

25-Meter Military Revolver

1. John Paine (United States) 442 points
2. Sumner Paine (United States) 380
3. Nikolaos Dorakis (Greece) 205
4. Ioannis Phrangoudis (Greece) --
5. Holger Nielsen (Denmark) --

Free Rifle

1. Pantelis Karasevdas (Greece) 2,320 points
2. Paulos Pavlidis (Greece) 1,978
3. Nikolaos Trikoupes (Greece) 1,713
4. Anastasios Metaxas (Greece) 1,701

5. Georgios Orphanidis (Greece) 1,698
6. Viggo Jensen (Denmark) 1,640
7. Georgios Diamantis (Greece) 1,456
8. A. Baumann (Switzerland) 1,294

Free Rifle, Three Positions
1. Georgios Orphanidis (Greece) 1,583 points
2. Ioannis Phrangoudis (Greece) 1,312
3. Viggo Jensen (Denmark) 1,305
4. Anastasios Metaxas (Greece) 1,102
5. Pantelis Karasevdas (Greece) 1,039

SWIMMING

100-Meter Freestyle
1. Alfréd Hajós (Hungary) 1:22.2
2. Otto Herschmann (Austria) 1:22.8

500-Meter Freestyle
1. Paul Neumann (Austria) 8:12.6
2. Antonios Pepanos (Greece) 9:57.6
3. Efstathios Choraphas (Greece) --

1,200-Meter Freestyle
1. Alfréd Hajós (Hungary) 18:22.2
2. Ioannis Andreou (Greece) 21:03.4
3. Efstathios Choraphas (Greece) --

100-Meter Freestyle for Sailors (members of the Greek Navy)
1. Ioannis Malokinis (Greece) 2:20.4
2. Spiridon Chasapis (Greece) --
3. Dimitrios Drivas (Greece) --

CYCLING

2,000-Meter Sprint (Scratch)

1. Paul Masson (France) 4:58.2
2. Stamatios Nikolopoulos (Greece) 5:00.2
3. Léon Flameng (France) --
4. Joseph Rosemeyer (Germany) --

Individual Road Race (87 kilometers)

1. Aristides Konstantinidis (Greece) 3:21.10
2. August Goedrich (Germany) 3:31.14
3. Edward Battel (Great Britain) --

One-Lap Race (333.33 meters)

1. Paul Masson (France) 24.0
2. Stamatios Nikolopoulos (Greece) 26.0
3. Adolf Schmal (Austria) 26.0
4. Edward Battel (Great Britain) 26.2
5. Theodor Flameng (Germany) 27.0
6. Frank Keeping (Great Britain) 27.0
7. Theodor Leupold (Germany) 27.0
8. Joseph Rosemeyer (Germany) 27.2

10-Kilometer Track Race

1. Paul Masson (France) 17:54.2
2. Léon Flameng (France) 17:54.8
3. Adolf Schmal (Austria) --
4. Joseph Rosemeyer (Germany) --

100-Kilometer Track Race

1. Léon Flameng (France) 3:08:19.2
2. Georgios Kolettis (Greece) --

12-Hour Race

1. Adolf Schmal (Austria) 295.3 kilometers/183.49 miles
2. Frank Keeping (Great Britain) 294.946/183.28

FENCING

Foil

1. Eugène-Henri Gravelotte (France)
2. Henri Callot (France)
3. Perikles Pierrakos-Mavromichalis (Greece)
4. Athanasios Vouros (Greece)
5. Henri de Laborde (France)
6. Georgios Balakakis (Greece)
7. Ioannis Poulos (Greece)

Masters Foil

1. Leon Pyrgos (Greece)
2. Jean Maurice Perronnet (France)

Sabre

1. Ioannis Georgiadis (Greece)
2. Telemachos Karakalos (Greece)
3. Holger Nielsen (Denmark)
4. Adolf Schmal (Austria)
5. Georgios Iatridis (Greece)

GYMNASTICS

Horizontal Bar
1. Hermann Weingärtner (Germany)
2. Alfred Flatow (Germany)

Parallel Bars
1. Alfred Flatow (Germany)
2. Louis Zutter (Switzerland)
3. Hermann Weingärtner (Germany)

Side Horse (Pommel Horse)
1. Louis Zutter (Switzerland)
2. Hermann Weingärtner (Germany)

Rings
1. Ioannis Mitropoulos (Greece)
2. Hermann Weingärtner (Germany)
3. Petros Persakis (Greece)

Rope Climbing
1. Nikolaos Andriakopoulos (Greece)
2. Thomas Xenakis (Greece)
3. Fritz Hofmann (Germany)
4. Viggo Jensen (Denmark)
5. Launceston Elliot (Scotland/Great Britain)

Vault
1. Karl Schumann (Germany)
2. Louis Zutter (Switzerland)
3. Hermann Weingärtner (Germany)

Parallel Bars—Team

1. Germany (Konrad Böcker, Alfred Flatow, Gustav Felix Flatow, Georg Hilmar, Fritz Manteuffel, Karl Neukirch, Richard Röstel, Gustav Schuft, Karl Schumann, and Hermann Weingärtner)
2. Greece (Panhellenic Club of Athens: Sotirios Athanasopoulos, Nicolaos Andriakopoulos, Petros Persakis, and Thomas Yenakis)
3. Greece (National Gymnastic Club of Athens: Ioannis Chrysaphis, Ioannis Mitropoulos, Dimitrios Loundras, and Philippos Karvelas)

Horizontal Bars—Team

1. Germany (Konrad Böcker, Alfred Flatow, Gustav Felix Flatow, Georg Hilmar, Fritz Manteuffel, Karl Neukirch, Richard Röstel, Gustav Schuft, Karl Schumann, and Hermann Weingärtner)

WEIGHT LIFTING

One-Hand Lift (Super Heavyweight—Unlimited Weight)

1. Launceston Elliot (Great Britain) 71.0 kilograms/156.5 pounds
2. Viggo Jensen (Denmark) 57.2/126.1
3. Alexandros Nikolopoulos (Greece) --

Two-Hand Lift (Super Heavyweight—Unlimited Weight)

1. Viggo Jensen (Denmark) 111.5 kilograms/246 pounds*
2. Launceston Elliot (Scotland/Great Britain) 111.5/246
3. Alexandros Nikolopoulos (Greece) 90.0/198.5
4. Karl Schumann (Germany) 90.0/198.5
5. Momcsilló Topavicza (Hungary) 90.0/198.5
6. Sotirios Versis (Greece) 90.0/198.5

* Jensen was awarded the championship based on style points.

TENNIS

Singles

1. John Pius Boland (Great Britain/Ireland)*
2. Dionysios Kasdaglis (Egypt)
3. Momcsilló Topavicza (Hungary)
4. K. Paspatis (Greece)
5. A. Akratopoulos (Greece)
6. E. Rallis (Greece)

* In the final, Boland defeated Kasdaglis 6-3, 6-1.

Doubles

1. John Pius Boland/Fritz Traun (Great Britain/Ireland/Germany)*
2. Dionysios Kasdaglis/Demetrios Petrokokkinos (Egypt/Greece)
3. Edwin Flack/George Robertson (Australia/Great Britain)

* In the final, Boland/Traun defeated Kasdaglis/Petrokokkinos 5-7, 6-4, 6-1.

Results from *The Complete Book of the Olympics*—1992 Edition by David Wallechinsky (Little, Brown and Company, 1991).

Acknowledgments

There were times when piecing together the story of the first American team was a solitary exercise of wading through archival materials and microfilm in big, cavernous libraries. In a sense, it was similar to all those long, lonely training runs I took as a former distance runner. How wonderful it was then to find a great team who believed in this project and made it happen, principally Doris S. Michaels and Delia Berrigan Fakis of the Doris S. Michaels Literary Agency, and Keith Wallman, Kristen Mellitt, and Joshua Rosenberg of Lyons Press. A big thank you and a laurel wreath to all for making this book better—and a lot more fun to put together.

NOTES

AUTHOR'S NOTE

viii According to . . . Fred R. Shapiro, ed., *The Yale Book of Quotations*, Yale University Press, New Haven, CT, 2006.

viii Note that Woodward . . . *Oxford English Dictionary* entry for "Ivy League," www.oed.com

viii particularly in 1954. . . http://www.princeton.edu/mudd/news/faq/topics/ivy_league.shtml

BEGINNINGS

1 A Harvard student . . . Ellery H. Clark, "The First Americans at the Olympic Games," 1911, based on his book, *Reminiscences of an Athlete: Twenty Years on Track and Field*, Houghton Mifflin Company, Boston, New York, 1911, 127-8.

1 James Connolly faced his own dilemma . . . James B. Connolly, *Sea-Borne: Thirty Years Avoyaging*, Doubleday, Doran and Co., Inc., Garden City, NY, 1944, 12-13. Excerpt reprinted in Rusty Wilson, ed., "The First Olympic Champion," *Journal of Olympic History*, January 2000.

2 Acknowledging the cramped conditions . . . Connolly, *Sea-Borne: Thirty Years Avoyaging*, 12-13.

2 seen off . . . *New York Times*, March 21, 1896; various unidentified March and April 1896 news clippings drawn from Francis Lane scrapbooks in the Mudd Archives at Princeton University.

3 olive boat . . . *Princeton Alumni Weekly*, June 2, 1964.

3 spirited but small send-off . . . The description of the start of the voyage of the SS *Fulda* is taken from several newspaper articles preserved in the scrapbooks of Francis Lane, stored in the Princeton archives. The information is from three articles—"In Ancient Athens: American Athletes to Contest in Olympic Games," "Athletes Off for Greece," and "Athens Their First Goal." The names of the newspapers are not preserved. The Garrett and Graham quotes are taken from the story "Athletes Off for Athens" in the *New York Herald* (March 22, 1896). Other information is taken from an article in the *New York Times*, "Princeton's Team for Athens" (March 20, 1896). The descriptions of the cheers are from the article "Cheers for the Princeton Boys" in the *New York Herald* (March 21, 1896), and Richard D. Mandell, *The First Modern Olympics*, University of California Press, Berkeley and Los Angeles, 1976, 116–17. Specific information on Solon J. Vlasto is taken from http://wiki.phantis.com/index.php/Atlantis_(newspaper).

7 Jamison was a last-minute substitution . . . Michael Llewellyn Smith, *Olympics in Athens 1896: The Invention of the Modern Olympic Games*, Profile Books, London, 2004,127; Charles B. Saunders Jr., "Olympic Princetonians: The Greeks Get Beat at Their Own Game When '97 Takes Off for Athens," *Princeton Alumni Weekly*, December 7, 1956.

8 "The trip will no doubt" . . . *Daily Princetonian*, March 1896.

8 On March 25, 1896 . . . "Princeton Track," *Trenton Times*, March 25, 1896.

8 That month alone . . . *New York Times*, March 1, 9, 18, 30, 1896.

8 About the same time . . . Saunders Jr., "Olympic Princetonians." Information also taken from "Monthly Record" in *Outing* magazine, May 1896, 21. The Connolly story is taken from the story cited above by Saunders.

9 Aboard ship . . . *Boston Morning Journal*, April 13, 1896.

11 Entering the Straits of Gibraltar . . . Connolly, *Sea-Borne: Thirty Years Avoyaging*, 12-13; Thomas B. Curtis, "High Hurdles and White Gloves," *Atlantic*, December 1956, 60–61 (this same article is taken from an earlier piece by Curtis, "Olympic Games of an Elder Day," that appeared in *Technology Review*, the MIT alumni magazine, in July 1924); team background and the "Fulton" quote is from Bob Fulton, "Our First Olympians," *American Heritage*, July/August 1996.

12 aboard the SS *Fulda* was another American. . . . *New York Times*, Burton Holmes obituary, July 23, 1958, www.burtonholmes.org/travelogues/travelogues.html.

14 It was a restful time . . . Connolly, *Sea-Borne: Thirty Years Avoyaging*, 12; Wilson, ed., "The First Olympic Champion." Connolly wrote years later that the team realized the schedule mix-up, not in Naples, but on the morning of April 5, while eating breakfast at their hotel in Athens. But considering Connolly's habit of sometimes stretching the truth when recalling the events of 1896, he may have fabricated that story. No other 1896 U.S. Olympians ever mentioned it in print.

15 The mix-up happened . . . Fulton, "Our First Olympians."

15 Thrilled that his sore back . . . Connolly, *Sea-Borne: Thirty Years Avoyaging*, 12.

17 Two long days . . . Curtis, "High Hurdles and White Gloves," 60–61. Curtis wrote that the man was a Frenchman named Albin Lermusiaux, who would finish a close third in the 1,500 Meters, which clearly indicated he knew what he was doing. In an interview in the July 27, 1932 issue of the *Boston Transcript*, Arthur Blake, who would edge Lermusiaux for second place, wrote that the man Curtis thought was the Frenchman was in fact Legoudaki, a Greek who had been studying in France. Blake's story is probably more accurate, in part because he'd had several conversations with Lermusiaux in and around the competition. Moreover, a Greek athlete would be more inclined than a Frenchman to wear white gloves for his king.

17 "we caught our first glimpse" . . . Ellery H. Clark, "The First Americans at the Olympic Games."

18 "were not exactly" . . . Curtis, "High Hurdles and White Gloves," 60–61.

CHAPTER 1

19 "Games at Athens?" . . . Ralph C. Wilcox, "The Literary Works of James Brendan Connolly, First Modern Olympic Victor," 1997; "The Works of James Brendan Connolly, First Modern Olympic Victor and Literator." *The Sports Historian. The Journal of the British Society of Sports History* 17: 1 (May), 63-92.

19 It was early 1896 . . . "Plans for the Olympic Games," *Harvard Crimson*, December 7, 1895; "International Sports: A Harvard Man Writes from Athens to Urge Their Support, *Harvard Crimson*, March 5, 1895; "Revival of Olympic Games," *Harvard Crimson*, January 28, 1896; "Freshmen Athletic Meeting: Contests Among Athletes from Ninety-Nine—List of Winners," *Harvard Crimson*, October 25, 1895.

21 The real decision-maker . . . http://en.wikipedia.orgwiki/Charles_ W._Eliot; www.1911encyclopedia.orgCharles_William_Eliot.

23 For Harvard students. . . David McCullough, *Mornings on Horse-back*, Simon & Schuster, New York, 1982, 196–97.

24 In 1874 . . . "Harvard Athletics—A Timeline of Tradition," www .gocrimson.com/information/history/traditiontimline.

25 simply loathed football . . . Bernard M. Corbett and Paul Simpson, "When Men Were Men and Football Was Brutal," *Yale Alumni Magazine*, November/December 2004. Adapted from their book, *The Only Game That Matters: The Harvard/Yale Rivalry*, Three Rivers Press, New York, 2005.

25 Perhaps no man . . . McCullough, *Mornings on Horseback*, 204–6.

26 bastion of the privileged . . . *Harvard University Class of 1897: Secretary's First Report*, The University Press, Cambridge, MA,1900.

26 his neighborhood . . . Wilcox, *The Literary Works of James Brendan Connolly*. Connolly's educational background and the story about Nathaniel Shaler is from Jonathan Shaw, "The Unexpected Olympians: How Harvard Dominated the First Modern Games—In Spite of Itself," *Harvard Magazine*, July 1996. The story about following to Savannah, Georgia, is taken from www.catholicauthors.com/Connolly.html.

33 a letter from March 18, 1896 . . . Shaw, "The Unexpected Olympians: How Harvard Dominated the First Modern Games—In Spite of Itself."

34 paid his own way to Athens . . . Wilson, ed., "The First Olympic Champion."

34 BAA wasn't as much a sports organization . . . Shaw, "The Unexpected Olympians: How Harvard Dominated the First Modern Games—In Spite of Itself."

34 Manhattan Athletic Club . . . Richard W. O'Donnell, "The Original Olympic Hero," *Olympic Review*, June-July 1996.

35 "Still the little hometown club for me" . . . Wilson, ed., "The First Olympic Champion."

CHAPTER 2

36 "welcoming us instantly" . . . Clark, "The First Americans at the Olympic Games."

37 No one in the Greek welcoming party spoke English . . . Wilson, ed., "The First Olympic Champion."

38 "The idea that this form of reception" . . . Thomas Curtis, "Olympic Games of an Elder Day," *Technology Review* (the MIT alumni magazine), July 1924.

38 "Our hosts scarcely understood" . . . Clark, "The First Americans at the Olympic Games."

38 Close to 9:00 p.m. . . . Wilson, ed., "The First Olympic Champion."

39 Hopping aboard was the intrepid Burton Holmes . . . Burton Holmes, *The Olympian Games in Athens, 1896: The First Modern Olympics*, Grove Press, 1984, 15–24. The book is based on Holmes's lectures in America about his experiences in Athens during the 1896 Olympic Games.

40 Seven photographers . . . *1896 Athens - Die Bilder der Spiele der I. Olympiade von Albert Meyer und anderen Fotografen. (1896 Athens - The Pictures of the First Olympiad by Albert Meyer and Other Photographers).* Edited by Volker Kluge, Berlin: Brandenburgiscjes Verlags-Haus, 1996.

41 "A small city built of very white houses" . . . Curtis, "Olympic Games of an Elder Day."

42 Watching the lines of the devout . . . Maynard Butler, "The Olympic Games," *Outlook*, May 30, 1896, reprinted in *The 1896 Olympic Games: Results for All Competitors in All Events, with Commentary*, by Bill Mallon and Ture Widllund, McFarland & Company, Jefferson, NC, 1998.

42 All that Saturday . . . Mandell, *The First Modern Olympics*, 122–24; Curtis, "Olympic Games of an Elder Day"; other details on this event are taken from David C. Young, *The First Modern Olympics*, The Johns Hopkins University Press, Baltimore, 1996, 143. Note: Averoff's age is from Maynard Butler, "The Olympic Games," *Outlook*, May 30, 1896, reprinted in *The 1896 Olympic Games: Results for All Competitors in All Events, with Commentary*, by Bill Mallon and Ture Widllund, McFarland & Company, Jefferson, NC, 1998.

43 "Up to this very moment" . . . Clark, "The First Americans at the Olympic Games."

43 "This stupendous structure" . . . Albert C. Tyler, "The Olympic Games at Athens," *Massey's Magazine*, July 1896.

43 A line of soldiers . . . Butler, "The Olympic Games."

44 Advance ticket sales had been practically nil . . . Young, *The First Modern Olympics*, 143.

45 all 60,000 or so of the seats . . . *Sports Illustrated*, August 2, 1896.

45 In some cases . . . http://e.wikipedia.org/wiki/1896_Summer_Olympics

45 The stands were full . . . Mandell, *The First Modern Olympics*, 122–25.

47 Angling into position for his heat . . . Curtis, "Olympic Games of an Elder Day"; Lane information is taken from the *Princeton Alumni Weekly*, June 2, 1964. Lagoudaki background is from Bud Greenspan, "How I Filmed the 1896 Olympics," *Journal of Olympic History*, Summer 1997.

47 Finding fellow marathoner Arthur Blake . . . *Boston Transcript*, June 27, 1932.

48 "The Committee in charge of the Games" . . . Tyler, "The Olympic Games at Athens."

48 yelled with gusto . . . Curtis, "Olympic Games of an Elder Day."

49 "Then, all at once" Clark, "The First Americans at the Olympic Games."

50 Even the king was transfixed . . . Curtis, "Olympic Games of an Elder Day."

51 It was the Triple Jump . . . Wilson, ed., "The First Olympic Champion." Descriptions of the history of the triple jump are taken from: http://trackandfield.about.com/od/triplejump/ss/illustriplejump.htm (Irish Games) and from www.Dunardry.net/ladies_lounge.html.

51 Some in the crowd objected . . . "Greater Boston Monuments: James Brendan Connolly," www.IrishHeritageTrail.com.

51 A more likely explanation . . . Wilson, ed., "The First Olympic Champion." The rabbit's foot story is taken from the *Boston Herald*, May 7, 1896.

52 The gesture. . . . Jack Wilkinson, "The Dauntless Dozen," *Stars and Stripes*, October 12, 1968.

53 "It's a miracle!" . . . Wilson, ed., "The First Olympic Champion." Event results throughout the book are taken from David Wallechin-sky, *The Complete Book of the Olympics—1992 Edition*, Little, Brown and Company, Boston, Toronto, London, 1991. Results of the Triple Jump are on page 103.

54 Connolly and the other Olympic victors would receive silver medals . . . Holmes, *The Olympian Games in Athens*, 88–89. Additional details about the Olympic medals are from E. M. Swift, "Athens Put on an Odd Show at the First Modern Olympics," *Sports Illustrated*, August 2, 2004. Background on the Olympic design is taken from www .olympic.org/content/Olympic-Games/All-Past-Olympic-Games/ Summer?Athens-1896-Collection/.

55 Connolly shook hands . . . Wilson, ed., "The First Olympic Champion."

Chapter 3

56 "A whiskered cat" . . . Mandell, 49–59.

59 "Well then, we are agreed" . . . Smith, *Olympics in Athens 1896*, 69–71. Courbertin's quote that begins "I just cannot understand the pedants," is from Mandell, *The First Modern Olympics*, 68.

59 In the summer of 1889 . . . Baron Pierre de Coubertin, *Univer-sités Transatlantiques*, Paris, Librairie Hachete et Cie, 1890, 363–64; Mandell, *The First Modern Olympics*, 62.

61 At some point during the next three years . . . Smith, *Olympics in Athens 1896*, 54–55.

63 Zappas had quite the resume ... "Timeline of the Modern Olympic Games" from www.zappas.org/timeline.html; Michael Llewellyn Smith, "The 1896 Olympic Games at Athens and the Princeton Connection," *Princeton University Library Chronicle* (date unknown, from Mudd Library at Princeton). The story about W. G. Grace winning the 400-meter hurdles at the 1866 "Olympic Games" in London is from http://en.wikipedia.org/wiki/W._G._Grace. The story about Greek professors objecting to the "open" Olympic Games is from the speech, "Imagine That! Olympic Games in Greece!" by Professor David Young at Columbia University, (www.greekembassy.org/Embassy/content/en/Article.aspx?office+1&folder+30&article+11574&hilite+David%20Young.

CHAPTER 4

67 The Discus was the pride of Greek athletics . . . Stephen R. Dujack, "Princeton in Athletics, 1896," *Princeton Alumni Weekly*, December 17, 1979.

67 Most famous was the ... Roman marble copy ... Francis Haskell and Nicholas Penny, *Taste and the Antique: The Lure of Classical Sculpture 1500–1900*, Yale University Press, 1981, 200; Townley background from Tony Kitto, "The Celebrated Connoisseur: Charles Townley, 1737–1805," *Minerva Magazine*, May/June 2005, in connection with a British Museum exhibition celebrating the bicentennial of the Townley purchase.

68 Raised in considerable wealth . . . Smith, "The 1896 Olympic Games at Athens and the Princeton Connection."

68 In early 1896 ... Robert Garrett, "I Was on America's First Olympic Team," *American Weekly*, November 15, 1956.

68 How exactly to prepare ... Frederic T. Fox, "Our First Olympian: Robert Garrett '97," *Princeton Alumni Weekly*, June 2, 1964.

69 "I was baffled" . . . Garrett, "I Was on America's First Olympic Team."

69 "part of a little outing" . . . Fox, "Our First Olympian: Robert Garrett '97."

70 Connolly had already taken the Triple Jump . . . Swift, "Athens Put on an Odd Show at the First Modern Olympics."

70 They had invented discus . . . Garrett, "I Was on America's First Olympic Team."

70 Asked as a middle-aged businessman . . . Fox, "Our First Olympian: Robert Garrett '97."

71 Born into a prominent Baltimore family . . . Neil Genzlinger, "They Had It and Flaunted It," *New York Times*, December 19, 2008.

71 Garrett's great-grandfather, also named Robert . . . John N. Ingram, *Biographical Dictionary of American Business*, Greenwood, 1983, 432–34.

72 A Confederate veteran winding up . . . Sumner Archibald Cunningham, "Real Americanism: Princeton Honors Blue and Gray Heroes," *The Confederate Veteran* (magazine), January 1922, 85–86.

73 history's first intercollegiate football game . . . http://etcweb .princeton.edu/CampusWWW/Companion/football.html.

73 In doing so, the team asked their fellow students to yell for them . . . Simon P. R. Jenkins, *Sports Science Handbook Vol. 2: The Essential Guide to Kinesiology, Sport & Exercise Science*, Multi-Science Publishing Co., Ltd., 2005, 289.

73 Robert Garrett's youthful escapade . . . Ingram, *Biographical Dictionary of American Business*, 432–34.

73 He collected rare coins . . . Max B. Spiegel, "The Garrett Collection: Coins, Medals, and Archives at the Am. Numismatic Society," *American Numismatic Society Magazine*, Winter 2006.

74 In 1888, Thomas even gave up a chunk . . . Ibid.

74 That same year, tragedy struck . . . Ingram, *Biographical Dictionary of American Business*, 432–34.

75 From its earliest years as a training ground . . . Dimitri Gondicas, "Modern Greek Literature at P-ton: Building a Program and a Collection," *Princeton University Library Chronicle*, Volume LVIII, 1996-97.

75 A late-19th-century snapshot . . . *Princeton Parents Handbook, 2006-07*, www.princeton.edu/pr/pub/ph/06/28.htm; information on eating clubs from "History of Eating Clubs" (http://diglib.princeton.edu/ead) housed in Princeton University, Department of Rare Books and Special Collections.

76 F. Scott Fitzgerald's debut novel . . . F. Scott Fitzgerald, *This Side of Paradise*, first published in 1920; this 75th-anniversary edition published by Forgotten Books, 2010, 29. Biographical information from Jon Blackwell, "1920: Fitzgerald's Own 'Paradise'," *Trentonian*, www.capitalcentury.com/1920.html.

77 The *Daily Princetonian* regularly featured ads . . . *Daily Princetonian*, April 8, 1896.

77 And unlike Harvard . . . "Association of Black Princeton Alumni History," www.princeton-abpa.org/dynamic.asp?id=history, and "Looking Back: Reflections of Black Princeton Alumni" in *Princeton Today*, Summer 1997.

77 Princeton differed from Harvard in another important way . . . http://etcweb.princeton.edu/Campuswww/companion/football.html.

78 Goldie arrived at Princeton in 1869 . . . Frank Zarnowski, *All-Around Men: Heroes of a Forgotten Sport*, Scarecrow Press, 2005, 64–69.

79 A peppering of talented, often colorful, and now largely forgotten stars . . . Information from displays at the Track & Field Hall of Fame Museum; for Myers, from the Internatonal Jewish Sports Hall of Fame, www.jewishsports.net/BioPages/LonMyers.htm; for Bennett, www.npg.si.edu/col/native/deerfoot.htm.

81 As the year's collegiate champion, Yale earned the right . . . "American Amateur Athletics in 1896," *Outing Magazine*, November 1896, 163.

82 "He is thoroughly positioned in all matters" . . . "Princeton Athletics: Those Who Have the Base Ball, Track and Other Athletic Teams in Charge," *Trenton Times*, February 15, 1896.

82 On February 9, 1896, at the sixth annual . . . "American Amateur Athletics in 1896," 163. The comment on Garrett's improvement and the quote are taken from articles (dates and publications unknown) in the Francis Lane files at Princeton, with additional detail from Smith, "The 1896 Olympic Games at Athens and the Princeton Connection."

83 Records vary . . . Baron Pierre de Coubertin, Timoleon Philemon, N. G. Politis, and Charalambos Anninos, *The Olympic Games: B.C. 776–A.D. 1896*, Charles Beck-Athens and H. Grevel and Co., London, 1897; Mallon and Widlund, *The 1896 Olympic Games*; and Smith, *Olympics in Athens 1896*.

83 Robertson had learned of the events . . . William Johnson, "The Taking Part," *Sports Illustrated*, July 10, 1972.

84 Robertson's enduring Olympic legacy . . . Young, *The First Modern Olympics*, 157–58.

84 In the Discus . . . Wilkinson, "The Dauntless Dozen." Tyler's quote is taken from his dispatch for The Associated Press, cited in Smith, "The 1896 Olympic Games at Athens and the Princeton Connection."

85 "Miserable duds" . . . Garrett, "I Was on America's First Olympic Team."

85 Garrett's form . . . Wilkinson, "The Dauntless Dozen."

86 Utilizing what the American photographer and writer . . . Holmes, *The Olympian Games in Athens, 1896*, 65–66.

87 "silent . . . as if the structure were empty." . . . Albert Tyler's letter to the *Princetonian*, April 14, 1896.

87 "The Greeks had been defeated" . . . Holmes, *The Olympian Games in Athens, 1896*, 66.

87 Looking back more than a half-century later . . . "History Shows 1896 Olympic Games Little More Than a Social Gathering," *Long Beach Press-Telegram*, April 15, 1948.

88 "Simply this" . . . George Robertson, "The Olympic Games by a Competitor and Prize Winner," *Fortnightly Review*, June 1, 1896, reprinted in Mallon and Widlund, *The 1896 Olympic Games*.

88 "Garrett devised an individual style" . . . Mandell, *The First Modern Olympics*, 127.

88 Meanwhile on the Princeton campus . . . *New York Times*, April 9, 1896.

Chapter 5

90 In its Tuesday, April 7, 1896, edition . . . *New York Times*, April 7, 1896.

90 "Americans win at Athens" . . . *New York Tribune*, April 7, 1896.

90 Of the major papers in New York . . . *New York Post*, April 8–11, 1896.

90 But the Olympic story was prominent clear across . . . *Galveston Daily News*, April 8, 1896; *Daily Northwestern* (Oshkosh, WI), April 7, 1896; *Daily News* (Salem, OH), April 8, 1896; *Morning Herald* (Titusville, PA), April 8, 1896; *Oakland Tribune*, April 7, 1896; *Weekly Wisconsin* (Milwaukee, WI), April 11, 1896.

91 The other prominent sports item that week . . . *New York Times*, April 7, 1896.

91 Included in the Francis Lane scrapbooks . . . Francis Lane scrapbooks, Mudd Library at Princeton University. According to Smith,

"The 1896 Olympic Games at Athens and the Princeton Connection," Tyler wrote from Athens for The Associated Press. Smith cites a dispatch quoted in Frank Presbrey and James Hugh Moffatt, eds., *Athletics at Princeton: A History*, Frank Presbrey Co., New York, 1901.

93 Of the bunch, Rufus B. Richardson, an archaeologist . . . Richardson obituary, *New York Times*, March 11, 1914; article information from Rufus B. Richardson, "The New Olympian Games," *Scribner's*, September 1896, 267–86.

94 Accompanying Richardson's article . . . Linson background from his obituary, *New York Times*, June 11, 1959, from www.liveauctioneers .com/item/1428114. Background on Linson and Stephen Crane from Linda H. Davis, *Badge of Courage: The Life of Stephen Crane*, Houghton Mifflin, 1998, 58–60, and from www.answers.com/topic/ stephen-crane.

96 Eugene Andrews, the man who had straightened out the king during the Triple Jump . . . Background on Eugene Andrews from his obituary in the *New York Times*, September 22, 1967; background on Benjamin Ide Wheeler from his obituary in the *New York Times*, April 4, 1927; information on the American School of Classical Studies at Athens from *The American School of Classical Studies at Athens Annual Report: 1900* (publisher is Managing Committee of the school, 1900); information on Cornell museum exhibit in the article by Carol Kammen, "Not the Most Isolated Place on the Eastern Seaboard," 2006, http://ecommons .cornell.edu/bitstream/1813/11117/6/Chapter1.pdf.

97 the presence of American academic expatriates . . . Background on Eben Alexander from his obituary in the *New York Times*, March 13, 1919; background on Charles Fairchild from http://political graveyard.com/geo/NY/lawyer.E-F.html.

97 the grandly named American . . . Background on Basil L. Gildersleeve from James Stimpert, "Hopkins History: First Greek Prof,

Basil Gildersleeve," *Johns Hopkins Gazette*, September 18, 2000, www
.jhu.edu/gazette/2000/sep1800/18greek.html, and "Gildersleeve,
Basil Lanneau," *Encyclopædia Britannica* (11th Edition), 1911. Gildersleeve's *Atlantic* February 1897 article, "My Sixty Days in Greece;
The Olympic Games, Old and New," is at www.theatlantic.com/
doc/200408u/fb2004-08-13.

100 There was another American in Athens . . . Dr. Don Anthony,
"The Remarkable Waldstein," *Journal of Olympic History*, Spring 1997,
18–19.

100 And yet, he joined Richardson and Gildersleeve . . . Charles
Waldstein, "The Olympian Games at Athens," *Field*, May 1896,
reprinted in Mallon and Widlund, 26–29.

100 Born in 1856 . . . Biographical information from Joseph Jacobs
and Frederick T. Haneman, *The Jewish Encyclopedia: 1901–1906 Edition*, Funk and Wagnalls, New York, 1906. Information on Waldstein
and his brother, Charles, from Isaac Markens, *The Hebrews in America:
A Series of Historical and Biographical Sketches* (first published in 1888
and republished by Cornell University Press, 2009). Background on
Waldstein's friendship with Coubertin from Anthony, "The Remarkable Waldstein," 18–19.

101 Details of Waldstein's evolving relationship . . . Anthony, "The
Remarkable Waldstein," 18–19.

101 Waldstein's star was rising quickly . . . Jacobs and Haneman, *The
Jewish Encyclopedia: 1901–1906 Edition*.

102 David Young believes Waldstein's role . . . Young, *The First Modern Olympics*, 89, 95, 98, 211.

102 The baron took Waldstein's advice . . . Olympic Movement—
Olympic Legacy.com, www.pe04.com/olympic/athens1896/index.php.

102 "Not only was the remarkable Charles Waldstein" . . . Anthony,
"The Remarkable Waldstein," 19.

103 wooded farm and estate in Newton Hall . . . *Times of London*, March 23, 1927.

103 In Athens, Waldstein spent a few days sick in bed . . . Anthony, "The Remarkable Waldstein," 18–19.

103 Waldstein competed in the 200-Meter Military Rifle . . . http:// en.wikipedia.org/wiki/Shooting_at_the_1896_Summer_Olympics_ _Men's_military_rifle.

103 At least his place . . . Mallon and Widlund, *The 1896 Olympic Games*, 20.

CHAPTER 6

104 all three had qualified . . . Wallechinsky, *The Complete Book of the Olympics—1992 Edition*, 3.

104 the 21-year-old native . . . *Daily Princetonian*, March 25, 1996; seasickness report from *New York Times*, April 7, 1896.

104 Curtis, a 24-year-old MIT graduate . . . Wallechinsky, *The Complete Book of the Olympics—1992 Edition*, 3.

105 the top sprinters had been running in the "10s" for most of the decade . . . Edward S. Sears, *Running Through the Ages*, McFarland, 2001, 94–95; Luther Cary and the "lonely Jersey byroad" story from the *New York Times*, November 29, 1895.

106 In the third heat of the 100 . . . Wallechinsky, *The Complete Book of the Olympics—1992 Edition*, 3.

106 The previous September at Manhattan Field . . . *New York Times*, September 22, 1895.

106 "Winning was more important to him than the making of a fast time" . . . *Boston Globe*, February 12, 1929.

107 "Greece will not soon forget this frank response from so remote a land" . . . Wilkinson, "The Dauntless Dozen."

107 The skies had cleared . . . *New York Times*, April 9, 1896.

108 Right from the outset . . . Curtis, "Olympic Games of an Elder Day."

109 Goulding was another matter . . . de Coubertin et al., *The Olympic Games.*

109 There was a 25-year-old Irishman named John Pius Boland . . . www.olympic.org, the official website of the Olympic movement, www.olympic.org/uk/athletes/heroes/bio.uk. Quotes on Launceston Elliot from Tom Hamilton, "The Incredible Story of the Scot Who Won Britain's First Olympic Gold," *Scottish Daily Record,* July 26, 2008.

111 Thomas Curtis actually did have reason to be concerned . . . *New York Times,* April 8, 1896.

111 For all his speed and the promise of Olympic glory . . . *Boston Globe,* March 19, 1896.

111 Chances are that Curtis had started running in his student days at MIT . . . Kathleen Rowe, "MIT Hurdler was Victor/Chronicler of 1896 Olympics," *MIT News,* http://web.mit.edu/newsoffice/1996/olymp1896-curtis.html, July 18, 1996.

111 Perhaps it was his upbringing as a son of the Army's Deputy General . . . Army Master Sgt. Bob Haskell, "Massachusetts Militia Soldier Was Olympic Pioneer," American Forces Press Service, August 5, 2008, and posted on the US Department of Defense website, www.defense.gov/news/newsarticle.aspx?id+50694; and Jeff Faraudo, "Curtis Won Hurdles in 1896 Olympics," *Oakland Tribune,* April 8, 2004.

112 Curtis was a wiry 145 pounds . . . *Boston Globe,* March 19, 1896.

112 Just why Curtis wasn't competing for Harvard . . . "Letters to the Editor" following Jonathan Shaw, "The Unexpected Olympians: How Harvard Dominated the First Modern Games—In Spite of Itself," *Harvard Magazine,* July 1996. "Letters" ran in the August 1996 issue.

112 In the mid-1890s, Curtis started applying his football skills to track . . . Rowe, "MIT Hurdler Was Victor/Chronicler of 1896 Olympics." Quotes from *Boston Globe*, March 19, 1896.

113 Part of Curtis's concern about the Englishman . . . Curtis, "High Hurdles and White Gloves," 60–61.

114 Meanwhile, there were no preliminaries in the . . . *Boston Globe*, March 19, 1896.

115 Connolly said he never heard Clark "indulge in a solitary exultant whoop of superiority" . . . Shaw, "The Unexpected Olympians: How Harvard Dominated the First Modern Games—In Spite of Itself."

115 jitters during the final countdown . . . Clark, "The First Americans at the Olympic Games." The quote, "It was little short of agony," is from Fulton, "Our First Olympians."

117 Landed 6.35 meters or 20.83 feet from takeoff . . . Wallechinsky, *The Complete Book of the Olympics—1992 Edition*, 97.

117 "(I) jumped and won" . . . Clark, "The First Americans at the Olympic Games," 136.

118 But curiously, in 1932 . . . Shaw, "The Unexpected Olympians: How Harvard Dominated the First Modern Games—In Spite of Itself."

119 But few events were as adversely affected by the soft, damp track . . . Wallechinsky, *The Complete Book of the Olympics—1992 Edition*, 20.

119 Nor was Jamison's qualifying time . . . NBC bio sheet for 1984 film, *The First Olympics: Athens 1896*, and from the *Daily Princetonian*, date unknown (from Lane files in Mudd Library at Princeton University).

119 Garrett had made a good choice. . . . *Princeton Alumni Weekly*, November 4, 1938.

119 In 1893 when Jamison was the Peoria (Illinois) High School track champion . . .
Robert Pruter, "Early Interscholastic Track and Field Meets," Illinois H.S.toric menu, http://ihsa.multiad.com/initiatives/hstoric/track_boys_early.htm.

120 Edgar Bredin of Great Britain . . . wasn't there . . . Wallechinsky, *The Complete Book of the Olympics—1992 Edition*, 20.

120 At the gun, Burke shot into the lead . . . Wilkinson, "The Dauntless Dozen."

120 Garrett and the 200-pound Goukos . . . "Letters to the Editor," following Shaw, "The Unexpected Olympians: How Harvard Dominated the First Modern Games—In Spite of Itself."

121 "Probably if the seven-foot circle had been allowed" . . . Tyler, "The Olympic Games at Athens."

121 So for the third time on day two of the first modern Olympiad . . . Wallechinsky, *The Complete Book of the Olympics—1992 Edition*, 107.

121 "Our boys are now called the 'American invincibles,'" . . . Holmes, *The Olympian Games in Athens, 1896*, 67.

121 Sitting nearby, Rufus Richardson marveled . . . Richardson, "The New Olympian Games," 277.

122 At Princeton, there was great joy . . . *Daily Princetonian*, April 8, 1896.

122 The US team had no weight lifters . . . Jensen background from www.sports-reference.com/olympics/athletes/je/viggo-jensen-2.html and www.absoluteastronomy.com/topics/Viggo_Jensen; weightlifting stats and controversy from Wallechinsky, *The Complete Book of the Olympics—1992 Edition*, 603; story about the prince from Greenspan, "How I Filmed the 1896 Athens Olympics."

123 Blake had been one of Boston's top distance runners since his student days . . . George A. Gipe, "The Hounds Were Rarely

Top Dogs in the Brief History of Paper Chasing," *Sports Illustrated*, December 9, 1974.

124 Blake took to hare and hounds, which prompted more formal success . . . *Boston Globe*, March 19, 1896.

124 For the record . . . Cordner Nelson and Roberto Quercetani, *The Milers*, Tafnews Press, 1984, 4–11.

124 For Blake, outdoor training . . . *Boston Evening Transcript*, July 22, 1932; additional biographical information from *Boston Globe*, March 19, 1896.

125 after the Games, the two men would retain a long, abiding friendship . . . Shaw, "The Unexpected Olympians: How Harvard Dominated the First Modern Games—In Spite of Itself."

125 Even so, Blake's route of Harvard was considerably easier . . . George E. Ryan, "American-Irishman Led First U.S. Olympic Team," *Boston Irish News*, July 1984.

125 At the BAA's 1896 amateur handicap games . . . Meet details from *Outing Magazine*, April 1996; Burnham story from Clark, "The First Americans at the Olympic Games," 124–25. The quote, "club pride revolted against such failure," is from an article (title, author, and date unknown) in the Lane files at Mudd Library, Princeton University.

126 Also set to run the 1,500 Meters at the Olympic Games . . . John Riley, "Edwin Flack: Our First Olympian," at www.victoria .org/au and on the City of Casey's website, www.casey.vic.gov.au/ olympic. Riley is the author of the articles and based much of his information on the book by Harry Gordon, *Australia and the Olympic Games: An Official History*, Queensland University Press, 1994. The Blake quote, "I almost broke my stride," is from an interview in the *Boston Transcript*, July 27, 1932. The Holmes conversation with the Greek spectators is from Holmes, *The Olympian Games in Athens, 1896*, 67.

128 More than a half-century later . . . the Emil Zátopek story is from "Olympics and History of the Modern Games Norway and Finland 1952," www.trivia-library.com/a/olympics-and-history-of-the-modern-games-norway-and-finland-1952.htm.

130 On Tuesday evening, giant spotlights streaked light across the Acropolis . . . Greenspan, "How I Filmed the 1896 Athens Olympics."

130 "I think it was on the third or fourth day of the Games that the Americanization of Europe began" . . . Curtis, "High Hurdles and White Gloves," 60–61.

130 On Wednesday, April 8, Americans back home woke up . . . *New York Tribune, New York Times, New York Evening Post*, all April 8, 1896.

CHAPTER 7

132 It had been nearly four years . . . *Report of the American Olympic Committee, 1920*, 77; Report taken from John A. Lucas, "Coubertin One Hundred Years Ago: His Second American Visit in 1893," *OLYMPIKA: The International Journal of Olympic Studies*, Volume II, 1993, 103–8.

132 "Total, absolute incomprehension" Baron Pierre de Coubertin, "Mémoires Olympiques," Bureau International de Pédalgogic Sportive 1931, 9.

132 But the Baron himself wasn't much better in his technical know-how . . . Lucas, "Coubertin One Hundred Years Ago," 103–8.

133 To some delegates, the Olympic concept was an idealized pageant . . . John A. Lucas, "Olympic Genesis: The Sorbonne Conferences of 1892 and 1894," based on a paper presented at 3rd Canadian Symposium on History and Sport (Dalhousie University, Halifax, Nova Scotia, August 19–31, 1974). Available at www.la84foundation.org/OlympicInformationCenter/OlympicReview/1974/.

133 "I was prepared for irony and protest, but not indifference" . . . de Coubertin, *Mémoires Olympiques*, 9.

133 He organized another Sorbonne conference . . . Lucas, "Olympic Genesis."

134 So in 1893, he had gone to America . . . Stephan Wassong, "Coubertin's Olympic Quest: His Educational Campaign in America," *OLYMPIKA: The International Journal of Olympic Studies,* Volume X, 2001, 59–72.

134 Arriving in the fall of 1893 in New York . . . Lucas, "Coubertin One Hundred Years Ago," 103–8.

135 They had met in either 1888 or 1889 in Paris . . . Sarah Kiernan, "William Milligan Sloane: Torchbearer of the Olympic Movement, Senior Thesis for the History Department of Princeton University, April 2005.

135 Coubertin spoke passable English . . . Jay Bavishi, "Forging Gold," Ivy League Sports/Ivy League Public Information, August 13, 2004.

136 Coubertin's Olympic dreams were still several years away . . . Kiernan, "William Milligan Sloane."

136 Sloane aptly demonstrated his worldview . . . William Milligan Sloane, "College Sports," *Harper's Weekly*, March 1, 1890.

136 "A man of many parts," the *Princeton Alumni Weekly* called Sloane . . . "A Man of Many Parts," *Princeton Alumni Weekly*, October 12, 1928.

137 Sloane's moral code and his aspirations . . . Kiernan, "William Milligan Sloane." Obituary information from the *Princeton Packet*, September 15, 1928, and "Professor W. M. Sloane Passes Away Here After Lengthy Illness," *Princeton Alumni Weekly*, October 18, 1928.

137 But in his 1890 article in *Harper's Weekly*, Sloane gave credit . . . Sloane, "College Sports."

137 At Princeton, Sloane's star rose quickly . . . Kiernan, "William Milligan Sloane." Background on Woodrow Wilson from *Woodrow Wilson at Princeton*, www.princeton.edu/mudd/news/faq/topics/wilson .shtml.

138 Sloane tackled his sports duties with gusto . . . Kiernan, "William Milligan Sloane." Sloan's quote on "weaken(ing) Princeton's 11" from "Princeton Makes Reply," *New York Times*, December 21, 1889.

139 So would the American impressionist painter, Mary Cassatt . . . Nancy Mowll Matthews, *Mary Cassatt*, Yale University Press, 1998, 210–11.

139 It was only fitting that the Sloanes and their four children lived on Bayard Lane in Princeton. . . *Princeton Herald*, January 30, 1930. Background on President Grover Cleveland from the *New York Times*, November 28, 1896, and http://en.wikipedia.org/wiki/ Westland_Mansion.

139 Sloane's best-known book . . . *Princeton Packet*, September 15, 1928; *Philadelphia Bulletin*, September 13, 1928.

140 On November 27 at Sloane's request, they met at the University Club . . . Robert Barney, "Coubertin and Americans: Wary Relationships, 1889–1925," a research paper published by "Research Team Olympia" of the Johannes Gutenberg (Center)-University of Mainz.

140 Sullivan in 1896 was a 34-year-old sports magnate . . . Allen Guttmann, contrib., Donald G. Kyle, ed., and Gary D. Stark, ed., *Essays on Sport History and Sport Mythology*, Texas A & M University Press, 1990, 64–65. Part of the Walter Prescott Webb Memorial Lectures.

140 In 1892, Sullivan hit the jackpot . . . *Spalding's Base Ball Guide and Official League Book for 1887*, A.G. Spalding & Bros., Chicago, New York, 1887 & reprinted by Horton Publishing Company under exclusive license from Spalding Sports Worldwide, 1988. Biographical information from "Al Spalding's career statistics," www.baseball-reference.com/players/s/spaldal01.shtml, 2009, and Mark Lamster, *Spalding's World Tour*, Public Affairs, 2006.

143 Sullivan and Coubertin, and by extension, Sloane, would never move beyond their early antipathy toward one another . . . Barney, "Coubertin and Americans."

143 On Saturday, November 30, they joined the multitudes squeezing into the Polo Grounds . . . *New York Tribune, New York Herald, New York Times*, all December 1, 1893. The quote, "The game was a gloriously confusing experience for Coubertin," is from John A. Lucas, "Coubertin One Hundred Years Ago," 39. Coubertin quote on ticket prices is from Lucas's bylined article, "The Re-establishment of the Olympic Games," in the *Chautaquan*, September 1894, 699.

144 In doing so, he described the Congress as a debate on amateurism . . . Kiernan, "William Milligan Sloane."

145 Mainstream America had little interest in an impending Olympic revival . . . "Athens Put on an Odd Show at the First Modern Games" by E.M. Swift, *Sports Illustrated*, August 2, 2004.

145 the *New York Times* . . . "Minor Sporting Matters," The *New York Times*, March 1, 1894.

145 Coubertin set an ambitious agenda . . . Smith, *Olympics in Athens 1896*, 311; and Kiernan, "William Milligan Sloane."

145 Some 2,000 people . . . John A. Lucas, "Olympic Genesis." The sentence that starts, "To no one's surprise" and some other details from the meeting are taken from David Miller, *Athens to Athens: The Official History of the Olympic Games and the IOC, 1894–2004*, Mainstream Publishing, 2005.

147 "As for myself," the Baron would say . . . John A. Lucas, "Olympic Genesis."

CHAPTER 8

148 Striding through the door . . . Shaw, "The Unexpected Olympians: How Harvard Dominated the First Modern Games—In Spite of Itself," *Harvard Magazine*, July 1996. Background on Gastine-Rennette Galleries from Frank Partnoy, *The Match King: Ivan Kreuger, The Financial Genius Behind a Century of Wall Street Scandals*, Public Affairs, 2009, 193. Information on event information from Bryan Kett, "Shooting at the First Olympic Games," *Olympic Review*, August 1991 (No. 286); information from an article about shooting competition in the Olympic Games in the May 1896 issue of *Shooting and Fishing* magazine.

149 Direct descendants of Robert Treat Paine . . . Biographical background from www.sports-reference.com/olympics/athletes/pa/sumner-paine-1.html and www.sports-reference.com/olympics/athletes/pa/john-paine-1.html. Background on Sumner Paine in the Civil War from Richard Miller, *Harvard's Civil War: The History of the Twentieth Massachusetts Volunteer Infantry*, University Press of New England, 2005, and from Earl J. Hess, *Pickett's Charge—The Last Attack at Gettysburg*, The University of North Carolina Press, 2000, 292–93.

151 John Paine was born less than two years later, in 1870 . . . Biographical background from Sarah Cushing Paine, comp., and Charles Henry Pope, ed., Paine Ancestry: *The Family of Robert Treat Paine, Signer of the Declaration of Independence*, D. Clapp & Son, Boston, 1912, printed for the family, 269. Background on Gross Medical College from the *Colorado Medical Journal*, Volume III, 1897, 166. The sentence that begins "On October 24, 1894, in a drenching rainstorm," is from the *New York Times*, October 25, 1894.

151 Deciding to study medicine . . . *Boston Globe*, May 30, 1901, June 8, 1901, and July 20, 1901. Death information from the *Boston Herald*, April 19, 1904.

152 "study in the hospitals" ... *Harvard College Class of 1890: Secretary's Report No. V: 1903–1909*, Boston, 1909; printed for use of the class.

152 The Paines cut it close ... Kett, "Shooting at the First Olympic Games."

153 To reduce the glare ... Holmes, *The Olympian Games in Athens, 1896*, 84. Background on the competition from Kett, "Shooting at the First Olympic Games."

153 Deciding to enter the remaining two pistol events ... Wallechinsky, *The Complete Book of the Olympics—1992 Edition*, 455–56.

154 His victory had seemed so effortless ... www.sports-reference .com/olympics/athletes/pa/john-paine-1.html.

154 A somewhat leisurely affair ... Wallechinsky, *The Complete Book of the Olympics—1992 Edition*, 446.

154 That Nielsen, a 29-year-old native of Copenhagen ... www .sports-reference.com/olympics/athletes/ni/holger-nielsen-1.html.

154 Sumner's exhaustive report ... Information from an article about shooting competition in the Olympic Games in the May 1896 issue of *Shooting and Fishing* magazine, and from Kett, "Shooting at the First Olympic Games."

155 Of the 3,500 rounds of ammunition ... Shaw, "The Unexpected Olympians."

155 So impressed by the Paines were their Greek competitors ... Holmes, *The Olympian Games in Athens, 1896*, 84–85.

155 On the final day of competition ... Wallechinsky, *The Complete Book of the Olympics—1992 Edition*, 444–72.

CHAPTER 9

156 Taking his place in a carriage ... *Boston Evening Transcript*, July 22, 1932. Event background from Wallechinsky, *The Complete Book of the Olympics—1992 Edition*, 51.

157 The tale of Pheidippides fed pride among Greeks ... Wallechinsky, *The Complete Book of the Olympics—1992 Edition*, 363, 374. Background on prizes and incentives from the *Boston Globe*, April 27, 1896.

158 The baron's friend, a French linguist named Michel Bréal ... Karl Lennartz, "Following The Footsteps of Bréal," *Journal of Olympic History*, Summer 1998.

158 medical experts warned it could be dangerous ... Charlie Lovett, "The Games of the I Olympiad: Athens, 1896," from the book, *Olympic Marathon*, Greenwood, 1997.

158 It was around the same time that pedestrianism or long-distance walking soared in popularity ... P. S. Marshall, *King of the Peds*, AuthorHouse, 2008, 1–12, 707–8.

159 Greek organizers announced that a team would be chosen from the top finishers of two time trials ... Lovett, "The Games of the I Olympiad" and Wallechinsky, *The Complete Book of the Olympics —1992 Edition*, 51. Background on the second trial race date from David Randall, "Olympics Special: The Original Marathon Man," the (London) *Independent*, August 8, 2004. Background on Louis from www.spiritus-temporis.com/spiridon-louis/the-marathon-race.html.

159 as BAA trainer John Graham would admit later ... *Boston Globe*, April 27, 1896. Blake's quotes on Boston's Blue Hill, the journey to Marathon, and pre-race preparations from the *Boston Evening Transcript*, July 22, 1932.

161 The Greek runners followed a different pre-race regimen ... www.spiritus-temporis.com/spiridon-louis/the-marathon-race.html.

162 There are very few descriptions of the weather during the last afternoon of track competition ... de Coubertin et al., *The Olympic Games*, 86.

162 The organizers had done their work as well ... Wallechinsky, *The Complete Book of the Olympics—1992 Edition*, 51, and David Randall,

"Olympics Special." Story on Carlos Airoldi from Lovett, "The Games of the I Olympiad." Blake quotes from the *Boston Evening Transcript*, July 27, 1932.

163 Greek journalists had grown ever more exasperated at the inability of Greeks to beat any Americans on the track . . . Holmes, *The Olympian Games in Athens, 1896*, 68–69.

164 Attention then shifted to the track . . . Richardson, "The New Olympian Games," 279.

164 In the day's first final, Burke, as expected, aced the field . . . Wallechinsky, *The Complete Book of the Olympics—1992 Edition*, 3, 62. Curtis quotes on Goulding from Curtis, "High Hurdles and White Gloves," 60–61. Clark's quotes on the final in hurdles from Clark, "The First Americans at the Olympic Games."

165 Around the same time . . . Clark, "The First Americans at the Olympic Games." Uniform information from Shaw, "The Unexpected Olympians."

165 Lost in the blizzard . . . First sentence of background from the *Boston Globe*, March 19, 1896. Background on making the team from Shaw, "The Unexpected Olympians."

165 Just where pole vaulting got its start is unknown . . . Mike Rosenbaum, "An Illustrated History of Pole Vault," http://trackandfield .about.com/od/polevault/ss/illuspolevault.html. Background on 19th-century American pole climbing from www.exampleessays.com/ viewpaper/88259.html. Background on changes in technique from "The History of the Vault" at www.texaspolevault.com/vaulthistory.html.

166 Hoyt and Tyler were among the five Olympic vaulters . . . de Coubertin et al., *The Olympic Games*, 85–86. Andrews quotes are from Wilkinson, "The Dauntless Dozen."

168 At 24, Tyler was older than most of his teammates . . . Various unidentified March and April 1896 news clippings drawn from Francis Lane scrapbooks in Mudd Archives at Princeton University.

168 "A splendid specimen of manhood" . . . "Ohio Boys in Athens," *Cincinnati Enquirer*, April 5, 1896 (probable date since the dateline is April 4 and the actual date is not recorded; preserved in Lane Archives, Princeton Library). The Franklin, Ohio, population figure is from the 1900 census, which listed a population of 2,724: http:// en.wikipedia/org/wiki/Franklin_Ohio.

169 both clearing the bar with ease . . . de Coubertin et al., *The Olympic Games*, 85–86. Ellery Clark's comments are from his *Reminiscences of an Athlete: Twenty Years on Track and Field*, 1911, 138. The story of the king's request to Hoyt is from Richardson, "The New Olympian Games," 279.

170 Atop "Coogan's Bluff," the crew of the USS *San Francisco* let loose with another dutiful cheer . . . Holmes, *The Olympian Games in Athens, 1896*, 71. Detail of Richardson's comment on the timing of the marathon runners is from Richardson, "The New Olympian Games," 280.

170 A man of simple tastes . . . www.spiritus-temporis.com/spiridon-louis/the-marathon-race.html.

171 Though Louis had run the route only six days before . . . Randall, "Olympics Special." Blake quote from the *Boston Globe*, April 27, 1896.

172 Soon, Blake was out as well . . . *Boston Globe*, April 27, 1896. Blake's quotes from the *Boston Evening Transcript*, July 27, 1932.

172 Lermusiaux clung gamely to the lead . . . Randall, "Olympics Special." Bicycle story from Lovett, "The Games of the I Olympiad."

174 With five miles to go, Louis pulled even with Flack . . . Randall, "Olympics Special." Ambulance story on Flack from Wallechinsky, *The Complete Book of the Olympics—1992 Edition*, 52.

175 Everyone in the stadium rose . . . Holmes, *The Olympian Games in Athens, 1896*, 72.

175 Breaking from the royal box . . . Lovett, "The Games of the I Olympiad."

175 Louis finished in 2:58:50 . . . Wallechinsky, *The Complete Book of the Olympics—1992 Edition*, 52.

176 But the pure relief and joy . . . Randall, "Olympics Special."

CHAPTER 10

177 Before 40,000 spectators . . . Background on Hajós from www .jewsinsports.org; event background from Wallechinsky, *The Complete Book of the Olympics—1992 Edition*, 474–75.

178 In reality, the Bay of Zea was a choice spot . . . Young, *The First Modern Olympics*, 154. Background on spectators from Curtis, "High Hurdles and White Gloves," 60–61.

178 If competitive swimming in open waters seems unusual . . . Mary Donahue, "History of Swimming," http://faculty.deanza.edu/ donahuemary/Historyofswimmingsection.

179 And what sports lover of the era could not help but admire the exploits of British Captain Matthew Webb . . . Kathy Watson, *The Crossing: The Curious Story of the First Man to Swim the English Channel*, Tarcher, 2001; obituary information from the story, "Captain Webb Missing Yet" in the *New York Times*, July 26, 1883. Detail on swimming in a pool at the 1912 Olympic Games from Donahue, "History of Swimming."

180 A boat ferried the swimmers out into the bay . . . Wallechinsky, *The Complete Book of the Olympics—1992 Edition*, 474–75.

180 Herschmann, another of the outstanding Jewish swimmers of the era, would swim and fence in future Olympiads . . . "Otto Herschmann Olympic Results" from www.sports-reference.com/ olympics/athletes/he/otto-herschmann-1.html and from Jews in Sports, www.jewsinsports.org. Race details from Wallechinsky, *The Complete Book of the Olympics—1992 Edition*, 474–75.

180 Ioannis Malokinis took the Greek Navy's exhibition 100-meter freestyle . . . Wallechinsky, *The Complete Book of the Olympics—1992 Edition*, 520. Background on Paul Neumann from The International Jewish Sports Hall of Fame/Yad Le'ish Hasport Hayehudi, www .jewishsports.net/BioPages/PaulNeumann.htm.

181 But of the 29 competitors . . . P. H. Mullen, *Gold in the Water: The True Story of Ordinary Men and Their Extraordinary Dream of Olympic Glory*, Macmillan, 2001, 41–42.

181 Boston native Gardner Williams was 18 . . . *Boston Morning Journal*, April 13,1896. Family background and information on Jeremiah Williams from the *Boston Herald*, June 24, 1916.

181 P. H. Mullen, the author . . . P. H. Mullen, *Gold in the Water*, 41–42. Thomas Curtis recollections from his "High Hurdles and White Gloves."

182 Common sense points to Mullen . . . Mullen, *Gold in the Water*, 41.

182 Hajós's strength-saving strategy worked . . . www.jewsinsports .org; event background from Wallechinsky, *The Complete Book of the Olympics—1992 Edition*, 474–75.

183 After the Games in Boston, he joined his Olympic and BAA teammates . . . *Boston Herald*, May 14, 1896.

CHAPTER 11

184 Baseball? . . . *Boston Herald*, May 10, 1896.

184 They would linger another week or so in Athens . . . Shaw, "The Unexpected Olympians."

184 On Sunday, April 12 . . . Holmes, *The Olympian Games in Athens, 1896*, 78–79. Story about "Informal Dress" from Young, *The First Modern Olympics*, 156.

185 preserved from Madame Schliemann's reception is a memorable photograph . . . Shaw, "The Unexpected Olympians."

185 On Monday April 13, Ambassador Alexander threw a reception . . . *New York Times*, May 3, 1896.

185 Though stormy conditions had canceled the sailing contests . . . Wallechinsky, *The Complete Book of the Olympics—1992 Edition*, 52 (Louis debate) and 458 (rifle results).

186 Then, on Tuesday afternoon in cycling's version of the marathon . . . Young, *The First Modern Olympics*, 155.

186 That evening at the Royal Palace reception . . . *New York Times*, April 13, 1896.

186 The baron was upset for several reasons . . . Young, *The First Modern Olympics*, 156–57.

187 At Tuesday's picnic, Ellery Clark was the baseball ringleader . . . *Boston Herald*, May 10, 1896.

187 "You may win this time," he teased Burke, "but we will beat you in 1900" . . . Holmes, *The Olympian Games in Athens, 1896*, 80, 82–83.

188 it's hard to believe the princes really had no idea what it was in light of the enormous attention generated by Albert Spalding's celebrated round-the-world tour of baseball all-stars . . . Eric Miklich, "Albert G. Spalding: 1850–1915," www.19cbaseball.com/players-albert-spalding.html.

188 First, they explained the functions of the pitcher and catcher . . . Most of this account is taken from Curtis' account as reported in the *Boston Herald*, May 10, 1896. The later account by Curtis in *MIT Technology Review* (and *Atlantic Monthly*) differs in some details, most likely because it was written more than 28 years later.

188 For all the easy informality at Madame Schliemann's reception, one American faced a crisis of etiquette. . . . *Boston Herald*, May 7, 1896.

189 So intense had the rain been on Tuesday morning . . . de Coubertin et al., *The Olympic Games*.

189 By 10:00 a.m. Wednesday, the Stadium was packed . . . Young, *The First Modern Olympics*, 157–59. Detail about the king handing out olive branches from de Coubertin et al., *The Olympic Games*.

190 To the victors went quite a stash. . . . de Coubertin et al., *The Olympic Games*.

191 Positioned with his camera near the royal box, Burton Holmes snapped photographs of the occasion, and imagined what it might feel like to be an Olympic champion. . . Burton Holmes, *The Olympian Games in Athens, 1896*, 83.

191 What happened next was a pleasant surprise . . . Tyler, "The Olympic Games in Athens."

191 Stadium cheers greeted the award winners . . . Young, *The First Modern Olympics*, 159.

192 "Almost the entire population (of Athens) was present at the Games" . . . Holmes, *The Olympian Games in Athens, 1896*, 91.

192 For Charalambos Anninos . . . de Coubertin et al., *The Olympic Games*.

193 But not everyone in the United States was impressed . . . Casper Whitney writing in an unknown publication; Lane Files, Mudd Library at Princeton.

193 "These Games, I believe, will create a great international interest in athletic sport" . . . *Boston Herald*, May 7, 1896.

194 "These intrepid pioneers" . . . Fulton, "Our First Olympians."

CHAPTER 12

195 Bounding off the ocean liner . . . *Boston Herald*, May 7, 1896.

195 Overjoyed to be home . . . *Boston Globe*, May 7, 1896.

196 the team had appealed to Collector of Ports . . . *Boston Herald*, May 7, 1896.

196 Not all the Americans had dawdled to party in Athens . . . Mandell, *The First Modern Olympics*, 159. Departure date and tour details from the *Daily Princetonian*, May 2, 1896. The name of the ship is from the *Princeton Alumni Weekly*, June 2, 1964. Dates of the voyage from the Lane files in Mudd Library at Princeton University.

197 In contrast to their Atlantic crossing six weeks earlier, the foursome spent a goodly portion of their trip in deckchairs . . . *Trenton Evening News*, May 2, 1896.

197 At the Princeton Inn, the four heroes took in a late lunch . . . *Princeton Alumni Weekly*, June 2, 1964, and Smith, "The 1896 Olympic Games at Athens and the Princeton Connection." Exam schedule from the *Daily Princetonian*, April 24, 1896.

198 "The enthusiasm displayed was in vivid contrast to that manifested on their departure six weeks ago" . . . *Daily Princetonian*, May 2, 1896.

198 "We met everywhere with the most hearty reception" . . . *Trenton Evening News*, May 2, 1896.

198 "Many of the records made were poor" . . . "Students Carried Olympic Heroes" from an article (date and publication unknown), May 2, 1896. The publication is in the Lane files of the Mudd Library at Princeton.

198 True to form, he and his fellow Princeton Olympians just got on with things . . . *Daily Princetonian*, May 4, 1896.

199 Back among the Bostonians . . . Curtis, "High Hurdles and White Gloves," 60–61.

199 Heading northwest toward Southampton . . . *Boston Globe*, May 8, 1896; John Paine story from Shaw, "The Unexpected Olympians."

200 Enjoying the splendors of Paris, he lingered and decided to go his own way . . . Trip logistics and dates from the *Boston Globe*, May 15, 1896. Other content and quote from O'Donnell, "The Original Olympic Hero."

200 Greeting them with enthusiastic front-page headlines. . . The headlines "Victors Return," "Champions Come Home," and "City's Tribute of Pride" from the *Boston Herald*, May 7, 8, and 14, 1896. The headlines "Triumphant Entry into Boston" and "Quintet of Blushing Athletes" from the *Boston Globe*, May 8 and 14, 1896. Travel information and quotes from Clark, "The First Americans at the Olympic Games."

201 Leaving Grand Central Station . . . *Boston Globe*, May 8, 1896. (Since 1913, Grand Central Station has been known as Grand Central Terminal).

202 At 9:00 p.m., May 7 . . . *Boston Herald*, May 8, 1896.

202 This time, Burke was first to the platform . . . *Boston Globe*, May 8, 1896.

202 Two days later, the BAA threw a formal dinner . . . *Boston Globe*, May 9, 1896.

203 Boston wasn't quite finished . . . *Boston Herald*, May 14, 1896.

ENDINGS

205 James Connolly slipped quietly into Boston. . . . *Boston Globe*, May 15, 1896; tea and apple pie story from the Irish Elk blog site: http://mcns.blogsport.com/search?q=james+connolly.

206 A few weeks later, South Boston honored Connolly . . . O'Donnell, "The Original Olympic Hero."

206 Joining the 9th Massachusetts Infantry . . . "American-Irishman Led First U.S. Olympic Team," *Boston Irish News*, July 1984.

206 By 1900, he was earning $25 a week . . . Wilcox, "The Literary Works of James Brendan Connolly."

206 Connolly and a friend, marathoner Dick Grant, paid their own way, in steerage, to the 1900 Games . . . Connolly, *Sea-Borne: Thirty Years Avoyaging*. Background on the 1900 Paris Games and results from Wallechinsky, *The Complete Book of the Olympics—1992 Edition*, Introduction, 103, 107, and 111.

208 Connolly skipped the 1904 Games in St. Louis . . . Wilson, ed., "The First Olympic Champion." Service in the US Navy from "American-Irishman Led First U.S. Olympic Team," *Boston Irish News*; July 1984. Background on congressional race from "The Political Graveyard—Massachusetts: U.S. Representatives, 1910s," http://politicalgraveyard.com/geo/MA/ofc/usrep1910s.html.

208 The author of many novels and short stories . . . Connolly, *Sea-Borne: Thirty Years Avoyaging*, 9–18.

208 Connolly settled in the Chestnut Hill section of Boston . . . Wilcox, "The Literary Works of James Brendan Connolly."

209 But the tale of how Connolly had left the school in the early spring of 1896 depended on the audience. . . . Shaw, "The Unexpected Olympians."

209 Critics compared Connolly's prose to Melville and Kipling, and Joseph Conrad called him "America's best writer of sea stories." . . . "American-Irishman Led First U.S. Olympic Team," *Boston Irish News*, July 1984. Conrad quote from *Colby College Magazine*, No. 2, 1985.

209 In 1948, about the time Connolly got his Harvard "H," the Eire Society of Boston awarded him its gold medal. . . . "American-Irishman Led First U.S. Olympic Team," *Boston Irish News*, July 1984. Background on relationship with Colby College from *Colby College Magazine*, No. 2, 1985.

210 Ellery Clark got over Connolly's spat . . . NBC bio sheet for 1984 film, *The First Olympics: Athens 1896*. Quote from Clark, "The First Americans at the Olympic Games."

210 So Clark returned to college . . . *Boston Sunday Herald*, May 17, 1896.

210 Clark's real talents emerged June 22 . . . *Boston Globe*, June 23, 1896.

211 He remains the only athlete . . . Wallechinsky, *The Complete Book of the Olympics—1992 Edition*, 85-91, 97-103, 167-172.

211 Clark would capture the national all-around championship twice more . . . *Boston Irish News*, July 1984.

211 practicing law, coaching, and penning a memoir . . . "American-Irishman Led First U.S. Olympic Team," *Boston Irish News*, July 1984.

211 the 1952 film . . . www.usatf.org/halloffame/TF/showBIO .asp?HOFIDs=31.

211 A well-known civic figure . . . "American-Irishman Led First U.S. Olympic Team," *Boston Irish News*, July 1984.

211 Tom Burke continued racing after Athens . . . *Boston Globe*, February 12, 1929.

212 In a 1932 interview in the *Boston Evening Transcript* **before the Los Angeles Games, Blake recalled** . . . *Boston Evening Transcript*, July 27, 1932. Biographical information from "American-Irishman Led First U.S. Olympic Team," *Boston Irish News*, July 1984. Falls, *The Boston Marathon*, MacMillan, 1975, 7, 165.

213 the "very 'first' New York Marathon" . . . Display at the Track & Field Hall of Fame, New York.

213 In 1924, the BAA moved the starting line several miles southwest . . . www.bostonmarathon.org/BostonMarathon/History.asp.

213 Those extra two-tenths of a mile added at the London Games would result in perhaps the most dramatic Marathon finish in history . . . R. J. (Bob) Wilcock, *The 1908 Olympic Games, the Great Stadium and the Marathon, a Pictorial Record*, The Society of Olympic Collectors, 2008.

214 Returning to the United States from Athens, Bill Hoyt was at a crossroads . . . "American-Irishman Led First U.S. Olympic Team," *Boston Irish News,* July 1984

214 Thomas Curtis was also touched by war . . . "American-Irishman Led First U.S. Olympic Team," *Boston Irish News,* July 1984; Rowe, "MIT Hurdler Was Victor/Chronicler of 1896 Olympics"; NBC bio sheet for 1984 film, *The First Olympics: Athens 1896.*

214 The post-Olympic career of Gardner Williams, the BAA swimmer, was practically set from birth. . . . Background on Williams from NBC bio sheet for 1984 film, *The First Olympics: Athens 1896.* John Paine information from "American-Irishman Led First U.S. Olympic Team," *Boston Irish News,* July 1984 with background on the bird sanctuary from the *New York Times,* August 3, 1951.

214 But for Sumner Paine, life took a hard turn. . . . NBC bio sheet for 1984 film, *The First Olympics: Athens 1896.*

216 Back at Cambridge University after Athens, Charles Waldstein resumed his life of scholarship . . . *Times of London,* March 23, 1927.

216 Married in 1909 to Florence, the widow of Theodore Seligman . . . *Times of London,* March 23, 1927; *New York Times,* March 23, 1927; *Columbia University Alumni Magazine* (1927?), courtesy Columbia University Archives. Name change information from biography of Dorothy Caroline (Shorr) at www.dictionaryofarthistorians.org/shorrd.htm.

216 How appropriate that after their boisterous lunch at the Princeton Inn . . . *Daily Princetonian* (date unknown) from Lane files, Mudd Library at Princeton. Tyler information from his "The Olympic Games at Athens."

217 Back on Princeton's football team . . . http://etcweb.princeton.edu/CampusWWW/Companion/football.html. Biographical and obituary information on Tyler and Jamison from "American-Irishman

Led First U.S. Olympic Team," July 1984, and NBC bio sheet for 1984 film, *The First Olympics: Athens 1896*. Additional background on Jamison from *Princeton Alumni Weekly*, November 4, 1938.

217 At graduation, his Class of 1897 elected him president ... Smith, "The 1896 Olympic Games at Athens and the Princeton Connection."

217 Ever the collector, Garrett in 1942 donated to the university's library his collection of Arabic manuscripts ... *Princeton Alumni Weekly*, June 2, 1964. Civic information from the *Evening Times* (Cumberland, MD), April 29, 1961. Story about employee gym from the *New York Times*, July 14, 1996. Wedding information from the *Washington Post*, May 2, 1907.

218 Garrett remained committed to Princeton's athletic programs ... Smith, "The 1896 Olympic Games at Athens and the Princeton Connection."

219 Continuing the legacy of their family's Olympic hero was very much on the mind of Garrett's descendants ... *New York Times*, July 14, 1996.

219 Today, the battered discus Garrett used to beat the Greeks in Athens ... *Princeton Alumni Weekly*, June 2, 1964. Obituary information from the *Evening Times* (Cumberland, MD), April 29, 1961.

219 The Olympic torch passed through Princeton en route to Lake Placid for the 1980 Winter Games ... Smith, "The 1896 Olympic Games at Athens and the Princeton Connection."

219 As of 2008, 86 Princeton students had participated in the Olympic Games ... "Current, Former and Future Tigers in Beijing for Summer Olympic Games," *Princeton News*, August 6, 2008, www .princeton.edu/main/news/archive/S21/80/47G06/index.xml.

220 There was no official US track and field team at the 1900 Olympic Games ... Wallechinsky, *The Complete Book of the Olympics—1992 Edition*, Introduction.

220 US trials launched in 1908 . . . "History of the U.S. Olympic Team Trials" from *The 2004 U.S. Olympic Team Trials—Track & Field Media Kit.*

221 The 1962 film, *It Happened in Athens,* **could have helped revive their accomplishments** . . . background on the film from www.imdb.com/title/tt0056109; Maltin quote from *Leonard Maltin's Movie and Video Guide 1995*, Signet, New York, 1994, 647.

221 Meanwhile, in 1987, Boston showed its gratitude to its native son Connolly . . . www.publicartboston.com/content/james-brendan-connolly.

222 But why is Clark the only team member enshrined in the National Track and Field Hall of Fame? . . . www.usatf.org/HallOf Fame/TF/showBio.asp?HOFIDs=31.

Index

A

Adee, George, 144
Airoldi, Carlo, 162
Alexander, Eben, 97, 185, 212
Alexander, Howard, 159, 160, 161
America
  competitive swimming in, 178–79
  coverage of Olympics in, 90–92, 94, 97, 130–31, 199, 200–201
  educational ideal in, 22
Ames, Oliver, 9, 126
Andreou, Ioannis, 181, 183, 227
Andrews, Eugene, 85, 96, 107, 167
Andriakopoulos, Nikolaos, 157
Anninos, Charalambos, 189, 192
Anthony, Don, 101
Aristodemocracy (Waldstein), 216
Arnold, Thomas, 58, 59
Art of Swimming, The (Webb), 179
Averoff, George, 43, 44, 158

B

Baker, Wendell, 24
Bancroft, George, 137
Barney, Robert, 140, 141
Barry, David, 203
Barry, Tom, 17, 38, 189, 199, 205
Battel, Edward, 186
Bauer, Rezső, 207
Baxter, Irving, 207
Belokas, Spiridon, 159, 174, 176
Bennett, Lewis, 79
Biddle, Nicholas, 75
Bikelas, Dimitrios, 146–47
Bingham, William J., 31, 32
Blake, Arthur, 5, 9, 123, 124–26
  after Olympics, 212
  baseball game, 188
  Marathon, 156, 158, 159–63, 171–72
  1500 Meters, 127–29, 223
  return home, 195, 196, 199, 201–2, 203
  trip to Athens, 10, 11–12, 37

274

Boland, John Pius, 109–10
Boston Athletic Association
    (BAA), 8–9, 34
    dinner for Olympians,
    202–4
    Olympians from, 4, 5, 6
    support for Blake, 125, 126
Boston Marathon, 212–13
Bréal, Michel, 158
Bredin, Edgar, 120
Briggs, LeBaron, 31, 115
Brookes, William Penny,
    62–63, 64
Burke, Fred, 195
Burke, Thomas, 5, 13, 26, 81,
    106–7, 221, 222
    after Olympics, 211
    at closing ceremonies, 191
    100 Meters, 46, 47, 104,
    106, 107, 164, 223
    400 Meters, 119, 120, 223
    return home, 196, 199, 201,
    202, 203
    trip to Athens, 10, 12, 37,
    38
Burnham, Arthur, 125, 126,
    201
Butler, Maynard, 42

C

Carlson, Alison, 219
Cary, Luther, 81, 105

Cassatt, Mary, 139
Chalkokondilis, Alexandros,
    104, 223
    Long Jump, 114, 116, 117,
    225
Chaplain, Jules-Clement, 54
Chase, Stephen, 113
Choraphas, Efstathios, 181,
    183, 227
Christopoulos, Dimitrios,
    172
Clark, Ellery, 5, 9, 12, 13, 25,
    26, 115
    after Olympics, 210–11
    arrival in Athens, 36, 37,
    38, 43
    baseball game, 187
    display in Track & Field
    Museum, 221
    High Jump, 165, 224
    on Hoyt, 169
    Long Jump, 114–19, 225
    return home, 199, 201, 202,
    203
    trip to Athens, 1, 12, 17, 18
Cleveland, Grover, 20
Colfert, James, 7–8, 119, 199
Colton, Trax, 220
Connolly, James, 9, 26–35,
    114–15, 185, 201, 221,
    222
    after Olympics, 207–10

dispute with Clark, 118–19, 209
at 1900 Games, 206, 207
High Jump, 165, 224
interest in Olympics, 19–20, 21, 31–35
Long Jump, 114, 116, 225
rabbit foot of, 188–89
relationship with Blake, 125
return home, 199, 200, 205–6
statue of, 221
Triple Jump, 50–55, 225
trip to Athens, 1–2, 11, 12, 15–17, 37, 38
Connolly, Michael, 29
Constantine, Crown Prince, 46, 102, 178, 203
interest in baseball, 187
and Olympic medals, 54
Cornish, Harry, 195, 200–201
Coubertin, Baron Pierre de, 44, 54, 56–62, 66
on closing ceremonies, 190
and 1904 Games, 220
Olympic plan of, 7, 61–62, 132–35
and Second Olympic Congress, 144–47
at shooting competition, 152–53

and Sloane, 135–36, 139–40, 143–44
and Sullivan, 141–42
and Waldstein, 101–2, 103
Courcel, Baron de, 133, 145
Cowan, Hector, 78
Crane, Stephen, 95
Cronin, Beverly, 51
Cuntz, Billy, 195
Curtis, Thomas, 26, 41, 111–13, 214
baseball game, 188
on his competition, 108, 109, 111
110-Meter Hurdles, 108, 164–65, 224
100 Meters, 46, 47, 104–5
return home, 201, 202, 203
trip to Athens, 10, 12, 17, 38
on Williams' race, 181–82

D

Damn, Peter, 215
Daní, Nándor, 223
Deliyannis, Demetrious, 159, 224
Delyannis, Theodore, 170
Discus, significance of, 67–68
See also Olympic Games, 1896
Dorakis, Nikolas, 153

Doubleday, Abner, 142
Dragoumis, Stephanos, 65,
   66

E

Eliot, Charles, 20, 21–24, 25
Elliot, Launceston, 110–11,
   230
   Weight Lifting, 122, 123,
   231
England. *See* Great Britain
Ewry, Ray, 207

F

Fairchild, Charles, 97
Farnam, Henry, 8
Fea, Carlo, 67
First Modern Olympics, The
   (Mandell), 88
First Olympians, The (film),
   125, 131, 221
Fitzgerald, F. Scott, 76–77
Flack, Edwin, 45, 127, 191,
   201
   Marathon, 162, 171,
   173–74
   800 Meters, 223
   1500 Meters, 127–30, 223
Ford, Malcolm, 79
Fulton, Bob, 13, 194

G

Gallohue, 28

Garrett, Alice Whitridge,
   12
Garrett, Robert, 4, 7, 76, 118,
   221, 222
   after Olympics and legacy
      of, 217–19
   at closing ceremonies, 191
   Discus, 67, 68–70, 84–89,
      226
   family of, 71–75
   at 1900 Games, 207
   High Jump, 165, 224
   Long Jump, 114, 116, 225
   return home, 196–98
   Shot Put, 119, 120–22, 225
   training with Goldie, 81–82
   trip to Athens, 10, 12
Garrett. Robert (grandson),
   219
George, King of Greece, 46,
   178, 187
   closing ceremonies and
      remarks, 186–87, 190,
      192
   and Marathon win, 174,
      175
   post-Games banquet,
      184–85
George, Prince, 51, 52, 116,
   123, 203
   interest in baseball, 187,
      188

George, Walter, 124, 138, 139

Gildersleeve, Basil Lanneau, 97–99

Gilman, Daniel Coit, 144

Gipe, George, 124

Gmelin, Charles, 120, 223

Goldie, George, 78–80, 81, 219

Goulding, Grantley, 108, 109, 111, 164–65, 224

Gouskos, Mitiados, 120, 121, 225

Grace, William Gilbert, 64–65

Graham, John, 4–5, 31, 34, 91, 112
  and Blake's marathon, 159, 160, 161, 171, 172–73
  and Boston Marathon, 212
  on Olympic coverage, 199
  return home, 203, 204
  trip to Athens, 10
  on US team's success, 193

Gray, George, 120–21

Great Britain
  1866 English Olympics, 64–65
  1908 Olympic Games, 213, 220
  1896 Olympic team, 45, 109–11, 192
  Wenlock Games, 62–63

Greece
  importance of Discus, 67–68, 82–83
  importance of Marathon, 156–58, 159
  war of independence, 63–64
  welcome for Americans, 36–39, 130
  Zappas Games, 63, 64, 65–66
  See also Olympic Games, 1896

Gregorious, Georgios, 172

Grigorou, G., 159

Grisel, Alponse, 83, 114

H

Hajós, Alfréd, 177–78, 180, 181, 182–83
  at closing ceremony, 191
  swimming results, 227

Hallahan, John, 106

Harris, William Torrey, 144–45

Harvard University
  competition with Princeton, 138
  Eliot president of, 22–24
  hare and hounds game, 123–24
  interest in Olympics, 19–21
  Olympians from, 9

student body of, 26
track team, 24, 25
Haxo, Thomas, 221
Hayes, Johnny, 213
Herodotis, 157
Herschmann, Otto, 180, 227
Hofmann, Fritz, 107, 120,
   164
   Olympic results, 223, 224,
   230
Holmes, Burton, 129, 155,
   185, 187
   on Americans' success, 92,
   164, 170
   at closing ceremonies, 191
   on Discus, 86, 87
   on Marathon finish, 175
   reaction to Athens, 39–40
   on success of Games, 121,
   192
   trip to Athens, 13–14
Hopkins, E. L., 210
Hoyt, William, 5, 9, 25, 26,
   164, 165–66
   after Olympics, 213–14
   encounter with Prince
   George, 52
   pole vault, 167, 168, 169,
   225
   return home, 202, 203
   trip to Athens, 10, 12, 37
Hughes, Thomas, 58

I

Innis, Nelson, 195
International Association of
   the Athletics Federations
   (IAAF), 24
International Olympic
   Committee, 146
It Happened in Athens (film),
   220–21

J

Jamison, Herbert, 7, 119–20,
   122, 217, 223
   return home, 196–98
   ribbon on uniform, 76
Jensen, Viggo, 83, 110, 186
   gymnastics results, 230
   Weight Lifting, 122, 123,
   231
Jordan, Gilbert, 106

K

Kalopothakes, Demetrius,
   20–21
Kasdaglis, Dionysios, 45,
   232
Kellner, Gyula, 162, 171, 173,
   176, 224
Kirby, Gustavus Town, 140
Kolletis, John, 64
Konstantinidis, Aristis, 186
Kraenzlein, Alvin, 207

L

Lagoudaki, 47–48, 113
Lambros, Ionnos, 158
Lane, Francis, 7, 76, 169, 217
 on Discus event, 87
 100 Meters, 46, 104, 105,
  164, 223
 return home, 196–98
 scrapbooks of, 91–92
 trip to Athens, 10, 12
Larkin, Frances, 81
Lathrop, James, 19, 21, 31,
 32
Lavrentis, Ioannis, 159
L'Education en Angleterre
 (Coubertin), 59
Lermusiaux, Albin, 127–28,
 130
 Marathon, 162, 163, 171,
  172
 1500 Meters, 224
Linson, Corwin Knapp,
 94–96
Lord, Fred, 112, 113
Louis, Spiridon, 41, 170–71,
 185–86
 at closing ceremonies,
  191–92
 Marathon, 159, 161–62,
  163, 172, 173, 174–76,
  224
Lucas, John, 133, 144

M

Maidstone (UK) Swim Club,
 178–79
Malokinis, Ioannis, 180, 227
Maltin, Leonard, 221
Mandell, Richard, 56, 88
Mansfield, Jayne, 220, 221
Mathias, Bob, 221
McCosh, Andrew, 80
McCosh, James, 77, 78, 80
 and Sloane, 138
McDermott, John J., 212–13
Merlin, Sidney, 103
Meyer, Albert, 40–41
Mitropoulos, Ioannis, 157, 230,
 231
Mooney, J. J., 116
Mullen, P. H., 181, 182
Mullen, Thomas, 203
Myers, Fred, 30
Myers, Lon, 79
My Stephen Crane (Linson),
 95

N

Napoleon Bonaparte, A History
 (Sloane), 139
National Track & Field
 Hall of Fame Museum,
 221–22
Neumann, Paul, 180–81,
 227

"New Education, The" (Eliot), 22

Nicholas, Crown Prince, 175, 187

Nielsen, Holger, 83, 154, 226

Notes sur l'Angleterre (Taine), 58

O

Olga, Queen of Greece, 42, 152

Olympic Games, 1896
  American spectators at, 92–94, 95–97, 98–103
  arrival of US team, 36–38
  closing ceremonies, 189–92
  complete results of, 223–32
  Discus, 83, 84–89
  High Jump, 165
  keeping track records, 24–25
  Long Jump, 114, 115–19
  Marathon, 156, 159, 162–63, 171–76
  medals for, 54–55
  110 Meter High Hurdles, 108, 113, 164
  100 Meters, 46–49, 104–5, 106, 107, 164
  400 Meters, 120
  1500 Meters, 127–29
  pole vault, 167–68, 169

shooting, 152, 153–55, 186
  Shot Put, 120–22
  stadium, 43–44
  start of, 42–43, 45–46
  swimming, 177, 178, 180–83
  Triple Jump, 50–54
  weather and crowds, day two, 107–9
  Weight Lifting, 122–23

Olympic Games, 1900, 206–7, 219–20

Olympic Games, 1904, 220

Olympic Games, 1908, 213, 220

"Olympic Games at Athens, The" (Tyler), 216

Orphanidis, Georgios, 186, 226, 227

Otto, King of Greece, 64

Owen, John, Jr., 105

P

Paine, Charles, 150, 151

Paine, John, 12–13, 26, 148–49, 151, 200
  after Olympics, 214
  shooting competition, 152, 153–55, 226

Paine, Robert Treat, 149–50

Paine, Salome Brigham, 152, 215

Paine, Sumner, 12, 13, 26,
    148–49, 151–52, 204
    after Olympics, 199–200,
    214–15
    shooting competition, 152,
    153–55, 226
Paine, Sumner (uncle), 150–51
Papasideris, Georgios, 120,
    225
Paraskevopolus, Panagiotis, 83,
    84, 85, 86, 87, 226
Paris Games. *See* Olympic
    Games, 1900
Persakis, Ionnis, 53, 225, 230
Peters, Jim, 129
Petros, Hadji, 189, 190
Pheidippides, 156, 157
Phrangoudis, Ioannis, 155,
    226, 227
Pietri, Dorando, 213
pole vaulting, origins of,
    166–67
    See also Olympic Games,
    1896
Powell, Foster, 158
Prefontaine, Steve, 125
Princeton University, 72–73,
    75–78
    competition with Harvard,
    138
    Olympians from, 3–4, 7–8,
    12, 219

Olympians' return,
    197–98
sports at, 77–78, 79–81

Q

Quincy, Josiah, 202,
    203

R

Randall, David, 175, 176
Red Badge of Courage, The
    (Crane), 95
Reichel, Frantz, 164
Reminiscences of an Athlete:
    Twenty Years on Track and
    Field (Clark), 118
Richardson, Rufus B., 93–94,
    121–22
Robertson, George Stuart,
    83–84, 87, 109
    ode by, 84, 190
Roosevelt, Theodore, 25–26,
    61
Rusie, Amos, 91

S

Saltonstall, Richard, 26
Samaras, Spiro, 45
Scaltsoyannis, Athanasios,
    114, 225
Schumann, Karl, 114, 225,
    230, 231

Sea-Borne: Thirty Years Avoyaging (Connolly), 208

Shaler, Nathaniel, 31, 33

Shaw, Jonathan, 33, 119

Sjöberg, Henrik, 83, 114, 225

Sloane, William Milligan, 19, 68, 131, 136–39, 219
  opinion of Sullivan, 143
  and Princeton athletes, 7, 138–39
  relationship with Coubertin, 132, 135–36, 139–40, 143
  at Second Olympic Congress, 144–45, 147

Smith, Michael Llewellyn, 59, 66, 218

Soutsos, Panayiotis, 63–64

Spalding, Albert, 140–41, 142, 188

Suffolk Athletic Club, 9, 35

Sullivan, James E., 140, 141–42, 143

Sullivan, John L., 27, 28

Sullivan, Joseph, 208

Szokoly, Alajos, 104, 223, 224, 225

T

Taine, Hippolyte, 58, 135

Tewksbury, John, 207

This Side of Paradise (Fitzgerald), 76, 77

Tocqueville, Alexis de, 61

Tom Brown's School Days (Hughes), 58

Townley, Charles, 67

Townley Discobolus (Myron), 67–68

track and field
  collegiate evolution of, 80
  format of trials, 220
  keeping records, 24–25
  National Track & Field Hall of Fame Museum, 221–22
  Olympic results of, 223–26
  See also Olympic Games, 1896

triple jump, history of, 50
  See also Olympic Games, 1896

Tuffère, Alexandre, 51, 53, 225

Tyler, Albert, 4, 7, 48, 76, 168–69
  after Olympics, 216–17
  coverage of Olympics, 91, 92
  on Discus event, 84, 85, 87, 88
  on Garrett's win, 121
  pole vault, 167, 226
  return home, 196–98

on stadium, 43
trip to Athens, 10, 12

U

United States. *See* America
US Olympic team
  athletes on, 3–5, 7–8,
    12–13
  cheers of, 48–49
  at closing ceremonies,
    190–92
  Discus event, 84–89
  first days in Athens, 36–40,
    41–43
  at 1900 Games, 207
  in Greece after
    competitions, 184–85,
    187–88
  High Jump, 165
  legacy of, 192–94, 219–22
  Long Jump, 114–19
  Marathon, 156, 159, 162–
    63, 171–76
  110 Meter Hurdles, 108,
    110, 113, 164
  100 Meters, 46–48, 104–5,
    106, 107, 164
  400 Meters, 119
  1500 Meters, 127–29
  pole vault, 167–68, 169
  results of Games, 223–32
  return home, 195–204
  shooting, 152, 153–55
  Shot Put, 120–22
  Triple Jump, 50–55
  trip to Athens, 1–6, 9–18
  See also specific individuals;
    Olympic Games, 1896

V

Vasilakos, Charilaos, 171, 173,
    174, 176, 224
  Marathon trial, 159
Velissariou, Petros, 64
Versis, Sotirios, 84, 85, 86, 88,
    226, 231
Vikelas, Dimitrios, 102, 103
Vlasto, Solon J., 6

W

Waldstein, Charles, 12, 13,
    100–103, 132–33
  after Olympics, 215–16
  shooting competition, 153
Wallechinsky, David, 157,
    232
Wassong, Stephen, 135
Webb, Matthew, 179–80
Wefers, Bernard, 81, 105
Wenlock Games, 62–63
West, Andrew Fleming, 89,
    136–37
Weston, Edward Payson,
    159

Wheeler, Benjamin Ide, 52, 96
Whitney, Casper, 193
Williams, Gardner, 12, 26,
    181–82, 183, 214
Williams, Jeremiah, 181
Wolcott, Roger, 202, 203

Y

Young, David, 65, 102, 187

Z

Zappas, Evangelis, 63, 64, 65
Zàtopek, Emil, 129

About the Author

Jim Reisler has written for a range of publications, including *Sports Illustrated*, the *New York Times*, and *Newsweek*. His books have been reviewed by the *New York Times* and *USA Today*, and he has been a frequent guest on sports radio shows, including Bob Costas's national satellite show and National Public Radio's *Morning Edition*.

Reisler is the author of eight baseball books, most notably *Babe Ruth: Launching the Legend*, which "finds new gold in an often-mined subject," the *New York Times Sunday Book Review* noted. Added *Sports Illustrated*: "Reisler casts a new and welcome light on the sudden, tremendous impact Ruth had on his game—and on all of American sports." A former cross-country, track, and marathon runner, he lives in Irvington, New York, with his wife, Tobie, and daughter, Julia.